Free Books
Hatfield

Crisis: Cause, Containment and Cure

Also by Thomas F. Huertas

CITIBANK, 1812–1970 (*with Harold van B. Cleveland*)
THE FINANCIAL SERVICES REVOLUTION (*co-edited with Catherine England*)

Crisis: Cause, Containment and Cure

Thomas F. Huertas

© Thomas F. Huertas 2010

All rights reserved. No reproduction, copy or transmission of this publication may be made without written permission.

No portion of this publication may be reproduced, copied or transmitted save with written permission or in accordance with the provisions of the Copyright, Designs and Patents Act 1988, or under the terms of any licence permitting limited copying issued by the Copyright Licensing Agency, Saffron House, 6-10 Kirby Street, London EC1N 8TS.

Any person who does any unauthorized act in relation to this publication may be liable to criminal prosecution and civil claims for damages.

The author has asserted his right to be identified as the author of this work in accordance with the Copyright, Designs and Patents Act 1988.

First published 2010 by
PALGRAVE MACMILLAN

Palgrave Macmillan in the UK is an imprint of Macmillan Publishers Limited, registered in England, company number 785998, of Houndmills, Basingstoke, Hampshire RG21 6XS.

Palgrave Macmillan in the US is a division of St Martin's Press LLC, 175 Fifth Avenue, New York, NY 10010.

Palgrave Macmillan is the global academic imprint of the above companies and has companies and representatives throughout the world.

Palgrave® and Macmillan® are registered trademarks in the United States, the United Kingdom, Europe and other countries.

ISBN: 978–0–230–23618–9 hardback

This book is printed on paper suitable for recycling and made from fully managed and sustained forest sources. Logging, pulping and manufacturing processes are expected to conform to the environmental regulations of the country of origin.

A catalogue record for this book is available from the British Library.

A catalog record for this book is available from the Library of Congress.

10 9 8 7 6 5 4 3 2 1
19 18 17 16 15 14 13 12 11 10

Printed and bound in Great Britain by
CPI Antony Rowe, Chippenham and Eastbourne

Contents

List of Figures   vi

List of Tables   viii

Acknowledgements   ix

Introduction   1

Part I   Cause

1   Rational Exuberance   7

2   Too Much of a Good Thing   17

Part II   Containment

3   Conditional Containment   39

4   Moving towards Meltdown   60

5   Unconditional Containment   76

Part III   Cure

6   Better Macroeconomic Policy   97

7   Better Resolution   109

8   Better Deposit Guarantee Schemes   123

9   Better Regulation   134

10   Better Supervision   168

Conclusion   182

Notes   197

References   207

Index   217

Figures

I.1   A $13 trillion cheque: official support to the
      financial system, 2007 to 2009   2
PI.1 Does monetary policy crank the asset cycle?   6
1.1   The financial system as transmission mechanism   8
1.2   Productivity parameters   10
1.3   A high wire act: the world economy, 2004–07   15
2.1   The great search for yield: responses to the challenge
      of falling spread on investment grade names   18
2.2   Shadow banking   19
2.3   Securitisation structure protects investors and
      funds sponsor banks   20
2.4   US securitisation issuance, 1996 to 2006   22
2.5   Credit derivatives, 2001–07   24
2.6   Money market mutual funds versus checkable
      deposits, United States, 2002–06   27
PII.1 A vicious cycle   38
PII.2 Containment of the crisis: three phases 3 month
      USD LIBOR-OIS spread in %, June 2007–November 2009   38
3.1   Crisis, what crisis? Official forecasts, fall 2007   40
3.2   Interest rate policy, Eurozone, UK and US, 2007–08   41
3.3   Conditional containment overview, August
      2007–September 2008   42
3.4   Northern Rock   45
3.5   Asset-backed commercial paper outstanding,
      July 2008–July 2009 in $ billions   49
3.6   Capital raised by 32 largest banks by type (cumulative),
      1 August 2007 to 15 September 2008 in $ billions   50
4.1   Moving towards Meltdown, 3-month $ LIBOR-OIS
      spread in %, 15 September to 15 October 2008   61
4.2   Federal Reserve pumps out liquidity post-Lehmans,
      10 September to 1 October 2008   66
5.1   Unconditional containment, 3-month $ LIBOR-OIS
      spread in %, October 2008–November 2009   77
5.2   The world economy goes into free fall – real GDP
      growth, advanced (OECD) economies quarter
      over quarter, annualised, in %, 2007–09   77

5.3   Governments prime the pump for further bank
      recapitalisations – capital raisings by 32 largest
      banks by type (cumulative) 15 September
      2008–26 November 2009, in $ billions equivalent   81
5.4   Fed floods the market with liquidity – central bank
      liquidity operations, September 2008–October 2009   82
5.5   Central banks slash interest rates effectively to zero   84
5.6   Massive fiscal stimulus – fiscal deficit/GDP
      in %, 2007–09   86
5.7   Possible recovery scenarios, end 2009 – GDP
      index 2008, 1Q = 100   91
PIII.1 A cure requires a comprehensive and
      consistent framework   94
6.1   Eligibility criteria for bank borrowing from
      the central bank   101
6.2   Economic scenarios   105
7.1   Official resolution policy   110
7.2   Resolution in practice   110
9.1   Regulation sets the stage for strategy at financial firms 135
9.2   The quality of capital has to improve   137
9.3   Pro-cyclicality   142
9.4   Good remuneration practice: bonus comes after
      profit, not before   159
C.1   Contingent capital can limit too big to fail and/or
      too complex to contemplate   188
C.2   Living wills   191
C.3   Calibrating the new regime: impact,
      probability and cost   194

Tables

7.1   Loss given resolution for various bank liabilities
      under different resolution methods to implement
      'constructive ambiguity'   118
8.1   Total deposit guarantees available to each person,
      selected countries, June 2009   124
10.1 Macro-supervision of financial infrastructures   179
10.2 Possible macro-prudential policy tools   180

Acknowledgements

This book is an expansion of the arguments made in a number of speeches and articles that I delivered during the course of the crisis, in particular the papers, 'The Rationale for and Limits of Bank Supervision', presented to the London School of Economics (LSE) conference on the crisis on 19 January 2009, and 'Too Big to Fail and Too Complex to Contemplate: What to do about Systemically Important Firms' at another conference at the LSE on 15 September 2009. I am grateful to the discussants at those conferences as well as to participants at presentations at the Institute for Law and Finance at the Johann Wolfgang Goethe University in Frankfurt.

Although the book does not necessarily represent the views of the Financial Services Authority, I am deeply grateful to my colleagues for discussion of the issues and for the opportunity to participate in the work of dealing with the crisis and laying the foundation for the future of financial regulation and supervision. Similarly, the book does not necessarily represent the views of the Committee of European Banking Supervisors, but it has certainly benefited from discussion with colleagues on that Committee, in particular the Expert Group on Prudential Requirements.

Finally and most importantly, I would like to thank my wife and son for their continuous encouragement and support. Without this, the book would not have been possible.

January 2010

Introduction

In 2009, for the first time in over fifty years, world output declined. At the start of the year economic output was declining at a rate faster than that experienced in the Great Depression. Even though this slide was arrested, the decline in output in the world's advanced industrial economies in 2009 was nearly 4% (IMF 2009a). In round numbers the fall in output amounted to over $4 trillion.

During the crisis that started in August 2007 and persisted into 2009, asset values also plummeted. For the first time in a generation, housing prices fell. Stock prices crashed. Bond prices declined sharply. Overall, the fall in household assets in the United States alone amounted to over $12 trillion.[1] Savings have been ravaged, and pensions are at risk.

Unemployment rose and will continue to rise. By June 2009 over 20 million people had lost their jobs as a result of the crisis. They have not all been bankers. Auto assembly workers, barkeepers, carpenters, delivery boys, editors, farmers, graphic designers, hotel workers and innumerable other occupations have all suffered. Forecasts made in mid-2009 predicted unemployment in 2010 to be above 10% of the labour force in most industrial countries (IMF 2009b).

To prevent these bad events from becoming even worse, central banks and governments around the world resorted to unprecedented stimulus measures. Central banks have slashed interest rates practically to zero, and governments ran budget deficits on a scale not seen since World War II. In the United States and the United Kingdom budget deficits in 2009 exceeded 10% of GDP and in the Eurozone they were about 6% of GDP, double the level permitted under the Maastricht Treaty (IMF 2009b).

In addition, central banks and governments took significant measures to stabilise the banking system. They guaranteed retail, and in some cases all, deposits. They guaranteed issues of securities by banks and other financial intermediaries. Central banks lent banks massive amounts of money, and they purchased securities directly in the open market. Governments and central banks capped the losses that banks need incur on so-called toxic assets through the provision of guarantees, non-recourse finance and/or so-called tail risk insurance. Finally, they provided substantial amounts of new capital to banks. Overall, central banks and governments provided over $13 trillion in support to banks, amounting to 85% of GDP in the United Kingdom, nearly 75% of GDP in the United States and nearly 20% of GDP in the euro area (see Figure 1).

Together the stimulus to the economy and the support of the banks appeared to be enough to arrest the downward debt – deflation spiral that had threatened the world economy in 2008 and early 2009 (IMF 2009a). But this escape from depression came at a very high cost, not only in terms of the trillions in output already lost and trillions already spent and trillions more in guarantees already given. The cost also came in mortgaging the future and in creating the threat of inflation down the road.

So finding a cure against future crises is paramount, both for society at large and for the financial institutions that are at the heart of the financial system. For these were the institutions that received the

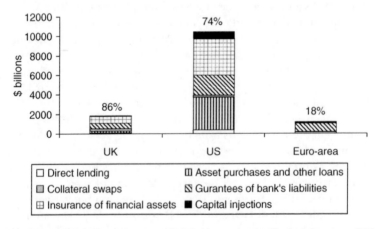

Figure I.1   A $13 trillion cheque: official support to the financial system, 2007 to 2009

Note: Figure in % above the column represents total support relative to GDP.

Source: Bank of England, Financial Stability Report June 2009.

bulk of the official support, and these are the institutions that need to provide assurance to society that they will not be the cause of crises in the future. Finding a cure requires that we understand the causes of this crisis, and why this crisis was so difficult to contain, and why this crisis ultimately required resort to stimulus on such an unprecedented scale.

That is what this book attempts to do. Part I examines the causes of the crisis and Part II, the efforts to contain the crisis. Although banks' sins of omission and commission play a leading role, macroeconomic policy plays a critical role as well, especially with respect to turning the cycle from boom to bust and for the duration of the crisis.

So the cure for crises must be comprehensive as well. It needs to encompass better macroeconomic policy, better resolution and better deposit guarantee schemes as well as better regulation and better supervision. In combination, these efforts can confront the difficult issues facing the financial system, including the most difficult of all, how to control institutions that are considered too big to fail.

The book does not address the question of who should implement the cure proscribed here. That is quite deliberate, as it keeps the focus on what should be done, not on who should do it.

Part I
Cause

The crisis of 2007 to 2009 (and possibly beyond) is a product of two factors: macroeconomic policy, especially the interest rate policy of the US Federal Reserve, and a financial system built on the premise that there would always be too much liquidity, never too little. Although either one of the two factors might have produced a downturn, it is doubtful that one without the other could have produced the calamity that actually occurred from 2007 to 2009.

In the opening years of the twenty-first century macroeconomic policymakers thought that they had discovered the way to dampen, if not entirely end, the business cycle. Acting under the so-called Taylor rule (Blanchard 2009: 568–9), monetary policymakers very actively managed interest rates so as to impact real economic activity and keep inflation under control. Although they recognized that the financial system was in effect the transmission mechanism for monetary policy, they reckoned that this transmission mechanism would remain largely unaffected by the success that they had had in controlling the business cycle.

Nothing could have been further from the truth. The Fed held interest rates at an extraordinarily low level for an extraordinarily long period of time after 2001. This low interest rate environment set the stage for a boom in asset prices, particularly in housing. After 2004 the Fed raised rates more sharply over a shorter period of time than at any time in the prior 25 years. In all likelihood, these increases in rates contributed to the reversal of the asset price bubble and to the onset of debt-deflation (see Figure PI.1).

Although Fed policy may have ignited and then reversed the asset price bubble, finance largely determined the magnitude of the bubble and finance largely determined the depths to which the debt-deflation spiral could go.

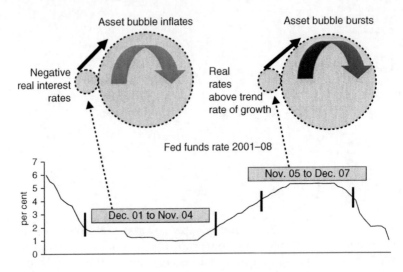

Figure PI.1   Does monetary policy crank the asset cycle?

None of these effects were anticipated, or even held to be remotely possible, and that is perhaps the true cause of the crisis. In macroeconomic policy, it was largely assumed that the transmission mechanism of the financial system would remain intact. One needed to worry about the interest rate, but not about default risk. The financial system would sort out relative prices and relative yields, but what counted for macroeconomic policy was the overall level of interest rates as determined by the short-term interest rate or policy rate. In the financial world, one came to believe the central banks' own press releases: if the risk of recession had largely vanished, it was safe to search for yield. It was not.

1
Rational Exuberance

In the opening years of the twenty-first century all economic signs were pointing in the right direction. Economic growth was faster. Economic growth was steadier. Inflation was under control. Confidence was growing among both policymakers and the public at large that the business cycle had been tamed, that central banks had mastered the art of guiding the economy to a soft landing.

In such circumstances a certain degree of exuberance was rational. As Alan Greenspan (2005b), Chairman of the US Federal Reserve Board, testified to Congress in February 2005,

> Over the past two decades, the industrial world has fended off two severe stock market corrections, a major financial crisis in developing nations, corporate scandals, and, of course, the tragedy of September 11, 2001. Yet overall economic activity experienced only modest difficulties. In the United States, only five quarters in the past twenty years exhibited declines in GDP, and those declines were small. Thus, it is not altogether unexpected or irrational that participants in the world marketplace would project more of the same going forward.

Starting in 2003 asset prices surged across the world. Policymakers recognised that this was a logical consequence of their success in taming the economic cycle. Policymakers, particularly in the United States, recognised that such asset-price bubbles could pose dangers, but they consciously chose not to puncture the bubble, reckoning that they could quickly clear up any problems that might result, as they had done in earlier episodes, most notably the aftermath of the 2001 terrorist attacks and the bursting of the dot com bubble.

More significantly, policymakers also assumed that they could keep the real economy stable by changing interest rates extraordinarily rapidly and by extraordinary amounts. The models central bankers used said that this would steer the economy away from deflation and enable the economy to escape inflation.

Effectively interest rate policy depended critically on the central bank's view as to whether output stood above or below the level determined by the trend rate of growth in productivity. Output levels above the trend line produced upward pressure on prices and inflation. Consequently, if prices were rising faster than the inflation target, the policy response was to raise interest rates so as to curb output growth and curtail price pressure. Such increases in rates had to be especially steep and rapid, if there were signs that higher rates of inflation could raise the long-term expected rate of inflation.

Conversely, if output stood below the productivity trend line, there was downward pressure on inflation. If prices were rising more slowly than the inflation target, the policy response was to lower interest rates so as to increase output and employment and put some upward pressure on prices. This was especially important at very low rates of inflation, lest the economy slip into deflation, for expectations that prices would actually fall could imply significantly positive real interest rates with adverse consequences for investment, output and employment.

The financial system played little or no role in the models that policymakers employed to decide changes in the interest rate. Although the financial system is the transmission mechanism for monetary policy, macroeconomic models generally ignored default risk, counterparty

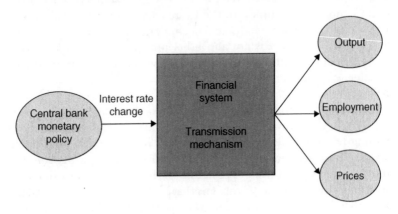

Figure 1.1   The financial system as transmission mechanism

risk and the possible changes in the financial system that changes in monetary policy could cause. Although central bankers acknowledged that monetary policy would affect prices and output with a long and variable lag, they generally regarded the financial system as a straightforward pass-through mechanism (see Figure 1.1). The dynamic stochastic general equilibrium models used as the basis for economic policy discussions and decisions generally ignored the possibility that the monetary policy could affect the transmission mechanism provided by the financial system as well as the possibility that changes in the financial system could affect output, employment or prices.[1]

Faster economic growth

The fall of Communism in 1989 ushered in some of the most rapid economic growth on record. Overall, the world economy grew at a rate of well over 4% per annum from 1990 to 2007, and nearly 5% per annum during the boom of 2003 to 2007.[2] Three forces lie behind that growth: (i) the entry of China, India and the former Soviet bloc into the market economy; (ii) rapid technological change, particularly in information and communications; and (iii) increasing globalisation. Together, these forces resulted in a rapid increase in productivity, not only in emerging economies, but also in advanced industrial societies, particularly the United States.

In the United States in particular conviction grew in official circles that the rate of growth in productivity had increased dramatically, from about 1.5% per annum to about 2.5% per annum. Officials at the Federal Reserve attributed this largely to the effects of widespread adoption of information and communications technology (ICT) in the US economy, including not only investment in tangible equipment such as computers and telecommunications devices, but also investments in intangible capital, such as the restructuring of work processes, so that maximum use could be made of the new technology (Greenspan 2002; Bernanke 2005). Gradually, the view took hold that the trend rate of growth in the US economy was 3 to 3.5% per annum.

Essentially, the new technologies permitted the economy to do more with the same amount of resources. How much more was difficult to say, and how rapidly the economy would realise the full potential of the new technologies was also difficult to say. Higher end levels of productivity with shorter transition periods (path A in Figure 1.2) would produce higher rates of productivity growth than longer transitions to somewhat lower levels (path B in Figure 1.2). But during the transition from the

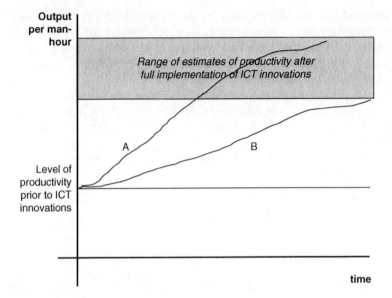

Figure 1.2   Productivity parameters

lower pre-ICT level of productivity to the higher level of productivity after full implementation of the ICT innovations, the economy would enjoy a burst, possibly a sustained burst, of higher growth in real output per hour worked. Similar effects had been observed in the twentieth century relating to the widespread adoption of the electric dynamo and the internal combustion engine (Greenspan 2002).

By 2005 the surge in productivity was into its second decade. Yet, there were good grounds for optimism that the surge in the growth of productivity still had some way to run. Although the pace of technological change may have faltered, the new technology was not as yet fully diffused. There remained a 'technology gap' between actual practice and what could be achieved, if the new technology were fully implemented. Closing this gap gave plenty of scope for further growth in productivity (Bernanke 2005).

Steadier economic growth

Economic growth was not only faster. It was also steadier. In the United States the variability of quarterly growth in real output had declined by half since the mid-1980s, and the variability of quarterly inflation had declined by about two-thirds (Blanchard and Simon 2001). The United

Kingdom experienced a similar marked improvement in economic performance (Haldane 2009). Growth remained positive year in and year out, and the belief grew that things could remain that way, that the world had put the risk of severe recession behind it.

Analysts (Shulman, Brand and Levine 1992) and then journalists spoke of the 'Goldilocks economy', – 'not too hot, not too cold'. Economists spoke of the 'Great Moderation'. They attributed the decline in variability in both output and inflation in no small measure to improved macroeconomic policies, especially monetary policy (Bernanke 2004).

The overwhelming goal of monetary policy was the establishment of price stability. Starting in 1979 the Federal Reserve had wrung inflation out of the economy, not least by taking pre-emptive action on various occasions to prevent the economy from overheating and inflationary expectations from building up. Indeed, the Fed ultimately acknowledged (Bernanke 2004) that it had been following something akin to the Taylor Rule, which called for the central bank to raise interest rates more than proportionately when there was a threat of an incipient increase in the rate of inflation above the target rate.

Conversely, when the economy showed signs of sagging, the Taylor Rule called for disproportionately large reductions in the rate of interest. This would prevent the inflation rate from sinking. Such rate reductions were judged to be particularly important in the aftermath of the September 11, 2001 terrorist attacks. The potential loss of confidence could, it was reckoned, have pushed the US economy into deflation, and radical reductions in rates were judged to be the appropriate countermeasure.

By 2003, it was widely considered that central banks had met the challenge of taming inflation and taming the business cycle. Indeed, the first promoted and perhaps even determined the second. Hitting the inflation target meant keeping the real economy on an even keel. Chairman Greenspan (1999) characterised price stability as 'a necessary condition for maximum sustainable economic growth', and in 2003 he declared that price stability had been achieved (Greenspan 2003). Bernanke (2004) noted that the achievement of price stability improved the ability of firms and individuals to make decisions about investment, consumption and inventories. Reductions in the expected variability of inflation had a positive feedback loop that promoted reductions in the variation of output. Price stability and economic stability went hand in hand. Indeed, Robert Lucas (2003), the winner of the 1995 Nobel Prize in Economics, went so far as to conclude in his presidential address to the American Economics Association that 'the central problem of depression-prevention has been solved for all practical purposes'.

Economists considered that the activist monetary policy embodied in a judicious application of the Taylor Rule would be sufficient to keep inflation low and steady and thereby preserve a high and fairly steady rate of economic growth. Recessions might occur, but they would be short and mild. Indeed, the 2001 recession was practically the mildest on record, at least in the United States. Policymakers had discovered how to make a 'soft landing'. They had one target (a low rate of inflation) and they reckoned that they could rely on one tool (the short-term interest rate).

Asset prices

Policymakers clearly recognised that the Great Moderation had a significant impact on asset prices and that changes in asset prices had an impact on macroeconomic activity. But policymakers considered these effects to be second order, compared to the direct effects of interest rates on real economic activity and on the rate of inflation. They saw no way to puncture the asset-price bubble short of engendering a recession – and that was a price they were determined to avoid if possible.

Clearly, the Great Moderation reduced risk. In particular, the establishment of price stability reduced the risk that the central bank would have to induce a recession to cool off the economy. In previous business expansions inflation was the primary reason why the expansion had come to an end. As the economy overheated, central banks had raised interest rates and killed off the boom in order to prevent inflation from spiralling out of control. But in the 1990s and the first years of the twenty-first century, there was little or no inflation. The party was well behaved, so from a central bank perspective, it could go on. There was little or no reason for central banks to 'remove the punch bowl'. As a consequence, recessions became rarer, and when they did occur, they were shorter and shallower.

The reduction in risk reduced the premiums that investors could charge for bearing risk, and that drove asset prices higher. For example, Greenspan (2005a) commented

> [T]he growing stability of the world economy over the past decade may have encouraged investors to accept increasingly lower levels of compensation for risk. They are exhibiting a seeming willingness to project stability and commit over an ever more extended time horizon.

The lowered risk premiums – the apparent consequence of a long period of economic stability – coupled with greater productivity growth have propelled asset prices higher.

Policymakers also recognised that elevated asset prices posed a risk to financial stability. As Chairman Greenspan (2005a) remarked,

> [T]his vast increase in the market value of assets ... is too often viewed by market participants as structural and permanent. To some extent, those higher values may be reflecting the increased flexibility and resiliency of our economy. But what they perceive as newly abundant liquidity can readily disappear. Any onset of increased investor caution elevates risk premiums and, as a consequence, lowers asset values and promotes the liquidation of the debt that supported higher asset prices. This is the reason that history has not dealt kindly with the aftermath of protracted periods of low risk premiums.

Although policymakers recognised that an asset-price bubble could flip into a downward debt-deflation spiral, they refrained from taking steps to puncture the bubble. In part, this was due to their belief that the only way to puncture the asset-price bubble was to raise interest rates to the point where a recession in the real economy would result. In other words, the only way to puncture the asset-price bubble was to reintroduce the risk whose absence had fed the bubble in the first place.

Effectively central banks wrote asset prices out of the script that determined monetary policy. The focus was on stability of prices of goods and services, for policymakers reckoned that achieving such stability would generate steadier and faster growth in output and employment.

Defeating deflation

Rather than asset prices, disinflation was the Fed's main concern, at least in 2003. The real economy was growing, but at a rate well below 3% to 3.5% (the rate that the Fed regarded as the trend rate of growth thanks to the increase in productivity). Prices were barely rising at all. The fear arose that prices might actually fall.

This created the spectre that the economy could be caught in a corrosive deflationary spiral similar to what had plagued Japan in the 1990s. Although the Fed regarded this possibility as remote, it stood 'ready to maintain a highly accommodative stance of policy for as long as it takes to achieve a return to satisfactory economic performance' (Greenspan 2003). To this end the Fed reduced the target rate for Fed funds from 1.5% to 1.25% in November 2002 and then from 1.25% to 1% on July 2003. In sum, the Fed reduced rates to an extraordinarily low level and kept them there for an extraordinary amount of time, until it was certain that growth could continue at or above its trend rate.

From 2004 to 2007: a high wire act

By the middle of 2004 Federal Reserve officials had gained sufficient confidence in the strength of the recovery to begin the process of removing 'the extraordinary degree of policy accommodation' that had been present since the middle of 2003. In plain English, the Fed began to raise rates.

And raise rates it did. From 1% in June 2004 the Fed repeatedly instituted 25 basis point increments in the Fed funds target rate until that rate stood at 5.25% in July 2006. The total increase in short-term rates amounted to four and one-quarter percentage points. The pace and extent of the interest rate increase was the largest since the early 1980s, when inflation had been in double digit territory and veering out of control.

This was effectively a pre-emptive war on inflation. As dictated by the Taylor Rule, the Fed moved interest rates up in order to head off any increase in inflationary expectations. Increases in commodity prices, especially oil, a pause in productivity growth, an increase in unit labour costs and high capacity utilisation created the risk in the eyes of the Fed that the hard-won reduction in inflationary expectations could be compromised. As actual inflation in 2004 and 2005 moved well above the 2% per annum rate that many thought should be the Fed's official inflation target, the rationale to keep raising short-term rates seemed robust.

The performance of real economy seemed to substantiate the Fed's policy of raising rates. Despite the steep increase in short-term rates, the economy continued to expand throughout 2004, 2005, 2006, and into 2007. These extraordinary macroeconomic results depended critically on various imbalances in the world economy continuing to offset one another (see Figure 1.3). Rapid growth in US consumer spending drove world demand. Production shifted to countries, which had a comparative advantage in manufacturing (e.g., China) or abundant raw materials (such as oil from the Middle East), as well as a high propensity to save. They channelled much of their savings to the United States

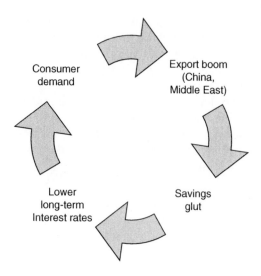

Figure 1.3   A high wire act: the world economy, 2004–07

as the country with the most liquid capital market, the still dominant currency and the strongest economic and investment outlook (thanks in no small measure to the pace of technological change and the potential profits from adopting such technology). This inflow of capital from abroad permitted the United States to run massive current account deficits. That in turn reduced the upward pressure on interest rates and promoted the rise in asset prices that allowed consumers to expand the borrowing that underpinned the boom in consumption spending.[3]

Overall, the Federal Reserve exhibited considerable confidence that this high wire act could be successfully sustained. Throughout the period 2004 to 2007 it expected that economic growth would continue at a good pace and that inflationary pressures could be contained. The Fed saw a series of threats to this forecast – oil prices, lapses in productivity growth, the federal government budget deficit – but expected that these obstacles could be overcome. Asset prices did not figure prominently as a threat to the economic outlook. Nor did the state of the financial system. Throughout the years 2004 to 2007 the central forecast was for continued growth and moderate inflation.

One soft landing does not guarantee another

Things turned out very differently. One soft landing did not guarantee another. The question is to what extent monetary policy was to blame.

Monetary policy does have a significant impact on economic activity. Maintaining interest rates below the rate of inflation tends to stimulate the economy; keeping rates very significantly above the rate of inflation tends to have the opposite effect. However, these effects are variable, and they take place with a lag. So it is entirely possible that the extraordinarily low interest rates of 2001 to mid-2004 stimulated the economic boom that followed from 2004 to 2007, and it is entirely possible that the extremely rapid and extremely steep increase in rates from mid-2004 to mid-2006 not only tempered the boom but also contributed to the crisis.

2
Too Much of a Good Thing

Although macroeconomic policy may have caused boom to turn to bust, finance itself contributed significantly to the amplitude of the boom and the amplitude of the subsequent contraction.[1] Finance built a superstructure based on two assumptions that would prove to be flawed: first, that recessions were a thing of the past (an assumption that markets shared with policymakers [see Chapter 1]), and second, that there would always be too much liquidity rather than too little.

Given those assumptions, finance as it evolved during the boom had a certain logic. The improved environment reduced the spread on investment grade names. This reduced potential profits, squeezed the rate of return on equity, and induced firms to engage in a great search for yield. This involved moving down the credit spectrum (lower rated borrowers still paid higher rates than more creditworthy names), riding the yield curve, increasing leverage, and increasing throughput so as to generate fees (see Figure 2.1).

Financial engineering was critical to all this. This enabled banks to create structures that splice and dice risk and return so as to enable investors and issuers to employ their capital most efficiently. Initially these structures made sense. They really did make risk management more efficient, and they added to the value that financial intermediation creates. This innovation was good for issuers, investors and intermediaries.

Nevertheless, during the course of the boom, financial institutions took things a step too far. Financial engineering constructed ever more complex structures, and financial institutions financed these structures though what amounted to a shadow banking system. Financial institutions shifted away from their traditional business models to 'originate-to-distribute' or 'acquire-to-arbitrage' models. Liquidity was the gas that

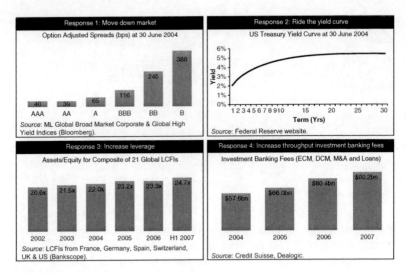

Figure 2.1   The great search for yield: responses to the challenge of falling spread on investment grade names

allowed these business models to expand, and illiquidity would bring it to an abrupt end in August 2007.

Shadow banking

With the benefit of hindsight it can be seen that the most dangerous aspect of finance during the boom was the development of the shadow banking system (see Figure 2.2). At its core stood an array of conduits and special purpose vehicles that were sponsored by the world's leading banks and which in some cases were provided with implicit or explicit liquidity support from those banks.

By and large these conduits invested in a variety of longer term securities and they financed themselves through the issuance of short-term, asset-backed commercial paper. At the peak of the boom a very large proportion of the securitisation issues underwritten by major investment banks were in fact purchased by the conduits and SIVs that those same investment banks had collectively sponsored and a very large proportion of the junior tranches of securitisation issues were sold to hedge funds, who refinanced these positions with collateralised credit from the very same pool of investment banks.

Many banks shifted to the so-called originate-to-distribute business model. Instead of holding the loans that they had originated to maturity,

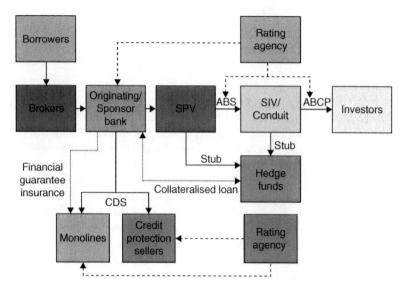

Figure 2.2 Shadow banking

the bank securitised the loans as quickly as they could be packaged into securities for onward sale to end investors. The ability to securitise allowed such banks to run their origination machinery at much higher speeds, since they 'knew' that they could fund the loans through the securitisation and/or covered bond markets.

Major banks engaged in what might be called an acquire-to-arbitrage model. They originated loans or bought loans from brokers and packaged these into securities. Although they distributed some of these securities to investors, they did not fully rid themselves of the risk. Either they kept some tranches of the securitisation on their own books or they granted liquidity puts to the investors who bought the securities or they promised to provide liquidity and/or capital to the vehicles that bought the securities. For some of the risk that they retained major banks sought to buy credit protection. However, the providers of such protection were few in number, and the amount of protection that they sold was so great, that there was a risk that if the protection had to be called upon, the providers would not be able to perform.

Six different elements all came together during the boom to create shadow banking: securitisation, derivatives (especially credit default swaps), financial guarantee insurance companies (monolines), non-bank institutional investors, rating agencies and the interaction between accounting and regulation. Singly, each of these elements was sound; in combination, they were not.

Securitisation

Securitisation effectively transforms loans into securities.[2] It allows investors to take a direct exposure to a set of assets without incurring the risk that the originator of those assets could fail. It allows issuers to raise funds based on the credit quality of the assets rather than the credit quality of the issuer. This can yield lower funding costs for the issuer.

In principle, the securitisation structure matches risk and reward. In the typical structure, the originating bank sells loans to a special purpose vehicle (SPV). The SPV then sells securities to investors differentiated into classes or tranches according the order of priority in receiving cash flows from the assets underlying the SPV (see Figure 2.3). Viewed from the vantage point of incoming cash flow, the securitisation structure operates like a waterfall. Cash goes first to the super-senior tranche, then to the senior tranche, then to the mezzanine and only then to the 'stub'. If the cash flows dry up before reaching the bottom of the waterfall, tranches at or below the point at which the cash flows dry up suffer losses. Conversely, in terms of loss absorption, the junior most security,

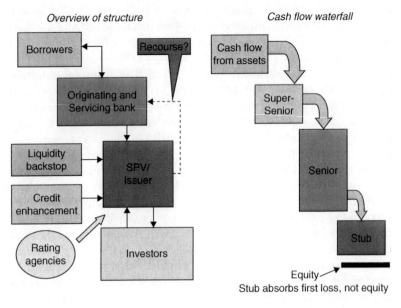

Figure 2.3   Securitisation structure protects investors and funds sponsor banks

or stub, absorbs the first loss; once this class of security is wiped out, the mezzanine securities bear loss; then the senior securities, and then finally the super-senior securities.[3]

This structure provides significant protection to the senior and super-senior tranches of the securitisation structure. Before the senior tranche could suffer a loss, the entire stub and mezzanine tranches would have to be wiped out. That protection was usually heightened further by 'overcollateralisation'. The SPV could draw on the cash flow from a pool of assets significantly greater in value than the aggregate value of the senior securities issued by the SPV. In addition, under many structures, the SPV had the right to put back to the originating bank a limited amount of non-performing loans. This sustained the quality of the underlying cash flows.

By increasing the proportion of assets or cash flows going to the senior tranches, it is possible to set the probability of loss on the senior tranche at very low levels. Rather than set an absolute level (e.g., 0.1% probability of loss), it made sense to set the level for probability of loss equal to the norm that the rating agencies (see "Rating Agencies" below) set for an AAA rating. That was ready shorthand with which investors were familiar from sovereign and corporate bonds, and the AAA rating conveyed to investors the impression that AAA-rated securitisation issues had similar probabilities of default.

Over the years a wide variety of assets had been securitised in great volumes. Starting with mortgages, securitisation gradually grew to encompass trade receivables, credit card receivables, lease payments and even future royalty payments. Total securitisation issuance for private (non-agency) issuers grew from approximately US$400 billion in 2000 to over US$1.6 trillion in 2005 and 2006 (see Figure 2.4). Securitisation had developed into a core component of the fixed income markets, greater in size than the corporate bond market. Banks routinely tapped the securitisation market for billions of dollars of funding.

Although securitisation generated significant benefits, it also carried certain risks. First, the securitisation issues were ultimately only as good as the cash flows that the underlying assets would generate. Low quality assets or assets with highly variable cash flows were not well suited to securitisation, for they would not produce the constant stream of cash necessary to service the debt issued by the SPV. Second, securitisation issues were somewhat opaque to end investors. Information about the performance of assets in the securitisation pool was not as readily available to investors as information about the earnings and business outlook for issuers of corporate bonds. The prospects for a securitisation

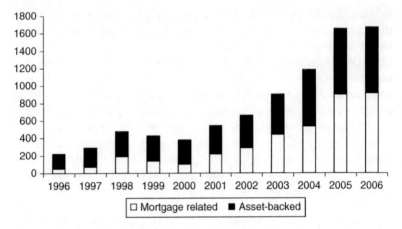

Figure 2.4   US securitisation issuance, 1996 to 2006 (non-agency, private issuers, $ billions)

Notes: Mortgage-related refers only to private issuance and excludes GNMA, FNMA and FHLMC mortgage-backed securities. Asset-backed includes securities backed by auto loans, credit cards, equipment, home equity, manufactured housing, student loans and other assets.

Source: SIFMA.

issue depended critically on the cash flows from the underlying assets. Analysing these required access to reams and reams of data as well as to considerable analytical modelling capability.

Re-securitisations or CDO-squareds were particularly complex to analyse, as these securities were in effect securitisations of securitisations. They pooled the mezzanine or stub tranches of standard securitisations and then set up the same waterfall for the cash flows that would come through. Provided the underlying loans in the original securitisations kept paying interest and amortisation, the cash would flow as modelled. But once the cash in the underlying securitisations was insufficient to service the stub or mezzanine tranche of that securitisation, the cash would stop flowing altogether to the CDO-squared. Estimation of the cash flows on a CDO-squared issue therefore required analysis of the cash flows on the underlying securitisation issues – a truly daunting task. Few investors had the time or capability to make such analyses on their own. They consequently depended on the rating agencies to do this job for them. That created a dependency on the rating agencies to get things right (see "Rating Agencies" below).

Thirdly, securitisation created what came to be known as 'warehousing risk'. Pending a securitisation issue, the sponsoring bank had to stockpile the loans that the SPV would ultimately purchase. These had to be financed until such time as the securitisation could be completed. As securitisation gathered steam, this warehousing risk grew. Finally, securitisation, like all forms of secured borrowing, including repurchase agreements, encumbered assets and effectively subordinated unsecured liabilities, such as deposits, that did not have specific assets pledged against them.

Credit derivatives

Credit derivatives allow an investor to take a position with respect to the possibility that the so-called reference entity (e.g., government, corporate or securitisation vehicle) will default. The investor can either buy protection, in which case s/he will receive a payment if the reference entity defaults, or the investor can sell protection, in which case s/he will make a payment if the reference entity defaults. In return for providing this protection, the seller of protection receives a premium from the buyer of protection.[4]

Essentially, credit derivatives allow the buyer of protection to exchange the credit risk on the reference entity for counterparty risk on the provider of the protection. This can make sense for the buyer of protection, if the credit risk of the counterparty is lower than the credit risk of the reference entity and/or the credit risk of the counterparty is not correlated with the credit risk of the reference entity.

Credit derivatives underwent extremely rapid growth during the 1990s and the first years of the twenty-first century (see Figure 2.5). From practically a standing start at the turn of the century, they grew to over $45 trillion in notional value by mid-2007. Critical to this growth was standardisation of various aspects of the credit derivatives transaction. This started with documentation. The International Swap Dealers Association (ISDA) led a multinational effort to standardise the contracts for all derivatives, including credit derivatives, so that transactions would have a common legal basis. This contract envisioned that the counterparties to a derivatives deal would be able, in the event of the default of one of the counterparties, to execute close-out netting. Under this procedure the two counterparties would aggregate all their derivatives contracts with each other, mark those contracts to market and net out the exposures that the counterparties would have to each other to arrive at one net figure that one counterparty would owe to the other. If the defaulting counterparty owed money to the non-defaulting party, the non-defaulting party would have a claim for the net amount of the aggregated contracts on the estate of the defaulting

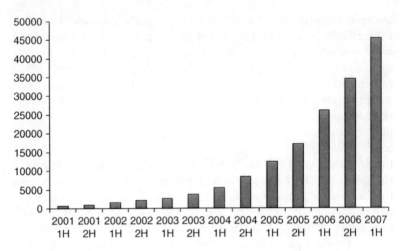

Figure 2.5   Credit derivatives, 2001–07 (notional amounts outstanding in $ billions)

Source: ISDA.

counterparty. These netting provisions would prevent the receiver of the defaulting counterparty from cherry-picking the contracts that the defaulting counterparty had with the non-defaulting counterparty, and they therefore reduced the risk that the non-defaulting counterparty had on the defaulting counterparty to the net amount of the exposure, rather than the gross amount of the contracts.

ISDA also worked closely with authorities in various countries to assure that such netting would be recognised under national bankruptcy statutes (and some countries changed such laws to assure that this would be the case), and regulators allowed banks to calculate capital requirements on the basis of net exposures, provided there were adequate legal opinions in place to assure that such netting would be legally binding on the counterparties to the transactions. In addition, ISDA worked with the major dealers to incorporate other risk-minimisation techniques, such as mutual margining above a threshold exposure limit. This effectively capped the counterparty exposure that could arise as a result of derivatives trading between two firms.

Yet as the credit derivatives markets grew, it became apparent that further improvements would be required, if credit derivatives were not to pose a threat to financial stability. Two problems ranked foremost in regulators' minds: unauthorised assignments and the growing backlog of unconfirmed transactions (Geithner 2006; Huertas 2006c). In

September 2005 regulators convened a meeting at the Federal Reserve Bank of New York with the principal dealers in derivatives to effectively order the industry to clean up its act. Unauthorised assignments had to stop, and the backlog of unconfirmed transactions had to be reduced and then eliminated.

This was a clear example of what would later come to be called macro-prudential supervision, and it succeeded. Firms changed their procedures so that assignments could be handled promptly and smoothly. Firms also devoted considerable resources to reconciling past trades and moving to electronic booking and confirmation processes so that backlogs would not build up in the first place. These efforts brought down the volume of unconfirmed transactions considerably. In 2006 and 2007 industry and regulators undertook further efforts to strengthen the infrastructure behind the credit derivatives market, including the introduction of a data warehouse that recorded all credit derivative transactions with major counterparties. It also began to make improvements in the procedures for settling payments to be made in the event of a default by a reference entity.

Yet this work was still incomplete in mid-2007. The infrastructure was not yet robust. There was no oversight over the aggregate amount of protection that a single counterparty had written. There was no assurance that trades would settle, if one of the major dealers or protection providers were themselves to fail. And there was no requirement that the counterparties to the defaulting entity would have to invoke close out netting upon default. Parties that would have owed the defaulting party money under the close out calculation had the option to let those contracts run further in the hope that the amount of money owed to the defaulting counterparty would decline.

Financial guarantee insurance (monolines)

Financial guarantee insurance performed a similar function to credit derivatives. In exchange for a premium, financial guarantee insurance companies (generally they only wrote this type of insurance and they were therefore known as monolines) provided protection against the possibility that an issuer would not be able to make timely payments of interest and/or principal on its securities. The financial guarantee insurance policy provided that the monoline would step into the shoes of the issuer and pay the interest and amortisation on the security on the originally scheduled basis. Hence, such policies provided cash flow protection to holders of the security, but did not protect against the decline in the market value of the security.

As long as the securities which the monoline insured were highly diversified, the monoline business model could and did work fairly well. The monoline received the premiums up front, and could invest these premiums and realise the investment returns pending the actual default of the issuer. If the issuer did default, all the monoline had to pay was the scheduled interest payment to the bondholder. At the same time, the monoline stepped into the bondholders' shoes in terms of negotiation during the bankruptcy or insolvency proceedings, so the monoline had ample scope to influence the restructuring of the issuer and to accelerate recoveries. Provided that the defaults were not highly correlated, the monoline should have had enough income and/ or capital to meet the obligations to bondholders from any defaulting issuers, particularly if the monoline exercised appropriate due diligence and credit discipline in deciding what securities to insure in the first place. That was essentially the rationale that led the rating agencies to rate the leading monolines AAA.

The trouble was that during the boom the monolines began to depart from this business model. They started to insure asset-backed securities as well as municipal bonds. These were much more likely than municipal bonds to go into default simultaneously. Moreover, the monolines also started to write protection via credit derivatives. This radically changed the nature of the protection provided, from substituting for the issuer in making scheduled cash payments to the investor, to compensating the investor for the capital loss that the investor would suffer, if the issuer defaulted. However, it was reckoned that this risk was limited, as the underlying reference entities for the credit derivative contracts were by and large the AAA-rated tranches of securitisations based on sub-prime securities.

Non-bank institutional investors

Non-bank institutional investors played a growing role in finance, especially in the United States. These ran the gamut from money market mutual funds to hedge funds, and during the first years of the twenty-first century they were key players in major markets.

By the turn of the century money market mutual funds in the United States had grown to the point where their assets dwarfed the amount of checkable deposits in the US banking system (see Figure 2.6). Originally money market mutual funds had been created as a means to provide investors with market-based returns on short-term funds at a time when there were limitations on the interest rates that banks could pay on time deposits and a prohibition on interest payments on demand deposits/current accounts. Although these

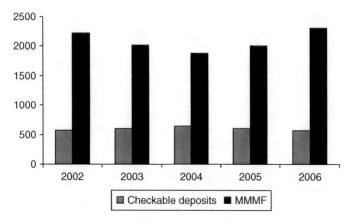

Figure 2.6 Money market mutual funds versus checkable deposits, United States, 2002–06 ($ billions, end of period, not seasonally adjusted)

Source: Federal Reserve Board, Flow of Funds statistics (11 June 2009), tables L 109 and L 121.

limitations had been lifted, money market mutual funds continued in operation.

The foundation of their success lay in a simple promise that the unit value of the money market mutual fund would always be $1. Earnings on the fund would be credited to the account in the form of additional shares, again each with a unit value of $1. This allowed the sponsors to market money market mutual funds to consumers as deposit equivalents, even though the funds were technically equity investments in which the investor bore the risk of loss in the underlying assets. Customers were even provided with 'chequebooks' that were effectively orders to sell some portion of their fund investment and transfer the proceeds to the beneficiary named on the cheque.

Regulations limited the assets in which money market mutual funds could invest to short-term, high grade investments (as determined by ratings) and limited the degree of concentration that the fund could have in any one obligor. Although it was recognised that losses could occur on one or more of the fund's investments, it was assumed that the requirements to maintain asset quality and limit concentration would be sufficient to assure that the loss on any defaulting asset would always be less than the overall interest accruing on the fund's investments. This would permit the fund to maintain a unit value of $1 at all times and to credit the net interest earned on the fund's investments as an increase in shares in the fund rather than a change in the unit value of the fund. Thus, to the consumer money market mutual funds appeared to be a deposit with a variable rate of interest rather than an equity investment in a portfolio of risky short-term securities whose principal value could rise or fall.

Given the ratings restrictions on eligible investments, money market mutual funds put a large proportion of their portfolio into the highly rated commercial paper issued by structured investment vehicles, conduits and holding companies of large, complex financial institutions. Any collapse in the value of such instruments would adversely impact the value of the money market mutual funds' portfolios and pose the threat that they would have to 'break the buck'. But money market mutual funds had been around for so long, and were supposed to have such a safe investment profile, that they were not considered a threat to financial stability. There was no consideration by the SEC, the authority responsible for regulating money market mutual funds, to require either the fund itself or the sponsor of the fund to put up capital to assure that the 'buck' could remain unbroken.

Quite a different attitude prevailed with respect to hedge funds. These were relatively new and extremely aggressive investors who were considered to pose a distinct threat to financial stability. Hedge funds played a critical role in the evolution of shadow banking since they were frequently among the largest investors in the junior tranches of the securitisation deals and/or the junior tranches of the debt issued by CDOs, conduits and SIVs. Hedge funds generally leveraged these positions by borrowing from prime brokers on a collateralised basis.

Hedge funds' investment strategies were very controversial, especially long-short strategies that took major positions in listed companies and sought to influence corporate strategy. Such activist investing raised hackles in many countries and posed questions as to whether the successful execution of such strategies relied upon market abuse – a suspicion heightened when a leading trader at a large hedge fund was in fact accused of market abuse.

Hedge funds themselves were generally not subject to regulation or supervision, as they were usually collective investment vehicles incorporated in tax-efficient jurisdictions such as the Cayman Islands. However, the managers of hedge funds were subject to regulation and supervision, at least in the United Kingdom. This required that the managers of the funds be 'fit and proper' and that they institute appropriate systems and controls to protect client assets, including the use of the third-party administrators and third-party custodians as well as controls to manage conflicts of interest and assure accurate valuations (FSA 2005a).

During the boom hedge funds grew dramatically in size, and the authorities examined whether or not they posed a threat to financial stability as opposed to the continuity of management at leading listed firms. The conclusion of these studies was that, although hedge funds did need to improve their practices, they did not, by and large, pose a threat to financial stability as long as the prime brokers lending to the funds continued to exercise appropriate credit controls over the funds (FSA 2005a; Nouy 2007). Hence, the control over the systemic risk that might be posed by hedge funds would be indirect, through the supervision of the major investment banks that provided credit on a collateralised basis to the hedge funds. To exercise this indirect control the UK FSA initiated a semi-annual review of the exposures of the major investment banks to hedge funds, but regulators could not reach an agreement on how to broaden this survey into a global one that might have provided a better overall picture of the exposure of major banks to hedge funds.

Rating agencies

Ratings and rating agencies were embedded in practically every aspect of finance.[5] The agencies provided the ratings critical to the success of securitisation. They rated the counterparties to derivative contracts and therefore triggered the margin calls for collateral under the ISDA contracts. They provided the ratings that allowed the monolines to run their business model effectively, and they provided the ratings that determined whether a security would be eligible for investment by money market mutual funds and other investors. Moreover, ratings were hard wired into regulatory criteria, such as capital requirements for banks and other financial institutions.

Thus, as far as the financial system was concerned rating agencies were potentially a 'single point of failure', much like the electricity grid. However, there was a view that ratings did by and large reflect risk, and that the independent rating agencies did a good job in rating securities. Moreover, the rating agencies were subject to 'recognition' by the US SEC and this was considered to provide some oversight to the ratings process.

Over time, the rating agencies had generally performed well. Risk ratings did in fact correspond to relative likelihood of default. A bond rated AAA was significantly less likely to default than a bond rated BBB, and a bond rated BBB significantly less likely to default than a bond rated B. The rating agencies cautioned that a rating is not forever, and that ratings could deteriorate or migrate over time, but they also published studies which showed a very slow downward migration in ratings, particularly for corporate bonds rated AAA.

Although some economists (Wakeman 1981) pointed out that ratings changes usually lagged rather than prompted changes in market prices (and so cast doubt on whether the rating agencies were really adding any new information or value to the market), the generally accepted view was that rating agencies performed a valuable service of initial and ongoing diligence on behalf on investors. The rating agency could evaluate on behalf of all investors the prospect that there would be a default on the security, and the issuer need only explain to a handful of rating agencies all the factors that could have an influence on the risk of default. To facilitate this diligence, rating agencies were granted insider status and exemption from fair disclosure rules. Rating agencies could have access to material, non-public information about the issuer and its prospects, and issuers could disclose information to rating agencies that they would not have to disclose more broadly to investors as a whole.

That approach had proved its worth over decades for corporate bonds. With very few exceptions, investment grade corporate bonds did not jump to default, and those that did, such as Parmalat or WorldCom, did so as a result of fraud. Virtually no AAA-rated security jumped to default, and generally AAA-rated sovereign and corporate securities were stable in price as well.

Initially ratings worked with respect to securitisation as well. Indeed, ratings were critical to the whole securitisation process. The agencies reviewed the proposed transactions prior to their coming to market, and placed their seal of approval on the deals in the form of a rating on the various tranches. The most critical rating was the one for the senior tranche. This was almost invariably AAA at inception. Indeed, deals were constructed so as to be sure that the senior tranche would get a AAA rating. To this end, the rating agencies had developed models of the cash flows underlying the various forms of securitisation based on data that the investment banks underwriting the issue had provided. Frequently, the rating agencies engaged in a dialogue with the investment banks with respect to the properties of the structure originally submitted for review, and investment banks sometimes changed the original proposal in order to meet the concerns of the rating agencies and assure that the senior tranche received the AAA rating.

Although the fine print of the ratings announcements pointed out that ratings for securitisation issues were not directly comparable with ratings on sovereign or corporate bonds, the use of the same ratings scale for securitisation issues as for sovereign and corporate bonds created exactly the opposite impression, and the use of the same ratings scale meant that AAA-rated securitisation issues would pass the same investment and regulatory screens as AAA-rated corporate bonds. Thus, the ratings from the agencies opened the door to selling securitisation issues to investors. Without ratings, it is doubtful that the securitisation market could have developed as far or as fast as it did.

The dependency of securitisation on ratings made the rating agencies' review of the proposed securitisation structures all the more important. Effectively, the rating agency models became a critical node in the financial system. Initially, the rating agencies' models were quite rigorous, taking into account a very wide array of factors that could give rise to default on the underlying assets. Moreover, initially many of the mortgages underlying the original securitisation issues were themselves guaranteed by a government-sponsored enterprise such as Fannie Mae or Freddie Mac. But gradually, investment banks started to present the rating agencies with deals where the underlying mortgages were 'non-conforming', either because they were too large to be purchased or insured by Fannie Mae or Freddie Mac, or because they lacked sufficient documentation (these were so-called Alt-A mortgages), or because the borrower was sub-prime.

Securitisation of sub-prime mortgages presented particular challenges to the rating agencies. The raw material for such securitisations was inferior to that which the rating agencies had otherwise encountered. Not only were the borrowers of lower creditworthiness, but most of the mortgages underlying the securitisation issues were originated by brokers rather than the sponsoring bank's own branch system or sales force. Initially, the rating agencies conducted fairly extensive samples of the documentation of the mortgages underlying the securitisation issues, but over time this sampling was scaled back. The rating agencies and the underwriters effectively relied on the sponsor bank's controls that brokers were in fact adhering to the sponsor bank's underwriting criteria, even though the originating bank was selling the mortgage outright to the securitisation vehicle. Even if the models had been perfect, there would have been the problem of 'garbage in, garbage out'.

However, the models were not perfect. They had difficulty in handling two very important issues: how correlated would possible defaults be, and what would be the loss given default? The first question was difficult to model, for one could not assume, as one could in the case of a coin toss, that the default on one mortgage was independent of the defaults on other mortgages. Indeed, there was a significant chance that if mortgages did actually start to default, they would all start to default at the same time. The second question was also related to the first, since loss given default would be greater, if the defaults were correlated, as this would likely depress the price of housing and delay resale of foreclosed properties.

Determining the probability that mortgages would default en masse was therefore critical to evaluating the risk of the senior tranches of securitisation issues. If mortgages defaulted en masse, losses would burn through the junior tranches of the securitisation structure and could be so large as to actually threaten the ability to maintain payments on the senior or even the super-senior tranches. If mortgages were largely independent of one another, the junior tranches would be more likely to be able to absorb any losses that might occur.

The proof of any model is whether it delivers accurate predictions, and one needs to test the model against actual outcomes to validate the model. Given the thousands of structures rated by the agencies and the millions of loans that in aggregate underlay the structures, this was a data management and analysis task of the first order. It was made even more difficult by the fact that the structures underlying the securitisation issues varied considerably from one issue to another. Validation of the models underlying the ratings on old issues lagged behind the work devoted to rating new issues.

In corporate bond issues, information about earnings and cash flows is generally available to end investors who have the opportunity to use this data to form their own view of the evolving creditworthiness of the issuer and to compare one corporate issuer against another. In the case of securitisation, this was more difficult, since the detailed information about the performance of the loans in the pools underlying the securitisation issues that would be required to model probability of default and loss given default was generally only available to the rating agencies and to investors in the security. It was not readily available to investors who had not originally bought the securities. This made it difficult for investors to evaluate prospective performance, and made investors generally dependent on the rating agency's evaluation of the performance of the loans against the model that generated the original rating.

Thus, it was only with a lag that information about the poor performance of securitisations based on sub-prime would come to the attention of investors. When it did, it became apparent that the deterioration in the underlying loans was far greater and proceeding far more rapidly than the original models anticipated.

That would undermine the credibility of the rating agencies, not just with respect to ratings of securitisations based on sub-prime, but ratings for all securitisations, and, to some extent, ratings overall. Investors could no longer trust the label AAA, and investors began to strike against the idea of buying any securitisation issues at all (see Chapter 3).

Accounting and regulation

The final element in shadow banking was the interaction between accounting and regulation. Accounting rules determined what was on and off the balance sheet for purposes of US GAAP, and therefore what counted towards the leverage ratio that the US authorities had imposed on US bank holding companies and, until 2005, on US-based securities groups. By selling to third-party investors instruments that assured that third-party investors would assume the expected loss in the vehicle, banking groups accounting under US GAAP assured that the conduits and SIVs that they had created would not be consolidated with the sponsor bank, even though the sponsor bank retained management control of the vehicle and supplied explicit or implicit liquidity support. This made it difficult for third-party investors to evaluate the risks that conduits and SIVs posed to banks reporting under US GAAP.[6]

Accounting also differed for assets that banks put into the trading book from the accounting for assets in the accrual book. Assets in the trading book were supposed to be marked to market and any changes in the market value of the asset taken immediately into profit and loss and so either added to or deducted from capital. In contrast, assets in the accrual book were valued at historic cost less impairments to the value of the asset. Impairments resulted from actual arrears at the individual asset level in the receipt of scheduled cash flows rather than as a general reserve for future losses.

Regulations treated the trading book very differently from the banking book. Since the trading book was marked to market, the capital requirements were calculated on the basis of the amount of capital that would be required to absorb the loss in the instrument during the period required for the bank to liquidate the instrument. For once the instrument was sold, no further capital need be held against it. In contrast, in the accrual book it was assumed that the bank would hold the asset to maturity, so that sufficient capital was required to enable the bank to sustain the level of impairments that might arise during the life of the loan. This could be a number of years in contrast to the number days or weeks that was reckoned to be the maximum time required for a bank to liquidate its trading portfolio. As a consequence of these differences capital requirements for the trading book were significantly lower than for the accrual book.

The actual amount of capital required for the trading book depended on the risk that the bank would incur a loss, and capital regulations allowed banks, subject to supervisory approval, to use their own models to estimate the risk of loss in the trading portfolio and therefore to establish the basis on which they would have to hold capital. This approach had been in place since the 1990s and had generally worked well.

However, the reason it worked well was that trading books predominantly contained assets, such as foreign exchange and government securities, that traded frequently in liquid markets. Such transactions established a market price to which each bank's position could be marked on a daily basis. There was no uncertainty about valuation, no uncertainty about profit and loss, and no uncertainty about what should be added to or detracted from capital. The factors influencing the price of such instruments could also be modelled fairly accurately, and the models validated relatively easily. Accordingly there was a high degree of confidence that capital held against trading book assets was sufficient to bear any unexpected losses that might arise.

That situation changed during the boom. Increasingly, banks elected to place complex credit derivatives and super-senior tranches of asset-backed securities into the trading book. This secured lower initial capital requirements but also posed the issue of how these positions should be valued in the absence of frequent transactions in the marketplace.

To some extent banks, accountants and regulators had already confronted this problem in the case of corporate bonds. Not every corporate bond trades every day, so there is not the same possibility to mark the corporate bond to market as there is with on-the-run US government securities or foreign exchange. Banks therefore used a model to value the corporate bonds that did not trade based on a matrix of prices of the corporate bonds that did trade that had similar ratings, maturities and coupons to the bonds that did not trade. These models were repeatedly validated with trade information as it became available, and mark to model became an accepted way to value securities in the trading book that did not trade all the time.

It therefore seemed natural to extend this approach to super-senior tranches of securitisation issues and to complex derivatives. The trouble was that this entire class of securities rarely traded at all, so it was much more difficult to obtain a matrix of comparable securities that actually did trade. To deal with this issue banks resorted to valuing their securities on the basis of the underlying market factors that should determine the value of the instrument, such as interest rates and default rates, as well as to the price of any index of similar securities – a process known as independent price verification (Derman 2001).

During the boom, both the market factors that drove the value estimates as well as the few transactions that took place pointed towards an increasing value for the assets subject to independent price verification. The banks readily marked up the entire portfolio of such assets to the higher value implied by the independent price verification and booked the gain to profit and added that profit to capital, even though they had not realised any cash at all from selling the asset. In many cases the banks then used the addition to capital as a basis for additional leverage, allowing them to book new trading book assets and to repeat the exercise. Effectively the combination of accounting and capital regulation encouraged greater leverage and created greater dependency on the models underlying independent price verification being correct and the market factors underlying the value of instruments such to such verification staying constant (Greenlaw et al. 2008).

Any downward lurch in the market factors driving the value of so-called Level III assets (assets subject to independent price verification) would have quite a destabilising effect. Leverage would operate in reverse. The bank would have to take an immediate write-down on the asset and deduct this write-down from capital. But the bank would then have to find new capital to back the asset since it would not have actually sold the asset. Such new capital could only come from selling truly liquid assets (thereby passing the price pressure onto those assets) or by depleting the bank's overall capital cushion. That in turn could create concerns about the bank's overall creditworthiness and cause funding difficulties for the bank as a whole unless it took steps to replenish its overall level of capital.

Summary

That is exactly the danger to which the world financial system became exposed in mid-2007. The great search for yield sparked by the extraordinarily long period of stable, rapid and non-inflationary growth led banks and other financial institutions to stretch each of the elements outlined here – securitisation, derivatives, monolines, non-bank institutional investors, rating agencies and accounting – to produce greater leverage. This offset the decline in margin and allowed firms to maintain, or even increase, their stated rate of return on equity.

Sustaining such rates, however, depended on all the underlying factors favouring finance remaining in place. If they had, the expansion of the financial system might have reached a natural limit, much as trees stop growing before they reach the sky. But the factors did not stay in place. Interest rates had escalated markedly over 2005 and 2006, substantially raising the rates which sub-prime borrowers would have to pay when their initial teaser rates expired. Housing prices had stopped rising, and in some cities were starting to fall. The music was about to stop, and banks that had shifted their business model to originate-to-distribute or acquire to arbitrage would soon find themselves under severe pressure.

Part II
Containment

The crisis broke on 9 August 2007, when BNP Paribas suspended withdrawals from three of its unit trusts on the grounds that they were no longer able to properly value many of the assets held in the funds. These hard-to-value assets were largely mortgage-backed securities. They were not unique to the BNP funds. They were held by institutions around the world. If BNP couldn't value them, why could anyone trust the values that anyone else was placing on these securities?

Thus began what would ultimately become a vicious cycle of debt-deflation (see Figure PII.1). Market liquidity of securitised assets declined. This created the potential for capital losses at institutions that held those securities, and cut off securitisation as a source of new funding. That in turn created funding difficulties at financial institutions and threatened to turn the financial crisis into an economic crisis where the real economy would decline.

Containment of the crisis fell into three phases (see Figure PII.2). The first was up to 15 September 2008, the date the US authorities allowed Lehman Brothers to declare bankruptcy. At that point, the nature of the crisis changed. The financial system lurched towards meltdown, as institutions toppled one after another on both sides of the Atlantic. The financial crisis became an economic crisis. The real economy went into reverse gear and began to slide downhill at a rate not seen since the 1930s.

That prompted a radical change in the approach to containment. Governments and central banks around the world moved very promptly to a policy of massive monetary and fiscal stimulus, coupled with programmes to sustain the capital and therefore the credit capacity of the major financial institutions. Containment became unconditional.

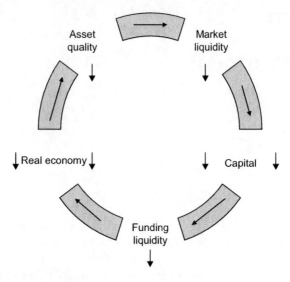

Figure PII.1 A vicious cycle

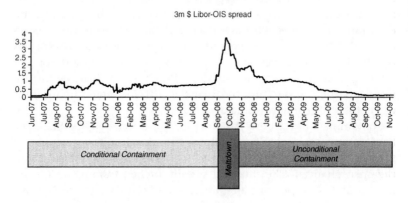

Figure PII.2 Containment of the crisis: three phases, 3 month USD LIBOR-OIS spread in %, June 2007–November 2009

3
Conditional Containment

The financial crisis started whilst the real economy was still showing vibrant growth, and growth continued for some time after the crisis started. So did inflationary pressures, especially from commodity prices. This economic environment conditioned containment of the crisis. Unlike prior crises in 1987, 1998 and 2001 the authorities did not counter the crisis with immediate reductions in short-term interest rates. The authorities kept interest rates relatively high in order to counter incipient inflation. Containment of the crisis centred on restructuring the so-called shadow banking system, recapitalising financial institutions, resolving particular institutions, and on limiting contagion to the rest of the financial system.

It was not enough. Although the authorities succeeded in defusing many situations that could have blown the financial system apart, they did not succeed in sustaining real economic growth. In the United States, United Kingdom and Continental Europe, real GDP peaked in the first or second quarter of 2008. Thereafter, the real economy started to shrink, and this put renewed pressure on asset prices, market liquidity, capital of major financial institutions and funding liquidity. Ultimately, this pressure caused the dam to burst on 15 September 2008, when Lehman Brothers declared bankruptcy.

Macroeconomic policy

For much of the first year of the crisis, the real economy continued to expand. The crisis appeared to be having little or no effect on economic activity. Indeed, during the latter half of 2007 and the first months of 2008, commodity prices surged. Many market participants expected that the crisis would be short-lived, with minimal disruption to real economic activity as had been the case in 1987, 1998 and 2001.

In fact, that is just what official forecasts were saying (see Figure 3.1). Forecasts made in the fall of 2007 for 2008 and 2009 showed that governments and central banks expected growth to continue despite the crisis. In the United States the November 2007 forecast by the Council of Economic Advisers called for real growth of 2.7% in 2008 and 3% in 2009, somewhat, but not significantly, below the forecasts made a year earlier in 2006. For the Eurozone, the ECB forecast in October 2007 that real growth would be 2.2% in 2008 and 2.1% in 2009. In the United Kingdom the Government predicted in October 2007 that real growth in 2008 would be 2% to 2.5% and that growth in 2009 would be 2.5% to 3%. The Bank of England made a similar forecast in its November 2007 Inflation Report. Its central forecast called for a slight fall in growth in 2008 to about 2%, before a pick up in growth to nearly 3% in 2009 and 2010. A fall in output was considered so remote a possibility that it did not even appear on the fan chart that the Bank used to present its economic forecasts. That meant the Bank considered the possibility of a recession to be less than 5%.[1]

Nor did price forecasts contain any hint of deflation. In the United States the Council of Economic Advisers forecast in November 2007 that prices would continue to increase at about 2% per annum in 2008, 2009 and 2010. If anything there would be a slight increase in inflation.

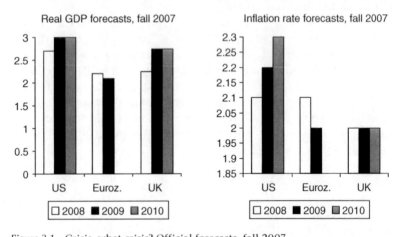

Figure 3.1   Crisis, what crisis? Official forecasts, fall 2007

Sources: For United States: Economic Report of the President forecast made in November 2007; for Eurozone: European Commission, Directorate General for Economic and Financial Affairs Affairs forecast made in October 2007; for UK: Pre-budget Report, October 2007.

The ECB forecast similar rates of inflation for the Eurozone for 2008 and 2009, as did the UK government and the Bank of England for the United Kingdom. If anything, the pressures on prices in the early stages of the crisis were strongly in the upward direction as a result of an ongoing boom in commodity prices, particularly oil.

Against this macroeconomic background, central banks in Europe kept interest rates relatively high for the first stage of the crisis (see Figure 3.2). In the United Kingdom the Bank of England left Bank Rate unchanged until December 2007, when it reduced the rate by 25 basis points from 5.75% to 5.5%. There were two additional rate cuts during the first months of 2008, but Bank Rate was still at 5% in October 2008, more than a year after the crisis started. The ECB kept its refinancing rate at 4% for practically the first twelve months of the crisis, and actually increased rates in July 2008 from 4% to 4.25%. It was not until October 2008 that the ECB cut rates below 4%.

Only in the United States did the central bank engage in significant reductions in interest rates. Soon after the crisis broke (September 2007), the Federal Reserve reduced the Fed funds rate by 50 basis points. It followed with further cuts in October (25 basis points), and December (25 basis points), but this still left the Fed funds rate at 4.25%. Only in January 2008 did the Fed start to cut rates aggressively, with two cuts totalling 125 basis points, taking the Fed Funds rate down to 3%. In 2001 in contrast, the Fed had already started to cut rates at the beginning of the year in response to the collapse of the dot.com bubble,

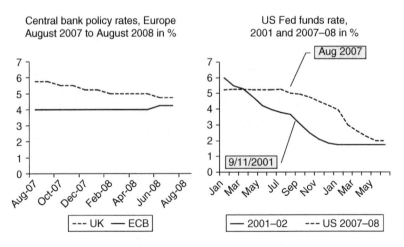

Figure 3.2 Interest rate policy, Eurozone, UK and US, 2007–08

and the Fed kept right on reducing rates after the 9/11 terrorist attacks. Correspondingly the economy is likely to have had considerably more monetary stimulus entering 2002 than it had entering 2008.

Conditional containment – an overview

Overall, therefore, actions to contain the crisis were largely limited to measures within the financial sphere (see Figure 3.3). That is where the crisis was perceived to have started, and that is where authorities attempted to resolve it. It was akin to defusing a series of bombs that could have exploded the financial system and derailed the real economy.

The most dangerous was the shadow banking system with all its tentacles, including conduits, SIVs, monolines, auction rate securities and the credit derivative market infrastructure. Defusing this was critical to keeping the core financial system intact and functioning. In addition, the authorities had to resolve specific institutions, including IKB and the Landesbanken (Germany), Northern Rock (UK), Bear Stearns (US), IndyMac (US), Fannie Mae (US) and Freddie Mac (US). Although the authorities in each of the countries took decisions based on the situation as they saw it at the time, a pattern gradually emerged from the resolutions that the authorities implemented: no retail depositor lost money, and few, if any, wholesale creditors experienced losses.

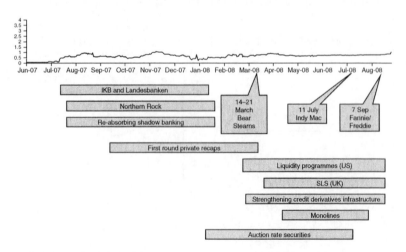

Figure 3.3   Conditional containment overview, August 2007–September 2008 (LIBOR-OIS spread in %)

July–August 2007: IKB and the German Landesbanken

The first casualty of the crisis was arguably Industrie Kreditbank (IKB), a German bank that specialised in lending to small to medium-sized enterprises at relatively low spreads. Although this business model supported the growth of the German Mittelstand, it did not generate much profit. To supplement the meagre profits generated by its core business IKB had established a subsidiary based in Ireland, called Rhineland Funding. This was effectively a structured investment vehicle whose main investment was CDOs of sub-prime asset-based securities (ABS). Rhineland Funding financed itself through the issuance of asset-backed commercial paper with a liquidity backstop from IKB. This back-up liquidity line was substantially in excess of the capital of IKB.

When liquidity in the asset-backed securities market started to dry up in July 2007, so did the ability of Rhineland Funding to issue new asset-backed commercial paper. Accordingly, it became apparent that Rhineland Funding would attempt to call on its back-up liquidity line with IKB. If Rhineland Funding did so, IKB would not have been able to perform. It did not have the cash required to meet the call, and, even if it had, it could not have booked the large exposure to Rhineland Funding that would have resulted from the line being drawn. Industrie Kreditbank faced the prospect of immediate failure, and the German authorities reckoned that this would have adverse consequences for the German banking system as a whole.

Accordingly, the German government took immediate steps to rescue IKB. The German state-owned development bank, Kreditanstalt für Wiederaufbau (KfW), was the controlling shareholder in IKB, and the German Finance Minister was the Chairman of the Supervisory Board of KfW. Over the weekend of 28–29 July, KfW resolved to provide liquidity assistance to IKB supplemented by a syndicate of banks doing business in Germany.

This initial liquidity assistance had to be supplemented several times with additional liquidity and capital, increasingly and then exclusively from KfW. In November KfW and a banking syndicate agreed to guarantee certain risks on IKB's balance sheet. In January 2008, KfW subscribed to a convertible bond issue and in February/March 2008 to issues of new equity. Upon completion of the final equity issue in August 2008, KfW held over 90% of the equity of IKB all of which it subsequently (October 2008) sold to a private equity investor, Lone Star, at a loss of over €8 billion. But no depositor and no creditor lost money.

A similar story and a similar fate applied to Landesbank Sachsen. Its business model also called for making loans to German enterprises at low spreads. To supplement its income Landesbank Sachsen had also formed an Irish subsidiary, Sachsen LB Europe plc, similar to Rhineland Funding, which invested in asset-backed securities and financed itself through the issuance of asset-backed commercial paper with a liquidity backstop from Landesbank Sachsen substantially in excess of the capital of Landesbank Sachsen. Again the prospect that this liquidity backstop would be called created the possibility that Landesbank Sachsen itself would fail.

This would have severely undermined the entire German system of Landesbanken, for this reversal came at the time when the Landesbanken had been stripped of their access to government guarantees. Originally, the Landesbanken were set up as 'central banks' for the German savings banks, and each of the Landesbanken enjoyed a guarantee from the German state in which they were headquartered. As the German states generally had high (usually AAA) ratings, this meant that the Landesbanken could borrow in the wholesale markets at or close to the government bond rate. Usually the Landesbanken passed most of this funding advantage on to their borrowers in the form of lower interest rates for credit. But in 2001 the European Commission had ruled that after 2005 the Landesbanken could no longer issue debt with a government guarantee. This led the Landesbanken to raise very substantial sums in the markets prior to the expiration of their ability to obtain guarantees – sums that they invested to a very significant extent in mortgage-backed securities or in vehicles, such as Sachsen LB Europe plc, that in turn raised further money in the markets to invest in such securities.

But when Sachsen LB Europe ran into liquidity trouble in August 2007, its owner and sponsor, Landesbank Sachsen, no longer had routine access to the guarantee of the state of Saxony. That meant that Landesbank Sachsen would have to seek funds in the market to meet the call for liquidity from its Irish subsidiary. The market was unwilling to provide such funds. To prevent the failure of the bank the German state of Saxony, the principal owner of Landesbank Sachsen, quickly provided an extraordinary credit guarantee and arranged for an emergency €17 billion liquidity line from the German savings banks (17 August). Rapidly thereafter (on 26 August) it agreed to a rescue merger for the troubled institution with Landesbank Baden Wurttemberg to take effect on 1 January 2008. This not only stabilised Landesbank Sachsen, but also created the impression that the German provinces and German federal state would find methods to save any future Landesbank that experienced similar difficulty.

August 2007–February 2008: Northern Rock

The closure of the securitisation markets in August 2007 created a funding squeeze on those institutions that had relied on securitisation for funding. Northern Rock was a perfect example of the so-called originate-to-distribute model (see Chapter 2). It used a combination of brokers and branches to originate residential mortgages, which it warehoused pending securitisation and funding through the market by investors. Although it had attracted approximately £20 billion in retail deposits, the bulk of its funding came through the proceeds of securitisation issues, especially those issued via its master trust arrangement Granite, and wholesale deposits sourced in the money market.[2]

The Northern Rock funding structure depended critically on maintaining a flow of unsecured wholesale deposits sufficient to finance the gap between retail deposits and the net proceeds from the securitisation issues. In terms of the assets to be financed, this included the mortgages in the warehouse pending securitisation, non-conforming mortgages that did not comply with the requirements of the securitisation programmes, and other assets, such as Treasury assets. But it also included the mortgages that effectively over-collateralised the securitisation issues. These assets remained on the Northern Rock balance sheet and had to be financed (see Figure 3.4), even though they were

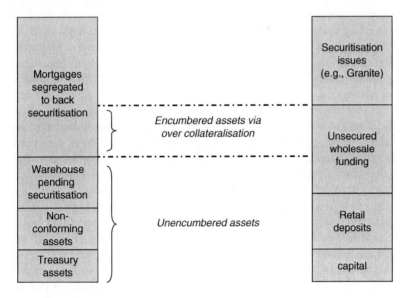

Figure 3.4 Northern Rock

encumbered (pledged to the bondholders in the securitisation and covered bond programmes).

Now from the standpoint of the wholesale depositor, only Northern Rock's unencumbered assets would be readily available to meet the obligations to the wholesale depositor. With the securitisation market out of commission, the ability of Northern Rock to turn its unencumbered assets into ready cash was severely compromised. Northern Rock had no back-up lines of liquidity, either with other banks or with central banks, such as the Bank of England. Northern Rock assumed that either the securitisation markets would reopen in time for it to execute its planned jumbo securitisation in mid-September, that it would be able to arrange repo facilities with another bank, or that the Bank of England would provide a bridging loan on the basis of Northern Rock's mortgage collateral.

The trouble was that Northern Rock's best assets were already encumbered to back its securitisation issues. The amount of unencumbered assets held by the bank was less than the amount of wholesale and retail deposits outstanding, and the quality of the unencumbered assets (particularly the Treasury assets) was such that private sector lenders were unwilling to take these assets as collateral.

By early September it became apparent that the securitisation market would not reopen in time for Northern Rock to complete the jumbo securitisation issue that it had planned for mid-September. Lloyds TSB indicated that it would be willing to execute a rescue acquisition of Northern Rock, provided the Bank of England provided a backstop liquidity line to Lloyds TSB. The Tripartite authorities refused to accede to this condition, and Northern Rock approached the Bank of England for a loan.

However, this loan could not be under the Bank's normal lending facilities. Northern Rock did not have sufficient collateral that met the Bank's eligibility requirements. The loan would be a lender of last resort facility. When the public learned of this in a BBC news flash on the evening of 13 September 2007, it alarmed rather than reassured the public. Depositors flooded the bank's call centre and internet banking facilities. These quickly became overloaded, and incited many people to get out early the next day to their branches to find out what was going on with the bank and their money. Although the Bank of England did in fact provide Northern Rock with emergency liquidity assistance on 14 September, queues quickly formed outside some Northern Rock branches. The media promptly flashed images of these queues of people demanding their money back across the nation and around the world, and that led to further queues. For the first time in 140 years there was a run on a British bank.

Fears for their money accelerated as it became apparent that the UK deposit compensation scheme (FSCS) at the time fully protected only the first £2,000 of the depositor's money and 90% of the next £33,000. Moreover, as the national newspaper websites pointed out, it could take months for the FSCS to process and pay the claims. Rather than take the chance that they would have to wait months to get 90% or less of their money back, depositors ran on the bank. This was entirely rational for them to do, and the run only stopped on Monday 17 September when the Chancellor of the Exchequer indicated that the Government would guarantee the deposits of Northern Rock and that no retail depositor would lose money from Northern Rock or from any other bank that got itself into a situation similar to that of Northern Rock.

Northern Rock had plainly failed, but there was no practical way to resolve the bank. Under UK law at the time, banks were to be resolved through the application of normal corporate bankruptcy or insolvency procedures. But putting Northern Rock into administration would have exposed the fact that the FSCS could not in fact rapidly compensate depositors. That would have undermined the entire deposit guarantee system and caused queues, not just at Northern Rock branches, but at many banks across the United Kingdom.

Consequently, the authorities had no alternative but to keep Northern Rock open and to prop it up with continued lending from the Bank of England. Efforts were made to sell the bank to private sector investors, but these demanded such large subsidies from the Government to take over the ailing bank that the Government eventually made the decision to take Northern Rock into temporary public ownership. This was done in February 2008 pursuant to the Banking Special Provisions Act.

August 2007 to February 2008: reabsorbing shadow banking

Shadow banking represented the greatest threat to financial stability. During the boom a very extensive shadow banking system had developed largely around conduits and structured investment vehicles (SIVs) sponsored by major financial institutions (see Chapter 2). These conduits and SIVs financed themselves largely through the asset-backed commercial paper market. They raised short-term liabilities to finance long-term assets. They performed the same type of maturity transformation as banks, and they were susceptible to the same type of liquidity pressures as banks, but they were not regulated as banks, nor did the conduits and SIVs have direct access to central banks as a back-up source of liquidity.

What conduits and SIVs did have, was access to their sponsor banks, either on a contractual or de facto basis. If the conduit or SIV could not raise funds in the commercial paper market, they could turn to their sponsor bank for funding if the sponsor bank had provided a back-up liquidity line, as many had done. Even if the conduit or SIV had not provided a formal back-up liquidity line, the sponsor bank still had an interest in assuring that the conduit or SIV did not collapse. This interest was twofold. First, the sponsor bank might wish to prevent the conduit or SIV from conducting a fire-sale of its assets, lest such sales depress the price of the very same securities that the bank held on its own balance sheet. Second, and more important, the sponsor bank might wish to avoid the risk to its reputation that could arise from the collapse of a vehicle that it had created, sponsored and managed.

So when it became apparent on 9 August 2007 that the market could no longer value accurately asset-backed securities and CDOs based on US sub-prime mortgages, liquidity pressure immediately spread to banks generally. Banks had either sponsored the conduits and SIVs that could no longer finance themselves, invested directly in CDOs and ABS based on sub-prime mortgages, or made loans to investors, such as hedge funds, that were collateralised by CDOs and ABS based on sub-prime mortgages. So a collapse in the market liquidity of CDOs and ABS quickly translated itself into a liquidity squeeze on practically all major banks.

As a consequence, the spread of LIBOR over the overnight index swap rate – the temperature gauge for the financial system – immediately spiked. The spread for one month $ LIBOR rose from less than 10 to more than 50 basis points practically overnight. To prevent a catastrophic collapse in the banking system, the ECB provided financing to banks in unlimited amounts on the basis of collateral that the banks had pledged with the national central banks that were members of the ECB. This was the classic central bank response to an incipient panic – lend freely to solvent banks on the basis of good collateral. The Federal Reserve (2008: 26) reduced the spread of the discount rate over the target Fed funds rate from 100 basis points to 50 basis points and extended the maximum term of a loan from the discount window to 30 days with an option for the banks to renew the loan as long as they remained in sound financial condition.

Ordinarily, such infusions of liquidity are sufficient to return a market to normal operation quickly. In this case, it wasn't. The securitisation market for mortgages had stalled, and it remained stalled. New issuance ceased, and investors refused to roll over a good portion of the asset-backed commercial paper issued by conduits and SIVs. Total asset-backed commercial paper (ABCP) outstanding peaked at $1.2 trillion on 8 August 2007 and went into a downward spiral immediately thereafter, falling $260 billion or 21% over the next seven weeks to the end of September and then falling a further $120 billion by the end of the year (see Figure 3.5).

Nor did liquidity return to the market for CDOs and asset-backed securities. This had never been high to begin with, and restrictions on the provision of information to anyone who was not already an investor in the security made it even more difficult to make a market in these securities. The little information that was available was not good. Defaults on the sub-prime mortgages underlying the ABS and CDOs were continuing to mount, and recoveries on the mortgages that had defaulted were continuing to fall. The few transactions that were being done were being done at what banks considered to be fire-sale prices below the long-term value of the cash flows that they considered would ultimately flow from the security. Consequently, many banks opted to continue to hold their inventory of CDOs and ABS and to sell positions in other instruments in order to help raise the liquidity that they needed in order to meet maturing liabilities. This spread the decline in prices from CDOs and ABS based on sub-prime to the market more generally.

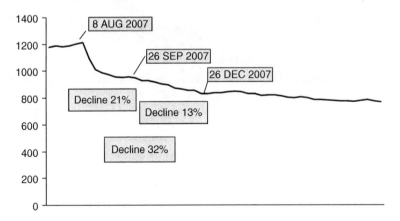

Figure 3.5 Asset-backed commercial paper outstanding, July 2008–July 2009 in $ billions

Source: Federal Reserve Board.

However, the core of the financial system held up. The major banks effectively took responsibility for assuring an orderly continuation or wind-down of the conduits and SIVs that they had sponsored. Either they took these conduits and SIVs onto the balance sheet or they reached agreement with investors on how the pain would be shared. For example, at the end of October HSBC announced plans to bail out two of the SIVs (total assets $45 billion) that it had sponsored, and in early December Citigroup announced a similar plan for six of its SIVs (total assets $49 billion). In practically all cases senior debt providers to the conduit or SIV came out whole.

The major banks also moved to replenish the capital that had been destroyed when they had to mark down their trading positions in CDOs, ABS and leveraged loans. Citigroup, Merrill Lynch, UBS, RBS, Barclays and other banks raised significant amounts of new capital in the final months of 2007 from third-party investors. In total major banks raised nearly $300 billion in new capital, predominantly from private sources, to offset losses and rebuild capital positions (see Figure 3.6).

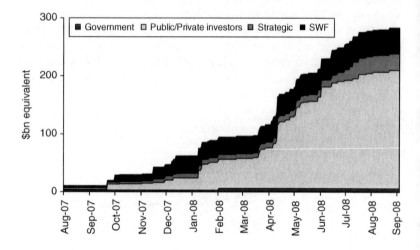

Figure 3.6 Capital raised by 32 largest banks by type (cumulative), 1 August 2007 to 15 September 2008 in $ billions

Note: The banks included are Bank of America, Barclays, Bayerische Landesbank, BNP Paribas, Citigroup, Commerzbank, Credit Agricole, Credit Suisse, Deutsche Bank, Dexia, Fortis, Goldman Sachs, HBOS, HSBC, IKB, ING, JPMorgan Chase, Lehman, Lloyds TSB, Merrill Lynch, Mitsubishi UFJ, Mizuho, Morgan Stanley, National City Corp., RBS, Santander, Société Generale, Sumitomo Mitsui, UBS, Wachovia, Washington Mutual and Wells Fargo.

Source: Bloomberg.

March 2008: Liquidity tightens and Bear Stearns fails

As February turned to March, liquidity tightened again in the money markets. In mid-February UBS announced a loss of over CHF 12 billion after taking write-downs of over CHF 15 billion on its portfolio of US mortgages and mortgage-backed securities, including a loss of over CHF 2 billion on Alt-A mortgages. Such mortgages were considered to be better than sub-prime, although they did not require documentation of the borrower's income. The markdown at UBS forced other firms across the industry to take similar markdowns and those with significant port-folios of or activities in sub-prime and Alt-A mortgages immediately experienced pressure in the money markets. These included in ascend-ing order of size, like dominoes poised to topple over, Peloton Partners, Carlyle Capital Corporation, Thornburg Mortgage, Bear Stearns, Lehman Brothers and Fannie Mae.

On 29 February Peloton Partners, whose 2007 performance had topped the hedge funds league table, failed. It had bet too early on a revival of the market for sub-prime asset-backed securities. On 5 March Carlyle Capital Corporation, a $22 billion hedge fund listed in Amsterdam that had invested extensively in US mortgage-backed securities, failed to meet margin calls. On 10 March Thornburg Mortgage, a non-bank mortgage provider that specialised in Alt-A mortgages, crumbled under a liquidity squeeze. Despite the introduction of two special liquidity programmes by the Federal Reserve on 7 March (see "March–April 2008: central banks open the liquidity taps wider" below) pressure mounted on the other major players in the mortgage-backed securities market, especially Bear Stearns. By 10 March major banks were refusing to roll over maturing funding lines to Bear Stearns and hedge funds were directing settlement of their trades away from Bear Stearns to reduce their free cash balances at the firm. A run was on (Cohan 2009).

This continued through the week, and the prospects grew that Bear Stearns would have to declare bankruptcy. That would have triggered losses at its counterparties around the world and, authorities thought, undermined the credit derivatives market, where Bear was a major counterparty. To avoid these repercussions the Federal Reserve stepped in to make funding available to JPMorgan Chase to facilitate the bank's takeover of Bear Stearns. Initially, the parties struck a deal at $2 per share on 16 March but this was raised to $10 per share during the course of the following week so as to be certain of obtaining the approval of the Bear Stearns shareholders.[3]

To support the transaction the Federal Reserve agreed to provide a $30 billion loan to JPMorgan Chase based on collateral comprising illiquid mortgage-backed securities. This loan was non-recourse to JPMorgan Chase beyond a first loss of $1 billion. The sole security for the Federal Reserve's loan was the portfolio of troubled securities that had been pledged as collateral. As this collateral declined in value, the losses incurred by the Fed could mount. Effectively, the Federal Reserve was putting what was ultimately $29 billion of taxpayers' money at risk in order to eliminate the possibility that Bear Stearns could fail in a disorderly manner and cause havoc in the financial markets. No stakeholder in Bear Stearns experienced any loss with the exception of Bear Stearns' management and stockholders. Even stockholders realised something.

The Fed had sent a signal that it would extend the safety net of the lender of last resort beyond commercial banks to non-bank firms whose failure was too complex to contemplate. Preserving financial stability had the utmost priority.

March–April 2008: central banks open the liquidity taps wider

Indeed, the Federal Reserve had confirmed the signal sent by the rescue of Bear Stearns by introducing on 16 March the Primary Dealer Credit Facility. This allowed non-bank primary dealers routine access to the Federal Reserve's discount window for the first time, ending the traditional distinction that the Fed had drawn between non-bank firms and banks. In addition, the Fed cut the spread of the discount window rate over the Fed funds rate to 25 basis points, effectively eliminating much if not all of the penalty rate that had been traditionally imposed on borrowing from the discount window. The Fed also extended the maximum term for such loans from 30 to 90 days. These measures supplemented the previously announced (11 March) Term Securities Lending Facility, whereby the Fed would extend credit for a period of up to 28 days rather than overnight. This became effective at the end of March. In addition, the Fed increased the amount of Term Auction Credit from $60 billion (12 March) to $100 billion (2 April) and then to $150 billion (28 May). All in all, the Fed initiatives sent a strong signal that the Fed stood ready to provide significant liquidity support to the markets, including non-bank primary dealers such as Lehman Brothers, who had come under funding pressures similar to that experienced by Bear Stearns.

In the United Kingdom the Bank of England and the Treasury also took steps to improve liquidity. On 21 April the Bank of England announced the introduction of a £100 billion Special Liquidity Scheme (SLS) which allowed banks to swap AAA-rated securities based on loans originated before 31 December 2007 for government securities. This window was to remain open for a period of six months, and it allowed the banks to obtain financing for their legacy loan portfolios for a period of up to three years. To protect itself against credit risk, the Bank of England insisted that the collateral have a AAA rating at inception and throughout the life of the loan. The Bank also imposed a healthy haircut on the value of the collateral. The banks utilising the SLS received Treasury securities which they could either sell or repo in the market to generate cash.

March–August: controlling credit derivatives

Credit derivatives were one of the key elements of interconnectedness that led the US authorities to make the decision to rescue Bear Stearns. This market had developed rapidly during the boom (see Chapter 2) and the authorities had early identified flaws in the structure of the credit derivatives market as something that could give rise to financial instability. As early as 2005 the authorities had identified that unauthorised assignments and unconfirmed transactions posed a significant risk, and they had put pressure on the leading participants in the market to eliminate these deficiencies.

Considerable progress had already been made prior to the onset of the crisis (see Chapter 2), but more remained to be done. The backlog in unconfirmed transactions was still too high, and the procedures for settling CDS after the failure of a major reference entity were still on a case-by-case basis. Nor was there an assurance that the market could survive the failure of one of the major dealers. Consequently, the authorities demanded that the industry accelerate its efforts to solve these problems or face the prospect that credit derivatives activity would be limited.

This regulatory pressure led the industry to adopt so-called 'tear-up' procedures that took thousands of transactions that might exist between two dealers and to net these down to a much smaller number of transactions. The old transactions were literally torn up and replaced with a new one. This consolidation led for the first time to a contraction in the volume of outstanding credit derivatives despite an ongoing growth in the volume of new transactions. The total notional value of credit derivatives outstanding fell from $62 trillion at the end of 2007 to $54 trillion in June 2008 and to $38 trillion at the end of 2008. The industry also initiated further improvements in credit event settlement and the procedures for close-out netting with a defaulted counterparty. Finally, the industry – with the encouragement of the regulators began to make preparations for creation of a central counterparty to clear credit derivative transactions (CRMPG 2008: 102–30).

May–June: minimising mayhem from monolines

Monolines were one of the main supports of the shadow banking system (see Chapter 2) and starting in May this support began to buckle as the rating agencies began to downgrade the leading monoline companies. This threatened to weaken the banks that had purchased protection from the monolines and to make it more difficult for municipal borrowers to raise finance, especially in the United States.

Originally, monolines were set up to insure a widely diversified portfolio of municipal bonds against default, and monolines were sufficiently well capitalised and their insurance protection sufficiently well diversified that monolines received a AAA rating. Consequently an issuer could, by buying credit protection from a financial guarantee insurance company, transform the rating of its issue from its own credit rating into the AAA rating of the monoline guaranteeing the issue. That allowed investors to buy the municipal bond issue with a minimum of due diligence on the municipality itself. They could rely on the credit of the monoline.

However, during the boom monolines expanded into writing financial guarantee insurance on CDOs and ABS based on sub-prime mortgages, and they had started to sell credit protection to major banks via credit default swaps with such securities as the reference entity. By the time the crisis broke, CDOs and ABS based on sub-prime accounted for a very large proportion of the total protection insurance written by the monolines. This was akin to a fire insurance company concentrating its coverage in a single town.

This brought the prized AAA rating of the monolines under threat. The rating agencies recognised that the deterioration in sub-prime mortgages made it more likely that the monolines would have to perform simultaneously on a large proportion of the guarantees that they had written. So as the rating agencies downgraded the CDOs and ABS based on sub-prime, they put the ratings of the monolines under review. Moody's started the ball rolling on 13 May following an announcement the previous day by MBIA that it had lost $2.4 billion in the first quarter of 2008.

This immediately raised alarm bells amongst insurance and bank regulators as well as the banks that had bought protection from the monolines. Without a AAA rating, the very basis for the monoline's ongoing business disappeared. It could no longer reasonably expect to insure new issues, and this would cut off the flow of new premiums. It would also trigger demands for collateral from the banks that had bought credit protection from the monolines under credit default swaps.

That potential demand raised the possibility that the monolines would have to allocate high-quality securities from their investment portfolios to serve as collateral for the swap contracts, leaving lesser quality securities as the only backing for the guarantees that they had provided to investors in municipal bonds. This could threaten the ability of the monolines to pay claims on municipal bonds, just at the time when some states, such as California, were experiencing budget shortfalls that made claims on municipal bonds more likely as well.

On 4 June Moody's formally placed Ambac and MBIA, the two leading monolines, under review for a downgrade, and the actual downgrade (initially to Aa3) followed on 19 June for Ambac and to A2 for MBIA along with the statement that the ratings outlook remained negative. The other monolines had suffered similar or worse downgrades.

Essentially, the ratings downgrades sent monolines into run-off. They wrote practically no new business, but continued to earn sufficient investment income and premiums from previously written policies to continue to be able to meet claims when due. To improve their position the monolines entered into commutation agreements with banks and other policyholders that released the monoline from the obligation to meet future claims in exchange for an upfront payment to the policyholder. So the position of the monolines deteriorated, but did so gradually rather than suddenly. This allowed banks to reduce progressively the value that they placed on the protection that they had purchased from the monolines and/or to commute or hedge the exposure that they had to default by a monoline. Again, values had fallen, but no default occurred. Through September 2008 monolines met all of their obligations in full and on time, but the banks that had purchased protection from the monolines had to take increasing losses and/or set aside increasing reserves to account for the increased probability that the monoline might not be able to perform at some point in the future. So the dam had not burst, but the pressure on the markets remained.

2 July–11 July: Countrywide and Indy Mac

Countrywide and IndyMac (a spin-off from Countrywide) had been two of the most aggressive mortgage lenders in the United States. They had high concentrations of sub-prime and Alt-A mortgages (mortgages that did not require borrowers to provide documentation on their incomes). The financial crisis undermined the viability of each of these institutions, and in early July each was resolved with limited or no losses to depositors.

Countrywide was the largest mortgage bank in the United States, originating at one point about 17% of all mortgages in the United States, many of which were non-conforming (ineligible for sale to Freddie Mac or Fannie Mae). Countrywide relied extensively on securitisation to finance these assets, and when the securitisation market froze in August 2007, Countrywide, like Northern Rock, began to experience liquidity difficulties. Unlike Northern Rock, however, Countrywide obtained new capital from another bank, Bank of America, first in the form of convertible preferred stock (August 2007) and then a full-scale acquisition. This had been announced in January 2008, and, after regulatory approvals had been secured, the merger was completed on 2 July 2008. This averted the possibility of major losses to creditors and depositors of Countrywide.

IndyMac had originally been a subsidiary of Countrywide, but was spun off to shareholders as a separate institution. It followed the same aggressive lending policies as its erstwhile parent, specialising in Alt-A mortgages. At the end of June 2008 IndyMac had assets of $30 billion and deposits of $19 billion, but concerns were being voiced – by Representative Charles Schumer of the House Banking Committee among others – about the quality of the bank's assets. On 11 July, after a week-long bank run, the Office of Thrift Supervision closed IndyMac FSB. The FDIC was appointed conservator and transferred substantially all of the assets as well as the non-brokered insured deposits to a new bridge bank that opened for business as usual on Monday 14 July, assuring that depositors continued to have access to their money. The FDIC also announced that it would make an immediate advance dividend payment to uninsured depositors equal to 50% of the amount over the insurance limit with further payments to come, depending on the speed and amount of the recoveries that the FDIC could make as the administrator of the estate of the failed bank.

This was the seventh and largest bank to have failed in the United States during the crisis, and the deposits of IndyMac were more than three times the value of the other six banks that had failed up to that point in the crisis. This would strain the FDIC's human and financial resources. Prior to resolution the FDIC had sent hundreds of staff to the bank's headquarters in Pasadena to sort out the data on IndyMac's accounts so that the resolution could be handled smoothly. Still the accounts were not in good enough shape to attract an outside bidder. That meant the FDIC had to establish a bridge bank. This would require further staff. The financial cost was also high. Originally, the FDIC estimated the cost of resolution to be $4 to $8 billion or about 10% to

20% of the total deposit insurance fund – enough to raise questions as to whether levies would have to be instituted to replenish the fund despite the ongoing crisis.

August: settlement of auction rate securities actions

In August, another element of the shadow banking market, the auction rate securities (ARS) market, posed additional pressure on major firms, including UBS, Citigroup, Merrill Lynch and Morgan Stanley. These firms agreed to settle charges that they had misled investors and issuers in connection with the origination and distribution of auction rate securities, and in connection with those settlements the affected firms had to take billions of assets onto their balance sheets and incur hundreds of millions of dollars in losses, further depleting their capital. This was damaging in and of itself, but it also raised the prospect that banks might be immediately held to account for other transgressions.

Auction rate securities were another example of off-balance sheet maturity transformation engaged in by investment banks during the boom, and by 2008 there were over $200 billion of such securities outstanding, largely in the hands of institutional investors and high net worth individuals. Auction rate securities were structured as a long-term bond or preferred stock but with a variable coupon equal to the rate that cleared the periodic Dutch auction for the security that the investment bank would hold among investors. The auction mechanism was presented to investors as a means of providing liquidity, and the perceived ability to get out of the investment at the next auction date induced investors during the boom to bid for the securities on the basis that they were effectively short-term instruments. This provided issuers with a long-term security at short-term (lower) rates.

However, this left both issuers and investors with a significant risk. What would happen if the auction failed? In such an instance the documentation envisaged that the rate payable on the security would revert to a punitive rate, usually significantly above the long-term rate that the issuer would have paid had it originally issued the security on a standard long-term fixed rate basis. So there was a sting in the tail for the issuer. There was also a sting in the tail for the investor, since s/he could not readily sell the security. Although the investor might benefit from the higher long-term rate, the security was effectively frozen, especially if the failure of the auction resulted from concern about the issuer's credit condition.

Previously, when auctions had failed, the investment bank sponsoring the issue acted as a reserve bidder. But as sell orders mounted relative to buy orders, acting as the reserve bidder became increasingly expensive – a cost that the principal underwriters (Merrill Lynch, Citigroup, UBS and Morgan Stanley) could ill afford to bear as they were coming under increasing capital pressure themselves as a result of trading losses. Consequently, starting in February 2008 these banks declined to act as reserve bidders as they had done in the past, and the interest rate on the bonds reverted to the punitive rate.

This provoked protests, particularly from the states and municipalities that had utilised this market for much of their financing. The shift to the higher reserve rate threatened to raise municipal financing costs and depress their ability to fund critical spending on roads, hospitals and other elements of the social infrastructure – just at the time when the municipal bond insurance companies were suffering downgrades that constrained their ability to insure new municipal bond issues.

Consequently both issuers and investors welcomed the initiative of Attorney General Cuomo of the State of New York to bring to justice the investment banks that had underwritten ARS. Rather than engage in a long and potentially losing battle, the investment banks settled, agreeing in August 2008 to purchase the ARS held by individual investors and bring them onto to their own balance sheet at a reduced rate of interest to the issuer and to employ best efforts to liquefy the holdings of institutional investors. Again, investors were protected, but pressure on the banks increased.

7 September 2008: Federal government places Fannie and Freddie under conservatorship

At the very heart of the US mortgage market stood two government-sponsored enterprises, Fannie Mae and Freddie Mac, and by the beginning of September 2008 both were buckling under pressure in the wholesale funding markets. These were government-sponsored enterprises with a mandate to promote the mortgage market in the United States. They held or guaranteed $5 trillion of mortgages on homes across the United States, about 40% of the $12 trillion of mortgages outstanding, and their bonds were held by central banks and other institutional investors around the world. As government-sponsored enterprises, it was commonly thought that the US government stood behind the two companies, even though there was no formal guarantee.

The government had strengthened that perception in July, when it announced that it had increased the credit line available to Fannie and Freddie and that it would seek authority to buy equity in the troubled companies if necessary. That calmed the markets temporarily, but by early September, doubts were again mounting that Fannie and Freddie would have sufficient resources to meet their obligations. Fannie and Freddie were staring at the prospect of default, and the US authorities had to consider the adverse consequences that such a default would have on the economy at large, the credit standing of the US government, the ability of banks across the country to continue to finance mortgages and the exchange rate of the dollar.

On 7 September the US authorities announced that they were putting Fannie Mae and Freddie Mac under the conservatorship of the Federal Housing Finance Administration. Effectively, the federal government took over both institutions. The Government promptly installed new management and it took a controlling stake in the equity of each company. The Government further stated that for the duration of the crisis Fannie and Freddie would continue their purchases of mortgages from banks around the country in order to promote the stabilisation of the mortgage market, although the long-term intent was to wind down each company's activity so that neither company represented such a contingent credit risk for the taxpayer.

August–September 2008: the limits of conditional containment

But the rescue of Fannie and Freddie illustrated the limits of conditional containment. This was a strategy that ultimately depended on economic conditions improving. They had not done so during the course of 2008, partly perhaps due to the macroeconomic policy that the authorities elected to pursue in the early stages of the crisis to combat inflation. The underlying economy was getting worse not better as the year 2008 progressed. That made it more likely that the losses that banks would have to take on both their trading books and banking books would grow, not shrink.

That economic background put increasing pressure on the financial system and made it more difficult for the authorities to continue to pursue resolution policies that protected creditors. The economic environment meant that more and possibly larger institutions would require resolution at the same time that past exercises had strained the capacity of the authorities to deal with further problems. Indeed, even the Federal Reserve was at the limits of what it could do without seeking further approval from Congress.

4
Moving towards Meltdown

On 15 September 2008 the nature of the crisis abruptly changed. Lehman Brothers failed. It was a leading stand-alone investment bank and one of the largest participants in equity and fixed income markets around the world. It had nearly $700 billion of liabilities to firms and individuals around the world. It was counterparty to practically every major financial institution. It had hundreds of thousands of trades due to settle in the US, UK and other markets.

The failure of Lehmans abruptly reversed the expectation that the US authorities had created in March 2008 when they rescued Bear Stearns on the grounds that it was 'too interconnected' to fail (see Chapter 3). Loss given resolution suddenly appeared to be quite significant. Risk premiums skyrocketed; market confidence evaporated. Market participants immediately focused on who the next candidates for resolution might be, and began to run on these institutions.

One institution after another required resolution (see Figure 4.1). Not all resolutions proceeded smoothly and some imposed unexpected losses, further destabilising the situation. Although central banks vastly expanded their liquidity support operations, these alone were insufficient to stem the tide. Governments were pushed into providing blanket guarantees of retail deposits or bank liabilities, only to see the market in some cases doubt their ability to fulfil such guarantees. In the United States, a lame duck administration could not get Congress to enact promptly the emergency measures that it had proclaimed to be essential, and after Congress finally did pass the measures, the administration could not immediately implement them. The global financial system moved towards meltdown.[1]

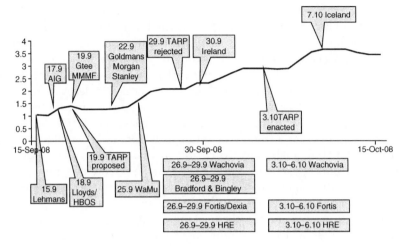

Figure 4.1   Moving towards Meltdown, 3-month $ LIBOR-OIS spread in %, 15 September to 15 October 2008

15 September: Lehmans fails

The failure of Lehmans caused immediate and severe disruption around the world. Suddenly, investors who had expected to receive either cash or securities from Lehmans had to face the fact that these would not be forthcoming on schedule or possibly not forthcoming at all. Suddenly, investors who had pledged securities to Lehmans as collateral for loans from Lehmans had to face the fact that they were at risk from the failure of Lehmans. Although the investor could offset the collateral against the value of the loan that it had received from Lehmans, the investor remained exposed for the amount of any excess collateral that it had pledged to Lehmans. At a minimum, the investor would have severe difficulty in regaining access to its securities, for they would be frozen whilst the administrator worked out the full details of Lehmans' assets and liabilities. And, if the investor had allowed Lehmans to re-hypothecate the securities pledged to Lehmans as collateral, the investor had to face the fact that it had effectively lost title to those securities and had become an unsecured general creditor of the Lehmans subsidiary to which it had pledged the securities.[2] In such cases (and they were many, for re-hypothecation was commonly called for in Lehmans' prime brokerage agreements), the investors were facing the potential of very serious loss.

In the United States, the authorities limited such disruption through keeping the US broker-dealer subsidiary, Lehman Brothers Inc., in operation for a few days following the declaration of bankruptcy by the parent holding company. This allowed the broker-dealer to complete settlement on trades that were in process at the time that the parent company declared bankruptcy. It also allowed Barclays to conduct some due diligence on the US broker-dealer so that it could buy the assets and assume some of the liabilities of the US broker-dealer – a deal which was announced on 17 September and completed on 22 September 2008.

But the quick resolution of the US broker-dealer subsidiary did not resolve Lehmans as a whole. For Lehmans was far larger and far more international than Bear Stearns. The US broker-dealer was a significant part, but only a part, of a much bigger and very complex group. In particular, the group had very extensive operations in the UK through Lehman Brothers International (Europe). This conducted the group's business in Europe and was the booking centre for much of the firm's global business, including its prime brokerage business. The group also had a bank in Germany, Lehman Brothers Bankhaus AG. Altogether it had subsidiaries in 20 different countries.

The failure of the US parent left the Lehmans subsidiaries in the UK and other countries with no alternative but to declare bankruptcy immediately. There was no scope and no cash available to permit the non-US entities to remain in operation so that trades in process of completion could be settled. So failure outside the United States was immediate and disorderly, and it is estimated that it will take several years to resolve the bankruptcy completely.

15–17 September: Fed rescues AIG

The failure of Lehmans had immediate and severe knock-on effects. On 15 September, the same day as Lehman Brothers declared bankruptcy, the Federal Reserve rode to the rescue of AIG, one of the world's largest insurance companies. Initially, the Fed provided $20 billion in secured funding to AIG's insurance subsidiaries. Two days later, on 17 September, the amount had grown to $85 billion, and it was clear that the Fed was acting as a lender of last resort. Collateral for the loan was a lien on the holding company's interest in its insurance subsidiaries around the world and the fee for the loan was the right to acquire up to 79.9% of the equity of AIG. Effectively, the US government had taken control of one of the world's largest insurance companies.

AIG had to seek this assistance because it could not meet, following its own credit downgrade the previous week, the requirement that it post collateral against the hundreds of billions of credit default protection contracts that it had written against various reference entities, including CDOs of sub-prime mortgage-backed securities. As long as AIG had had its AAA rating, practically all of its counterparties were willing to accept its credit on an unsecured basis. They reckoned that AIG would be good for the payment that it would have to make, if the reference entity were to default. But if AIG lost that AAA rating, counterparties would wish to assure themselves that they would still receive the protection that they had bargained for. So it had been quite common for counterparties under the ISDA contracts that documented the credit default swaps to demand that AIG collateralise its exposure to them if AIG lost its AAA rating.

AIG's counterparties were the world's leading financial institutions. If they could no longer count on receiving the protection that they had bought from AIG, they would have had to take extensive losses on the assets that they had insured with AIG. Such losses would have significantly reduced the capital of many financial institutions under-mining their own ability to attract funding and raising the prospect that they too would fail. The Federal Reserve's emergency liquidity assist-ance to AIG enabled AIG to survive and to make good on the promises that it had made to other financial institutions to provide credit protec-tion. Shortly after receiving the emergency liquidity assistance from the Fed, AIG Financial Products began to unwind the credit default swaps that it had concluded with major counterparties around the world. This effectively immunised the rest of the financial system from further deterioration in the condition of AIG. The risk of AIG now rested with the Federal Reserve rather than the financial system as a whole.

18 September: global liquidity support

On 18 September the world's central banks announced coordinated measures to address continued elevated pressures in US dollar short-term funding markets. The Federal Reserve increased its total swap lines with foreign central banks by $180 billion via an increase in pre-existing swap lines with the ECB and the Swiss National Bank and the introduc-tion of new swap lines with the Bank of England, the Bank of Canada and the Bank of Japan to facilitate these central banks' providing dollar financing to banks headquartered in their respective jurisdictions. This brought the total amount of dollar funding supplied by the Fed to foreign central banks to over $300 billion. Each of the foreign central banks promptly announced that they stood ready to lend dollars to banks within their own jurisdictions. The Bank of England for example announced that it would make the $40 billion available to UK banks in the form of overnight lending with allocation awarded via an auction process against the provision of eligible collateral.

18 September: Lloyds rescues HBOS

Outside the United States the knock-on effects of the Lehman's failure were quite severe. Institutions dependent on funding from US wholesale markets were particularly affected. The institution that felt the most immediate impact was HBOS, a bank with £680 billion in assets but only £260 billion in customer deposits. HBOS had financed a significant portion of its assets through the issuance of commercial paper and other securities in the US dollar market and swapped the proceeds of these issues back into sterling. When the US dollar market dried up in the wake of the Lehmans failure, the funding squeeze on HBOS became enormous, and the stock price plummeted. There was concern that HBOS might require lender of last resort assistance or even resolution.

However, Lloyds TSB intervened to make an offer to take over HBOS in an all share transaction. This took HBOS out of the line of fire and preserved financial stability. Indeed, just that result was what prompted the UK Government to provide an exemption from the anti-trust restrictions that had previously blocked such in-market mergers among the big UK banks. The Lloyds TSB management reckoned that this was a very significant and unique opportunity to improve their market position in the United Kingdom despite the fact that they would not have the opportunity to do any significant amount of due diligence before announcing the transaction. The merger proposal temporarily calmed the market.

19 September: the United States backstops money market mutual funds and opens the liquidity tap

Yet another knock-on effect from the failure of Lehmans was 'breaking the buck' at money market mutual funds. This occurred at the Primary Reserve Fund which had invested a portion of the fund's assets in Lehman Brothers commercial paper. The markdown in that paper reduced the value of the fund, so that the fund's unit value could no longer be held at $1. The fund had to break the buck. This threatened to destroy the very premise on which money market mutual funds had been created and marketed in the United States (see Chapter 2).

'Breaking the buck' punctured the myth that US regulation had allowed to develop that money market mutual funds were the equivalent of deposits. Accordingly, breaking the buck at one fund threatened to provoke widespread withdrawals from money market mutual funds generally and to force such funds to sell their assets at fire-sale prices. This would have aggravated the downward spiral. It would have made it more difficult for banking organisations to raise funds (money market mutual funds invested an appreciable portion of their assets in commercial paper issued by bank holding companies and conduits associated with banks). It could also have caused the commercial paper market for non-financial companies to contract and for those companies to draw upon their back-up lines of credit at commercial banks, just at the time that commercial banks were themselves experiencing severe liquidity difficulties.

Consequently, the US Treasury announced on 19 September a programme to guarantee, in exchange for a fee from money market mutual funds that elected to participate, that the unit value of a money market fund would not fall below $1. In addition, the Federal Reserve announced on 19 September a temporary liquidity programme for US money market mutual funds, whereby the Fed would make loans to money market mutual funds that had experienced severe redemption outflows. Money market mutual funds could post asset-backed commercial paper (ABCP) as collateral for the loan. Loans under the program were non-recourse, so that the money market mutual fund could meet its obligation under the loan by simply surrendering the collateral to the Fed. The credit risk of the ABCP remained with the Fed (beyond the initial haircut that the Fed imposed on the collateral). By the 1st of October there was over $150 billion in credit outstanding under this facility.

In addition, the Fed provided another $100 billion of credit through the discount window to banks and through the dealer facility to primary dealers and other broker-dealers. Altogether, during the two week period ending 1 October the Fed increased its provision of credit to the financial system by nearly $300 billion (see Figure 4.2).

19–20 September: the United States announces TARP

On 19 September Secretary Paulson also announced that the United States would take a more comprehensive approach to removing toxic assets from banks' balance sheets. The first leg of this programme was to order the two government-sponsored enterprises, Fannie Mae

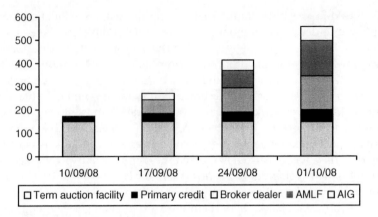

Figure 4.2   Federal Reserve pumps out liquidity post-Lehmans, 10 September to 1 October 2008 (in $ billions)

Source: Federal Reserve Board.

and Freddie Mac (now that they were under government conservatorship), to increase their purchases of mortgage-backed securities. The Treasury also announced that it would expand the mortgage-backed securities purchase programme that it had announced earlier in the month.

The following day, 20 September, Treasury Secretary Paulson announced that the government was seeking authority from Congress to spend up to $700 billion to buy troubled assets directly from the banks so that they could clean up their balance sheets and remove doubts in investors' minds about their condition.

This was a radical proposal, and it was presented in a radical way – in the form of a simple three page memo asking that the Treasury be given practically unlimited authority to dispose of $700 billion in taxpayers' funds with few, if any, checks or balances. Failure to grant the Treasury this extraordinary authority would, the Treasury and Fed warned, produce economic catastrophe, for without the Troubled Asset Relief Program (TARP), the Treasury and Fed had reached the limit of their authority and capability to combat the crisis.

Congress was sceptical, and so was the nation. The two Presidential candidates restrained their enthusiasm for the plan. Rather than a quick passage through both Houses of Congress, an intense debate began. For the time being, the Treasury's bold proposal was producing talk not action. This unsettled markets further.

22 September: the end of stand-alone investment banking

Alongside AIG, the most immediate knock-on effect from the failure of Lehman was a threat to the other three remaining stand-alone international investment banks, Merrill Lynch, Morgan Stanley and Goldman Sachs. Market participants could no longer reckon that such firms would be rescued or resolved without loss to creditors, if they got into trouble. Accordingly, market participants aggressively shifted their business, especially their free cash balances, away from such firms. This created a funding squeeze on the firms and threatened to force the firms into fire-sales of assets that would have destroyed capital and further fuelled their liquidity problems.

Merrill Lynch had already seen the writing on the wall and decided on 13 September to throw itself into the arms of Bank of America in an agreed merger transaction, which the authorities immediately sanctioned. This brought Merrill Lynch into the arms of the nation's largest deposit taker, and market participants reckoned that Bank of America would support Merrill Lynch and, if need be, the Fed would support Bank of America.

Morgan Stanley needed a capital injection as well as liquidity. To secure the former, it quickly completed negotiations with Mitsubishi UFJ Financial Group whereby the Japanese bank injected $9 billion into Morgan Stanley in exchange for up to 20% stake in Morgan Stanley on a fully diluted basis. To secure liquidity, Morgan Stanley converted itself – with the active encouragement and support of the Federal Reserve – into a bank holding company. This assured that Morgan Stanley's bank subsidiaries would have full access to the discount window of the Federal Reserve and that this liquidity would be available to support the entire enterprise. Goldman Sachs quickly followed suit and converted itself into a bank holding company as well. In addition, it raised capital from Warren Buffett and other outside investors.

The announcement of bank holding company status for Morgan Stanley and Goldman Sachs came on the morning of 22 September. The stand-alone investment bank model was dead, but the major invest-ment banks would live on as bank holding companies or as part of bank holding companies. Henceforth the Federal Reserve would assure that they had access to liquidity if needed and henceforth the Federal Reserve would exercise consolidated official supervision over the entities engaged in investment banking. This prospect stabilised the situation of the remaining stand-alone investment banks and averted further contagion.

25 September: Washington Mutual fails

It did not, however, spell the end of the crisis. On Thursday 25 September, one of the largest deposit-takers in the United States, Washington Mutual, failed, and the least-cost resolution method mandated under US legislation (FDICIA) imposed serious losses on unsecured senior creditors of the bank. JPMorgan Chase bought the insured deposits as well as certain assets and liabilities of the insured bank subsidiaries of WaMu in an auction conducted by the FDIC. The premium paid was $1.9 billion. Left behind were the assets and liabilities of the parent holding company as well as the unsecured debt of the operating bank subsidiaries, including uninsured deposits over the coverage limit of $100,000.

This unexpected imposition of loss on senior creditors further aggravated the concern of market participants about loss given resolution and made investors nervous about placing funds in troubled banks, even on an overnight basis. Interbank spreads immediately widened. This created further funding pressures on banks around the world, prompted governments to extend guarantees to deposits and other bank liabilities and pushed banks in the United States, United Kingdom, Belgium, Germany and Iceland into resolution.

26–29 September: Wachovia requires resolution

The funding pressure created by the failure of Washington Mutual immediately toppled over Wachovia, the third largest bank in the United States (ranked by domestic deposits). It had $812 billion in assets and $448 billion in deposits, over 3,000 bank branches in 21 states and a very extensive securities business. By the close of business on Friday 26 September it had run out of liquidity and it had to be resolved.

The US authorities scrambled to do this over the weekend, and they invoked for the first time the systemic risk exemption to the least-cost resolution requirement in the FDICIA legislation. The authorities agreed to provide open bank assistance to Wachovia to facilitate its sale to Citigroup. The proposed deal resolved Wachovia in a manner that protected depositors and other creditors from losses, and it considerably augmented Citigroup's deposit base and strengthened this troubled institution as well.

26–30 September: Fortis and Dexia

Wachovia was by no means the only bank to require immediate resolution. In Belgium the government had to step in to resolve two of the country's largest banks, Fortis and Dexia. To do so it had to arrange for burden-sharing agreements with the other principal countries in which Fortis and Dexia did business. Belgium alone did not have the capacity to save both banks at the same time.

Fortis was the larger and more complex of the two. Fortis had extended itself to buy the Dutch retail operations of ABN Amro. Although it had raised €1.5 billion in additional equity in July to finance this acquisition, losses in the bank's trading books ate up much of the newly issued capital. By mid-September, Fortis was facing a funding squeeze, and the flight to quality on 26 September was effectively a flight away from Fortis and other similarly situated banks. The initial solution announced early in the morning of Monday 29 September was an injection of a total of €11 billion in equity from the three Benelux governments (Belgium, Netherlands, and Luxembourg) into the respective national entities within the Fortis Group. Each national government would wind up with a 49% stake in the subsidiary headquartered within its borders.

The following day, Belgium, France and Luxembourg announced that they were making a €6.4 billion equity injection into Dexia. Dexia was also headquartered in Belgium and had significant subsidiaries in France and Luxembourg. The French subsidiary, Credit Locale, was a principal lender to municipalities across France and heavily reliant on wholesale funding. This prompted the French authorities to be actively involved in the rescue.

26–29 September: Hypo Real Estate/Depfa

In Germany, Hypo Real Estate (HRE) also ran into severe liquidity difficulties on 26 September, and the authorities initially arranged for a consortium of German banks to provide a €35 billion line of credit to HRE with the government providing a guarantee for 100% of the first €22 billion and for 40% of the remainder of the facility.

There were two reasons for this support. First, HRE was one of the leading issuers of Pfandbriefe, or covered bonds. This had long been the primary method by which German financial institutions refinanced mortgages. They had originally been introduced in the nineteenth century, and there had never been a default by an issuer of Pfandbriefe, not even in the Depression. The authorities did not wish to risk the knock-on effects on other Pfandbrief issuers (many of whom were themselves having difficulties) that could result from the failure of HRE.

Second, the failure of HRE would have meant the failure of Depfa as well. HRE had acquired Depfa in October 2007. Although Depfa was headquartered in Ireland, it specialised in providing finance to German municipalities. So there was concern that if Depfa failed, municipalities would have found themselves short of financing.

26–29 September: Bradford & Bingley

In the United Kingdom the authorities moved to resolve Bradford & Bingley, a lender with £50 billion in assets and approximately £22 billion in retail deposits[3] that had specialised in providing mortgages collater-alised by buy-to-let properties and that had sourced its mortgages from brokers and by buying portfolios from originators with a weak track record. Although the bank had succeeded – thanks in some measure to the intervention of the authorities – in raising new equity earlier in the year, the rapidly declining housing market did not allow the new B&B management installed at the time of the equity issue sufficient time to turn the troubled institution around. When the bank ran out of liquidity at the end of September the authorities invoked the Special Provisions Act, took the institution into temporary public ownership and sold the retail deposits and branches of the bank at an auction to Abbey for a premium of £612 million.

29 September: the US Congress rejects TARP

Although the 29th of September had started on a positive note with the announcements of the resolution of Wachovia, Fortis, Bradford & Bingley and HRE, it ended dismally. Congress rejected the US govern-ment's proposed TARP. This appeared to underline the inability of the US authorities to act in the election interregnum. Would the disaster forecast by the president if Congress failed to pass the bill now actually come to pass?

The Administration and Congressional leaders resolved to try again to pass TARP, but the proposal would require revision and there was no guarantee they would succeed. Without TARP the Fed and the Treasury were running out of ammunition. They did not have the authority to spend taxpayers' funds on the scale required to combat, much less contain, the crisis. That fact alone potentially pushed participants in the market further towards panic. If the Fed and Treasury had no further money to mount the rescue of a troubled institution, then the prudent thing for an investor to do was to get out of any institution deemed to be troubled before it actually slid into resolution. But as each investor individually tried to do the rational thing, the collective rush for the exit could bring about the very crash that one was trying to avoid.

Indeed, in the following week more firms would require resolution and some of the rescues announced at the conclusion of the weekend of 27–28 September would have to be redone the following weekend, further weakening confidence in the effectiveness of resolution regimes.

30 September: Ireland issues a blanket guarantee

The following day Ireland issued a blanket guarantee of all deposits, debt and lower Tier 2 capital at its banks for both existing and new debt. This was done to stabilise the funding position of Irish banks, as the market had become concerned about the quality of their assets (these typically included large concentrations of land and development loans).

Although this stabilised the position of the Irish banks, it posed significant competition issues within the EU. Other member states felt pressure to do something similar for their banks. As the initial guarantee appeared to be restricted to the liabilities of Irish banks headquartered in Ireland, it raised the prospect that proliferating government guarantees could undermine the single market.

3 October: passage of TARP

On 3 October the US Congress finally passed TARP and President Bush signed the bill immediately into law. The original 3-page memo asking for authority to spend up to $700 billion to support the US banking system had ballooned into a 451 page tome, entitled the Emergency Economic Stabilisation Act of 2008. In the intervening week between the defeat of the bill on 29 September and its passage on 3 October a host of provisions had been added to the bill, including authorisation for the Fed to pay increased interest on required reserves and excess reserves, a temporary (to 31 December 2009) increase in the ceiling for deposit insurance from $100,000 to $250,000 per account, limits on executive pay, assistance to homeowners to avoid foreclosure and various tax changes.

What the bill did not contain was a blueprint of how the Treasury would actually implement its intent to take troubled or toxic assets off the books of the banks. Setting too high a price would amount to a gift of taxpayers' money to the banks, and this was politically unacceptable and economically wrong. Forcing banks to sell at too low a price would create further losses and aggravate the banks' capital and funding problems as well as be subject to challenge in the courts. So after all the storm and fury about the passage of TARP, it was not apparent that Treasury could quickly or effectively implement the new weapons at its disposal. Although the passage of TARP removed a threat to confidence, it did not actually restore confidence.

3–6 October: Fortis round 2

In fact, confidence was put sorely to the test once again over the weekend of 3 to 6 October. The rescues of Fortis, HRE and Wachovia concluded the previous weekend had to be done again.

Fortis was the most difficult and most controversial. Although the announcement by the Benelux countries of the equity injection into Fortis on 29 September appeared to stabilise the situation, the deal did not complete immediately. Cash did not promptly flow from the three governments into Fortis. Wholesale funds continued to flow out of Fortis, and, as September turned into October, Fortis Belgium found it necessary to draw tens of billions of euros of emergency liquidity assistance from the National Bank of Belgium.

A new rescue had to be negotiated. On 3 October Fortis concluded an agreement with the Dutch government. The Dutch government agreed to pay €16.8 billion to obtain complete control of Fortis Netherlands. Under the terms of the agreement €12.8 billion was used to recapitalise Fortis Bank Nederland and €4 billion was transferred to Fortis Group in exchange for the Dutch insurance operations of Fortis. The agreement accorded Fortis Bank Nederland the right to receive the Dutch retail operations of ABN Amro that Fortis had agreed to acquire as part of the consortium acquisition of ABN Amro.

On 6 October, after a weekend of further extensive negotiation, the Belgian government agreed to acquire the remaining 51% in Fortis Bank Belgium from Fortis Group for an additional consideration of €4.7 billion. This left the Belgian government in complete control of Fortis Bank Belgium. The Belgian government further agreed to sell a 75% stake in Fortis Bank Belgium to BNP Paribas. Separately, Fortis Group agreed to sell its Belgian insurance operations to BNP Paribas for a consideration of €5.7 billion. As a result of these two transactions the Fortis Group had completely exited the banking business. It was left with an international insurance group and a two-thirds interest in a €10 billion structured products portfolio that had been separated out from Fortis Bank Belgium. This restructuring proved effective, although shareholder suits in Belgium delayed the closing of the sale of Fortis Bank Belgium to BNP Paribas until May 2009.

3–6 October: HRE round 2

In Germany the deal to rescue Hypo Real Estate also had to be redone. As conditions in the money markets deteriorated, it became apparent that HRE could not survive, if assistance were limited to the €35 billion life line that had been originally agreed. The Finance Ministry agreed to increase its guarantee by a further €15 billion and it indicated that further steps would be taken to support the bank.

The rationale for stepping up the level of support was twofold. First, the arguments about Pfandbriefe and municipal finance continued to hold. Second, and much more importantly, it was correctly recognised that the state could not afford to see a rescue operation fail. Once the decision had been taken to protect the bank's creditors, the state had to make good on that promise. Otherwise confidence would be completely undermined. So the German government increased the support.

At the same time the German Government sought to provide assurance to the population that their savings would be safe. In a joint television statement the Chancellor and the Finance Minister promised that no German retail depositor would be allowed to lose her savings. This calmed consumers' concerns but further aggravated concerns that the Irish guarantee had raised about consistency with the letter and spirit of EU law.

3–6 October: Wachovia round 2

Fortis and HRE were not the only rescues that had to be redone during the weekend of 4–5 October. At the time of the announcement of the Citigroup-Wachovia transaction (29 September), all the parties had was a heads of agreement. They did not have a definitive purchase and assumption agreement. This made it possible for Wells Fargo, which had also been negotiating with the authorities over the weekend of 27–28 September to take over Wachovia, to trump Citigroup's offer. On the same day (29 September) as the Citigroup-Wachovia deal was announced, the US Treasury changed a clause in its tax regulations improving the ability of an acquirer to make use of the tax losses of the acquired company. That allowed Wells Fargo to make an offer for all of Wachovia on 3 October without the need for federal assistance, and the Wachovia board accepted this higher offer without hesitation.

This put the Citigroup transaction into limbo, creating further confusion about the effectiveness of US resolution policy. Although the transaction was undoubtedly good for Wachovia shareholders and did hold out the promise of a lower-cost resolution for the FDIC, it created doubts that the authorities would stick to a resolution deal if they could get a better one. It also unsettled market expectations with respect to Citigroup, since the market had reckoned that the Wachovia transaction would have provided significant funding and liquidity support to Citigroup through the acquisition of Wachovia's domestic deposit base without the bulk of Wachovia's troubled assets.

7 October: Iceland implodes

On 7 October Iceland's banks and Iceland's economy imploded. Under the provisions of the European Economic Area (EEA) treaty Iceland's banks had had the right to establish branches and subsidiaries throughout the EEA (the 27 Member States of the EU plus Iceland, Norway and Liechtenstein). Iceland's banks had made extensive use of these rights and had built up banking businesses in the United Kingdom, Netherlands, Germany and the Nordic countries. Although the banks did engage in local business in these economies, a very significant portion of their assets were leveraged loans to Icelandic entrepreneurs to facilitate their purchases of businesses throughout Europe, but especially in the United Kingdom.

As the crisis deepened, these loans ran into difficulty, as did other assets in the Icelandic banks' portfolios. Losses mounted and the banks' capital position weakened. This created funding pressures. Although these could be partially offset through raising insured retail deposits via branches and subsidiaries in EU countries, the Icelandic banks ultimately had to look to the Icelandic central bank for liquidity support and/or the Icelandic government for capital support. The central bank could not provide the former – what the banks needed was sterling or euro liquidity, and the amounts required were far in excess of the central bank's reserves. Nor did the government have the resources necessary to offset the capital losses that the Icelandic banks had incurred. The country was too small to save its banks, and one after another – Landsbanki, Kaupthing, Glitnir – they failed.

Resolution of the failed banks differed from country to country, illustrating again that banks may be global in life, but they are national in death. In Iceland, the government nationalised the domestic operations and protected the domestic depositors in full. The international operations of the bank were left to be resolved on a country-by-country basis.

The resolution of the banks' UK operations – where the Icelandic banks had the largest operations – caused the most controversy, both domestically and internationally. With respect to retail depositors, the UK government provided protection far in excess of the amount required by law.[4] It protected all retail depositors and stated that they would be reimbursed in full via the UK compensation scheme, the FSCS. However, that is where the protection stopped. Wholesale depositors, including UK local authorities and UK building societies, received no protection and were left to seek to recover what they could from the insolvency proceedings. This was a harsher treatment than provided to the depositors in Bradford & Bingley and further confirmation that loss given resolution could be high indeed. This uneven treatment caused some controversy.

But the real controversy was international. Although the UK government opted to protect all retail depositors in the UK branches and subsidiaries of the Icelandic banks, in doing so it assumed the right of those depositors to seek recovery from the estate of the failed bank. To implement that right the UK government used the Terrorism Act to seize the assets of the UK branches of the Icelandic banks. This disrupted diplomatic relations between the two countries and threatened the basis of the EEA treaty.

On the verge of meltdown

Despite all the work to rescue one institution after another, the financial system at the start of October 2008 was looking decidedly bleak. Lehmans had unleashed a chain reaction in the financial markets, taking down a series of very large institutions. The European Union was squabbling amongst itself and the single market seemed under threat. The United States seemed out of ideas and possibly out of resources to fight the crisis. Meanwhile, the pressures from the market continued to mount. Interbank markets had again frozen, and if funds could be obtained at all, they were prohibitively expensive – indeed, banks were facing the prospect of paying far more for their funds than they could expect to receive on their assets. The world financial system and with it the world economy was moving towards meltdown.

5
Unconditional Containment

Meltdown did not happen, but the world came close. Following the failure of Lehman Brothers the world economy went into a free fall. Output declined at an even faster rate than it had at the start of the Great Depression. The prospect of a downward debt-deflation spiral loomed.[1]

Containment of the crisis became unconditionally the first priority for governments around the world (see Figure 5.1). First, authorities implemented measures to stabilise the banking system, chiefly through the infusion of capital and liquidity and through providing protection against losses that could arise from troubled assets. Secondly, the authorities unleashed massive monetary and fiscal policy stimulus to support the real economy.

Although these measures did not prevent the world economy from suffering a rapid and wrenching contraction in the fourth quarter of 2008 and the first quarter of 2009, there were signs by November 2009 that these policies had arrested the rate of decline and put the world economy back on the path to recovery.

The economy goes into free fall

The collapse of Lehmans and the subsequent havoc in financial markets pushed the world economy into free fall. Spending on consumer durables and investment goods dried up, and companies slashed their inventories. Industrial production plummeted, and unemployment began to climb dramatically.

The fall in GDP was faster and steeper than anything since the Great Depression. Indeed, in some respects the economy was falling even more rapidly than it had at the start of the Great Depression. In the

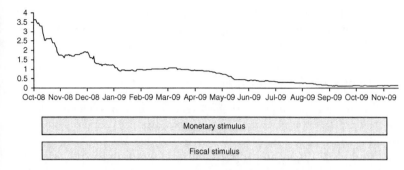

Figure 5.1 Unconditional containment, 3-month $ LIBOR-OIS spread in %, October 2008–November 2009

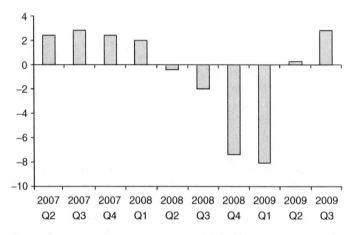

Figure 5.2 The world economy goes into free fall – real GDP growth, advanced (OECD) economies quarter over quarter, annualised, in %, 2007–09
Source: OECD 2009.

fourth quarter of 2008, the world's leading economies contracted at a 6% annual rate, and in the first quarter of 2009 the rate of decline was nearly as bad (see Figure 5.2).

The decline was quite widespread, affecting not just the United States, where the crisis had originated, but economies throughout the world. In Japan real GDP fell at double digit annual rates in the fourth quarter of 2008 and the first quarter of 2009. Other export-oriented economies were severely affected as well, particularly those, such as Germany, that specialised in investment goods and consumer durables. Central and Eastern Europe was extremely adversely affected as were Ireland, Spain, Italy, Russia and Mexico (IMF 2009a; OECD 2009).

Stabilising the banking system

Unlike the decision makers in the Great Depression, policymakers in 2008 recognised immediately the gravity of the situation and the need to take action. The first priority was to stabilise the banking system. The European Union and the United Kingdom pointed the way. On 6 October, the French Presidency convened a meeting of the 27 EU heads of state and government. They collectively declared that each of them would take 'whatever measures are necessary to ensure the stability of the financial system' (PFUE 2008).

The following day the finance ministers of the EU Member States (ECOFIN 2008) filled in the details. Effectively the ECOFIN gave the green light to member states to provide capital and liquidity support to their banks but drew the line at allowing member states to provide unconditional and unlimited guarantees for all bank liabilities as the Irish had done. This assured that member states could take emergency measures but also assured that such measures would be consistent with the maintenance of the single market. The ECOFIN statement concluded:

> We have agreed to support systemic financial institutions. We commit to take all necessary measures to enhance the soundness and stability of our banking system and to protect the deposits of individual savers. ... The liquidity of the financial system shall be ensured by all authorities in order to preserve confidence and stability. ... To protect the depositors' interests and the stability of the system, we stress the appropriateness of an approach, including, among other means, recapitalisation of vulnerable systemically relevant financial institutions. We are prepared to act accordingly in this context.

The G-7 finance ministers and central bank governors came to a similar conclusion a few days later in Washington (G-7 2008).

October 2008: bank recapitalisation

In accordance with this approach, the United Kingdom (HMT 2008a) announced the next day (Wednesday 8 October) a comprehensive

£500 billion programme to stabilise the UK banking system. The plan addressed both capital and funding liquidity together, not one in isolation from the other. The plan had three components:

1. It doubled the size of the Bank of England's Special Liquidity Scheme to £200 billion.
2. It instituted a guarantee programme (the Credit Guarantee Scheme) of approximately £250 billion for new wholesale debt issuance by banks that either already had adequate capital or could put in place a plan for raising Tier I capital to an amount and in the form the Government considered appropriate.
3. It indicated that the UK Government had allocated £50 billion to act, if need be, as an underwriter or capital provider of last resort (the Bank Recapitalisation Fund) to enable banks to meet the capital standard required for participation in the Credit Guarantee Scheme.[2]

This plan pointed a way out of the quagmire, but by the end of that same week (10 October), the market's initial enthusiasm for the plan had waned. Market participants were unwilling to give the UK authorities the benefit of the doubt. The difficulties experienced in the United States with respect to enacting TARP and the delay that the United States was likely to have in implementing TARP made investors sceptical about the ability of the UK government to implement its scheme quickly and effectively. By Friday 10 October UK banks were experiencing severe funding difficulties, and two banks, HBOS (since 1 October) and RBS (since 7 October) were receiving emergency liquidity assistance on a covert basis from the Bank of England (BoE 2009c).

This prompted the Tripartite authorities to implement the 8 October plan quickly. Over the weekend of 11–12 October, the authorities conducted a rapid capital review of the major British banks and determined the amount of capital that each would require in order to survive the stress implied by a marked deterioration in the economy below the then current economic forecast. For RBS and the merged Lloyds/HBOS group the Government agreed to underwrite £20 billion and £17 billion of new equity respectively in fulfilment of its commitment to act as a capital provider of last resort. At the same time, the authorities confirmed that the other major banks either had sufficient capital or had in place credible plans to raise sufficient capital from the markets so that they would be able to withstand the stress that might result in the world economy.

This prompt action arrested the panic that had started to grip the British banks the previous Friday. Effectively, the Government had declared that it would not let any major UK bank run out of capital. Managers might be thrown out. Shareholders might suffer death by dilution. But depositors and debt-holders would be safe. If need be, the Government would provide enough equity to enable the banks to absorb the losses that could result from their bad portfolios. Together with the introduction of the Credit Guarantee Scheme and the extension of the Special Liquidity Scheme the recapitalisation program began to restore confidence in the markets, allowing RBS and HBOS to begin to repay the emergency liquidity assistance that they had received from the Bank of England (BoE 2009c) and setting the stage for shareholders of HBOS and LloydsTSB to approve the merger of the two institutions.

Other countries promptly followed with bank recapitalisation programmes of their own. On 14 October the United States (UST 2008) announced that it would utilise $250 billion of the TARP money to purchase capital instruments in US banks, starting immediately with an injection of $125 billion of capital into nine banks, including Citigroup, Bank of America, JPMorgan Chase, Wells Fargo, Goldman Sachs and Morgan Stanley. These initial transactions took the form of preferred stock with warrants that would allow the government to buy common stock in the bank at some future point in time (and therefore enable the government to participate in the upside as institutions recovered). The initial capital infusions were deliberately structured to include institutions that did not need immediate assistance, so as to avoid the programme stigmatising those institutions that did apply for capital assistance. Although the headlines continued to focus on the major banks' participation in the programme, by March 2009 the Treasury had provided capital to over 500 US financial institutions.

In addition, the US government invoked the systemic risk exemption in the FDICIA act governing deposit insurance and bank resolutions and authorised the FDIC to temporarily guarantee the senior debt of all FDIC-insured institutions and their holding companies as well as deposits in non-interest bearing deposit transaction accounts. This step complemented the liquidity programmes that had been implemented by the Federal Reserve (see "October – November 2008: Unleashing Liquidity" below).

European countries took similar measures. On 17 October Germany enacted a Financial Market Stabilisation Act. This provided for up to €400 billion in loan guarantees and up to €80 billion in possible capital investments. Under this programme the government made investments in Commerzbank/Dresdner and HRE. France announced a €360

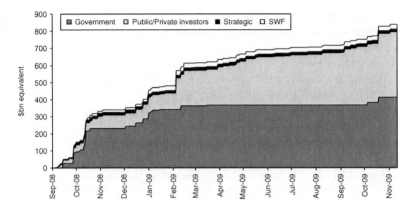

Figure 5.3 Governments prime the pump for further bank recapitalisations – capital raisings by 32 largest banks by type (cumulative) 15 September 2008–26 November 2009, in $ billions equivalent*

Source: Bloomberg.

*Gross capital injections (buybacks not considered). Gross capital injections denominated other than $ converted as of June of the year that took place.

billion programme of loan guarantees and capital support measures. Under the latter France would provide capital to both Société Générale and BNP Paribas. Austria initiated a €100 billion programme of loan guarantees and capital injections (under the latter it would take a stake in Erste Bank, a large Austrian savings bank with extensive investments in Central and Eastern Europe). Spain indicated that it would guarantee up to €100 billion in bank debt. The Netherlands stated that it would provide up to €220 billion in loan guarantees and capital injections (under the latter it would take stakes in ING and Aegon). Switzerland provided a capital injection into UBS and strengthened its deposit guarantee scheme. All in all, by the end of October governments had announced support for the financial system totalling well over $1 trillion, and the direct capital infusions into banks primed the pump for banks' raising significant further amounts of capital in the private markets (see Figure 5.3).

October–November 2008: unleashing liquidity

In addition to governments' injecting capital directly into banks, central banks developed alone or in conjunction with their respective finance ministries, supplemental liquidity programmes as well as asset purchase schemes to support the financial system. As noted above, the

UK expanded its Special Liquidity Scheme and introduced a Credit Guarantee Scheme. In addition, the Bank of England revised the terms on which it would normally provide liquidity to banks by introducing a Discount Window Facility. This broadened the range of eligible collateral and reduced the rate charged for short-term borrowing (BoE 2008).

In the United States the Federal Reserve continued the very rapid expansion in reserve bank credit that it had initiated following the Lehmans' collapse. From $1.7 trillion on 15 October total reserve bank credit increased $500 billion over the course of the next month, reaching a total of nearly $2.2 trillion on 19 November, an amount nearly two and one half times the level of $890 billion that had prevailed on 10 September shortly before the Lehman's failure. This was liquidity creation on an unprecedented scale, and the Fed has kept this liquidity in place through the end of October 2009 (see Figure 5.4).

The composition of reserve bank credit also shifted markedly towards direct provision of credit to the private sector. The Fed more than doubled the term auction facility from $150 billion (8 October) to over $415 billion (12 November). This allowed the Fed to direct liquidity to the banks that were most in need of it. From 27 October the Fed started to buy three-month commercial paper directly from issuers in order to foster liquidity in short-term funding markets and increase the

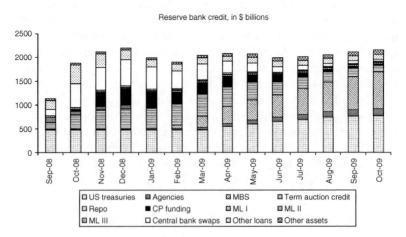

Figure 5.4 Fed floods the market with liquidity – central bank liquidity operations, September 2008–October 2009

Source: Federal Reserve Board. ML I refers to Bear Stearns, ML II and ML III to AIG.

availability of credit to businesses and households. By 12 November it had bought nearly $250 billion of such paper.

The Fed also used its balance sheet to support the mortgage market. Starting in September 2008 it began to buy Federal agency debt securities, and by July 2009 the Fed had amassed over $100 billion in such paper. From January 2009 the Fed started to buy mortgage-backed securities directly. By mid-March 2009 it had accumulated $225 billion of this paper, and by the end of October 2009 it had acquired over $775 billion in such securities, nearly all of them long term (over ten years maturity). This massive purchasing programme can be reckoned to have provided both a certain degree of liquidity to this depressed market as well as some underpinning of the prices in that market.

October 2008–March 2009: massive monetary and fiscal stimulus

The rapid and wrenching decline in economic activity that followed the bankruptcy of Lehman caused central banks and governments to rethink their policies towards containing the crisis. Deterring deflation and depression became the order of the day.

At the G-20 meeting in Washington on 15 November the heads of state of the 20 largest economies in the world concluded that 'more needs to be done to stabilize financial markets and support economic growth'. In addition to 'whatever further actions are necessary to stabilize the financial system', the G-20 stressed the importance of monetary policy support and the use of 'fiscal measures to stimulate domestic demand to rapid effect' (G-20 2008). This effectively unleashed an unprecedented counter-cyclical package of monetary and fiscal measures by practically all advanced economies.

Monetary policy

Following the bankruptcy of Lehmans central banks moved quickly to slash interest rates practically all the way to zero (see Figure 5.5) and to provide additional stimulus through outright money creation or quantitative easing. On 8 October (the same day as the United Kingdom announced its liquidity and capitalisation programme) the Bank of England, the ECB, the US Federal Reserve, the Bank of Canada, the Swedish Riksbank and the Swiss National Bank all announced significant reductions in their policy rates. This underlined the central bank commitment to follow through on the stabilisation policy that the EU and G-7 had mandated.

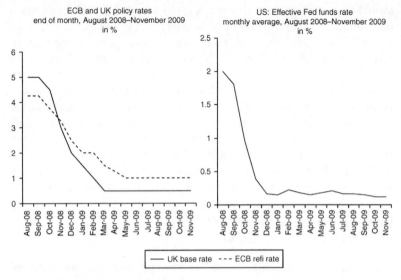

Figure 5.5   Central banks slash interest rates effectively to zero
Source: Federal Reserve Board.

Each of the central banks cut rates much further in the following weeks and months. In the United States, the Federal Reserve cut the target Fed funds rate two further times before the end of the year, by 50 basis points on 29 October to 1% and by 75 basis points to 25 basis points on 16 December. Effectively, the United States had adopted a zero interest rate policy.

The United Kingdom started much further away from zero than the Fed, but quickly caught up. At the point Lehmans failed the UK base rate was still 5% as it had been since April 2008 (and it was only 75 basis points below the level that had prevailed in August 2007). Following the initial 50 basis point cut on 8 October, the Bank cut rates a further 150 basis points on 6 November (to 3%), another 100 basis points on 4 December (to 2%), another 50 basis points on 8 January 2009 (to 1.5%), a further 50 basis points on 5 February (to 1%) and another 50 basis points on 5 March (to 0.5%). This was the lowest rate in the Bank's 300-year history. For all practical purposes, the short-term interest rate was close to zero.

The ECB also slashed rates, in many cases on the same day as the Bank of England. But the ECB started from a lower level and proceeded in smaller steps. Following the initial 50 basis point cut on 8 October, the ECB cut rates another 50 basis points on 6 November (to 3.25%), a further 75 basis points on 4 December (to 2.5%), another 50 basis points on 15 January 2009 (to 2%), a further 50 basis points on 5 March (to 1.5%) and another 25 basis points on 2 April to 1.25% and a further 25 basis points on 13 May to 1%.

Not content with the stimulus that zero interest rates would provide, central banks and governments in the United Kingdom and the United States also initiated quantitative easing or the outright purchases by the central bank of government and corporate debt in massive amounts (BoE 2009a). Ordinarily, central banks conduct open market operations in order to maintain interest rates at a certain level. The change in the interest rate is what stimulates or constricts the economy. However, when interest rates fall to zero or close to zero, this policy is no longer as effective. To stimulate the economy further than the adoption of zero interest rates alone would do, it is necessary for the central bank to buy securities outright, and to buy them in massive quantities.

That is exactly what the Bank of England started to do. In January 2009 it received authorisation from the Treasury to buy up to £50 billion (subsequently raised to £150 billion) of government and private securities in the open market. The Bank promptly initiated several asset purchase programmes encompassing not only gilts (government debt) but also corporate bonds and commercial paper. By the end of October 2009 the Bank had bought £175 billion in bonds, a sum greater than 8% of UK GDP.

In the United States, the Fed began to engage in 'credit easing'. This effectively meant an expansion of the Fed's balance sheet (see "October – November 2008: unleashing liquidity" above). At its core was the provision of dollar liquidity to the global banking system – directly to domestic institutions through collateralised lending and term auction facilities, and indirectly to foreign institutions through central bank liquidity swaps with foreign central banks so that they could on-lend dollars to their own institutions. But credit easing went beyond this to direct lending to firms via the purchase of commercial paper and providing backstops to money market mutual funds and to the direct purchase of agency and mortgage-backed securities. This mix of liquidity support and asset purchases was aimed to correct the 'dysfunctional' dispersion of credit spreads in US financial markets so that the Fed could continue to 'push down interest rates and ease credit conditions in a range of markets, despite the fact that the federal funds rate is close to its zero lower bound' (Bernanke 2009).

Fiscal policy

Governments for the first time in the crisis also moved to use fiscal measures to combat the crisis. In part, fiscal stimulus was already flowing into national economies through automatic stabilisers such as progressive income tax rates (as GDP falls tax revenues fall more quickly) and unemployment benefits (an example of spending that shoots up as GDP falls). But what the summit recommended was more stimulus. Generally, governments opted to spend more rather than provide tax rebates (the fear was that the rebates would simply be saved and would not stimulate the economy).

The United States was quick off the mark. Even before it was sworn into office, the new Obama administration identified hundreds of 'shovel-ready' projects worthy of federal government support. Soon after the Inauguration in January 2009 the new administration introduced and Congress enacted a stimulus package of nearly $800 billion. This brought the budget deficit for the United States to approximately 10% of GDP, a proportion not seen in the United States since World War II (see Figure 5.6).

The United Kingdom engaged in fiscal stimulus on a similar scale. The consensus forecast (November 2009) for its budget deficit in calendar 2009 was nearly 13% of GDP. In the Eurozone, the aggregate fiscal deficit for 2009 is estimated to be nearly 6% of GDP or nearly twice the 3% ceiling set under the Maastricht Treaty, with some countries, such as Spain and Ireland at three to four times the 3% ceiling. Japan also envisioned a budget deficit of about 10% of GDP for 2009.

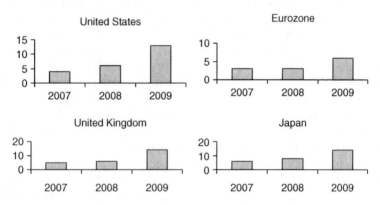

Figure 5.6   Massive fiscal stimulus – fiscal deficit/GDP in %, 2007–09
Source: IMF World Economic Outlook, October 2009.

November 2008–November 2009: asset-protection schemes

In addition to providing capital and liquidity to banks, governments around the world provided asset-protection or tail-risk insurance against losses that could arise from the 'toxic' assets in banks' portfolios. The idea behind such programmes was to 'clean up' the bank so that it could again attract funding and support new lending to the real economy.

Although there was much discussion of establishing a 'bad bank' that could purchase some or all of the bad assets in a banking system, governments found it difficult to put this into practice. Buying assets at above market prices would have been and been seen as an outright gift from the taxpayer to the bank; offering to buy assets at or below market prices provided little inducement to banks to sell. Sales at a fire-sale price would have meant additional losses (and a requirement to replace the capital that such losses would have eradicated) as well as giving up the possible upside from that fire-sale price.

Instead of purchasing toxic assets outright, governments provided tail-risk insurance against extreme losses on such assets. During the fourth quarter of 2008 and the first months of 2009 governments engaged in a series of bilateral transactions with banks that were under the most pressure. Each transaction was tailored to the specific situation of the bank, but overall a pattern emerged whereby the government took the vast majority (generally 90%) of the risk that losses on a segregated volume of assets would exceed a certain threshold amount (the first loss or deductible in insurance parlance that would be retained by the bank). In exchange the government demanded an insurance premium that in many cases was payable in the form of a capital instrument (e.g., common stock, warrants to buy common stock or preferred stock) issued by the bank to the government. In some cases the government provided funding for the assets in the form of a non-recourse loan collateralised by the assets; in other cases, the protection took the form of an insurance contract with the bank remaining responsible for the funding of the assets protected under the scheme. In some cases the government provided new capital to the bank in question so that it could pay the insurance premium and/or absorb the first loss requirement under the asset-protection scheme.

Notable deals included transactions of the US government with Citigroup (covering $294 billion of assets) and Bank of America (covering $118 billion in assets), of the Swiss National Bank with UBS covering $60 billion in assets and of the Dutch government with ING covering $24 billion in Alt-A mortgages. In addition the UK reached heads of agreement in March 2009 on the largest deals of all: with RBS to cover £325 billion in assets (subsequently reduced to £280 billion) and with Lloyds Banking group to cover £260 billion in assets (subsequently cancelled in exchange for an exit fee of £2.5 billion). Finally in July 2009 Germany introduced a 'bad bank' scheme that would allow banks to exchange toxic assets for government bonds and to amortise the losses on the underlying assets over a 20-year time frame. All in all, government guarantees for troubled assets amounted to over $1.5 trillion.

Stress tests and promoting new lending

Although this three-pronged programme of capital infusion, liquidity and asset protection prevented an outright implosion of the financial system, the question remained whether sufficient credit would be available in the economy to arrest the debt-deflation spiral. During the boom households and non-financial corporations obtained credit from many sources, including direct issuance into the securities markets, trade credit, foreign banks as well as domestic headquartered banks. During 2007 and 2008 some of these sources of credit began to dry up or even contract. This contraction in non-bank credit implied that bank credit would have to grow quite rapidly indeed in order to sustain total credit to households and non-financial corporations.[3]

Consequently, public intervention to prop up the banking system was designed to assure not only that the banks could survive, but that they would continue to function as providers of credit to the economy, particularly to small to medium-sized businesses and to households. Although large, investment grade corporates could and did access the corporate bond markets to refinance themselves, smaller firms and individuals had no such access, and it was critical that sound enterprises and households remain able to finance themselves.

Policymakers were concerned that the banks would attempt to rebuild their capital ratios by cutting back on lending to institutions and individuals who were still in sound financial condition. If the banks did so, this would force those entities to curtail spending, leading to a further decline in the economy. Consequently, as a condition of granting liquidity, credit and capital support to the banks, governments required banks to make sure that they had enough capital to sustain lending. To determine this, the regulators submitted the banks to rigorous stress testing. Furthermore, governments required banks to make commitments with respect to new lending.

Stress testing

Although regulators had emphasised the importance of stress testing before the crisis,[4] it was only during the crisis that regulators moved to integrate stress testing into the supervisory framework for banks. The United Kingdom was perhaps the most explicit in this regard. As a condition for admission to the government's credit guarantee scheme, banks had to be able to demonstrate to the FSA that they would have core Tier I capital greater than or equal to 4% of their risk-weighted assets, even under a severe economic stress. This effectively became the minimum ratio, and banks were given to understand that they should operate prior to the stress materialising with ratios significantly above that level so that they would have a buffer that could be run down, if the stress did materialise (FSA 2009h). Effectively, banks had to either have the capital that would enable them to meet the stress test, or have credible and rapidly executable plans to raise that capital. Otherwise the banks would have to take tail-risk insurance from the government under its asset protection scheme. In evaluating the banks' ability to meet the stress test, the FSA took into account measures that the firms were taking to sell certain businesses (such as Barclays proposed sale of iShares) or to raise capital in private markets (such as the fully under-written offer by which Lloyds Banking Group would raise £22.5 billion in private capital markets, including the issuance of contingent capital instruments in exchange for existing hybrid and Tier 2 instruments). RBS received an additional capital infusion from the government and concluded an asset protection agreement with the government.

The United States also employed stress testing in connection with TARP. Prior to allowing any bank to repay the TARP money that they had received from the US government, the US banking regulators subjected each of the 19 largest US bank holding companies (BHCs) to a supervisory capital assessment programme. This was designed to assure that each of the firms would have a 'one time buffer' so that 'market participants, as well as the firms themselves [have] confidence in the capacity of the major BHCs to perform their critical role in lending, even if the economy proves weaker than expected. The actual buffer was set at a 'Tier I risk-based ratio of at least 6% and a Tier I common risk-based ratio of at least 4% at the end of 2010 under a more adverse economic scenario than is currently anticipated'. The results of the test were announced on 7 May 2009. Banks that had excess capital under the test were allowed to repay the TARP funds (and to escape from some of the constraints that came with the acceptance of TARP funds). Banks that had to raise capital to meet the test had to file a detailed capital plan with the authorities within a month (by 8 June 2009) and they had to raise the additional capital within six months (9 November 2009).[5]

The European Union requested that the Committee of European Banking Supervisors (CEBS) conduct a stress test to determine the resiliency of the European banking system. This was to build on the tests conducted by national supervisors, but not to identify capital shortfalls at individual institutions. That would remain the purview of national authorities, who would remain responsible for assuring that any capital deficiencies were remedied, either by the institutions themselves in the market or through injections of public funds.[6]

New lending

From the standpoint of an individual bank, reducing lending in a crisis is potentially an attractive course of action. It trims exposure to clients who may subsequently default, and it reduces the assets for which funding must be found and capital must be maintained. However, if all banks take this course of action, even sound companies and households may find it difficult to roll over maturing credits. This could lead to a liquidity squeeze, not just on banks, but on the economy more generally, and that would aggravate the decline in output and employment.

To prevent this authorities in many countries have arranged for banks to engage in collective action to sustain the level of lending in the economy. The purpose is to assure that creditworthy companies and households can continue to receive credit (i.e., to keep banks' making 'good' loans to 'good' borrowers) rather than asking banks to bail out failing companies.[7] To this end the authorities have required banks to make new lending commitments as a condition for access to various government and central bank programmes (capital assistance, credit guarantees, asset-protection schemes and/or liquidity assistance). In the United Kingdom, for example, the authorities formed a lending panel consisting of the eight leading UK banks and received commitments from each of these institutions regarding the amount of new lending that they would make over and above what had originally been called for in their business plans.

This enforced collective action countermanded the credit contraction in which each individual institution might have been tempted to engage in order to improve its balance sheet. Had each individual institution been left to contract credit as it saw fit, overall credit in the economy might have contracted sharply and the downturn would have been steepened and/or been lengthened.

Back from the precipice

Taken together, the monetary and fiscal policy measures undertaken by the G-20 central banks and governments amounted to stimulus on an unprecedented scale. Such massive stimulus has been needed to counteract the unprecedented speed with which the world economy deteriorated in the fourth quarter of 2008 and the first quarter of 2009. This stimulus complemented the measures taken by the authorities to stabilise the banking system, and by the time of this writing (November 2009) the crisis was well on the way to containment. The economy was no longer in free fall. Preliminary results for third quarter GDP are starting to come in for various countries and it is apparent that the recession has ended at least temporarily in a number of countries (see Figure 5.2).

Debate was beginning to shift to the timing and shape of the recovery: would it be a 'V' as in previous recessions, a 'square root' where the economy stalled after an initial recovery, or would there be some type of relapse (a 'W'-shaped recovery)? Although it was too early to say anything definitive, anxiety was diminishing that the recovery would only start in a few years time (a 'U'-shaped recovery) or that the economy would not recover at all (an 'L'-shaped recovery (see Figure 5.7).

Financial markets were also beginning to return to 'normal'. The LIBOR-OIS spread had fallen to approximately the same level as it

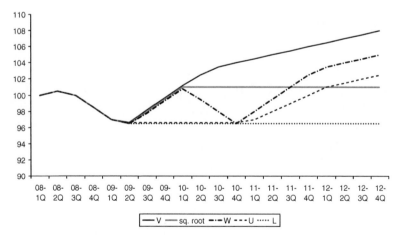

Figure 5.7 Possible recovery scenarios, end 2009 – GDP index 2008, 1Q = 100

had reached at the start of the crisis. Equity markets had rallied, and investment grade corporates were raising record amounts in the bond markets. Some major banks had returned to profitability, and attention was turning increasingly to what reforms would be necessary to assure that such a calamity as the crisis of 2007–2009 would never occur again.

Part III

Cure

In August 2009 the crisis entered into its third year. It had already cost society trillions in lost output. It had already cost millions of workers their jobs. It had destroyed people's savings and put their retirement at risk. It had prompted governments and central banks to resort to stimulus on a scale unprecedented in peacetime. The crisis has therefore exposed the taxpayer to a heavy burden both immediately and in the future.

How can society prevent such a calamity from recurring? There is no single solution. We must build a consistent framework among macroeconomic policies (including the provision of liquidity by the central bank), resolution, deposit guarantee schemes, regulation and supervision (see Figure PIII.1).

In designing the new financial system, there are many, many choices to be made, akin to the many choices that must be made in designing a building. Some determine the overall purpose (apartment house/block of flats or detached house with garden); others determine how well the building functions (e.g., design of the heating system). Whether the building 'works' depends on whether the overall design suits the building's site and whether the individual design choices are consistent with one another.

The most important choice to be made in the design of the future framework for finance is what the system should seek to protect. Should protection be limited to the assets that consumers could be expected to have? Should protection differ among different types of firms, or should the protection extend to the liabilities of all systemically relevant firms?

Prior to the crisis, there was a view that consumer assets, especially consumer deposits, should be protected via guarantee schemes such as

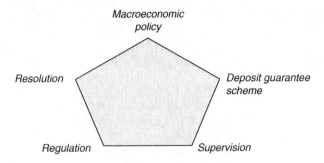

Figure PIII.1   A cure requires a comprehensive and consistent framework

FDIC insurance. There was also a view that deposits – as the lynchpin of payment and settlement systems and the repository of society's liquid wealth – made banks special (Corrigan 1987). Banks therefore deserved special protection. Banks and banks alone had access to central bank lending facilities. It was assumed that controlling the credit extension by banks to non-banks would safeguard the banking system and therefore the economy from the failure of non-banks. It was further assumed that the failure of non-bank firms, however large, could be resolved through normal bankruptcy procedures.

As the recipients of special protection, banks therefore had special regulation, particularly of capital. The Basel Accord was established in 1988 and its risk-based update, Basel II, was in the process of being implemented as the crisis broke in 2007. Banks also had special resolution, at least in the United States. This empowered (indeed forced) the authorities to intervene whilst a bank still had positive net worth and to resolve the bank in a manner that resulted in the least cost to the deposit guarantee fund.

As to exactly what course the resolution should take, the pre-crisis doctrine held that there should be 'constructive ambiguity' even for the very largest banks. Indeed, the US legislation put barriers in the way of 'open bank assistance'. Although the legislation envisaged a 'systemic risk exemption', the legislation also assured that invoking that exemption would be extremely difficult to do.

All this amounted to a bank-centric framework for finance. Banks would be subject to special protection (deposit guarantees and access to the discount window and lender of last resort facilities), but also subject to special resolution and very extensive regulation, especially of capital. Banks would control credit to non-bank firms and exercise market discipline over them. Non-bank firms would be allowed to fail and they would be resolved according to normal bankruptcy proceedings.

The crisis exposed many fault lines in the implementation of this bank-centric design for financial regulation. In many countries, notably the United Kingdom and Germany, there was no special resolution regime for banks, and this made it difficult to handle troubled banks. In many countries, again notably the United Kingdom, the deposit guarantee scheme lacked the ability to pay out insured depositors promptly. This constrained the resolution options open to the authorities and weakened market discipline. Regulation focused too much on capital and not at all on liquidity.

The cure will require a framework that is both comprehensive and consistent. It has to encompass macroeconomic policy, resolution, deposit guarantee schemes, regulation and supervision. It has to be consistent, not only across the components in the framework, but internationally. Finally, it has to be able to deal with the very largest firms. Such a framework will restore the ability of financial intermediation to contribute to growth.

6
Better Macroeconomic Policy

Macroeconomic policy set the stage for the crisis (see Chapter 1), and reforming macroeconomic policy must be part of any cure that would prevent future crises. In the first years of the twenty-first century macroeconomic policymakers had effectively assumed that the financial intermediaries would function as passive transmitters of policy measures to the broader economy. Indeed, monetary policymakers' economic models usually made little or no reference to finance (Adrian and Shin 2008a: 301; Economist 2009b).

That must change. The crisis has shown that finance is far more than just a passive transmission mechanism. Policy does not affect output, employment and prices directly. Instead, policy affects financial markets, and financial markets affect the availability of credit and the decisions that consumers and corporations make about consumption, savings and investment. That in turn drives output, employment and prices. So what happens in financial markets matters to macroeconomics.

Even if short-term interest rates remain the primary policy tool of macroeconomics, the method by which central banks control short-term interest rates may also need rethinking. Exclusive focus on buying and selling risk-free government securities is not the only way to implement monetary policy. Monetary policy can also be implemented during normal times through refinancing the assets of the banking system, as the practice of the European Central Bank amply demonstrates (ECB 2008), as well as in dire times, when 'credit easing' may be necessary (Bernanke 2009). Such implementation methods for monetary policy also afford the central bank a much more direct involvement in the operation of financial markets. It also sets a somewhat different stage for resolution, regulation and supervision.

Towards a new macroeconomics

With the benefit of hindsight, it is abundantly clear that the financial system must become a significant factor in the models that policymakers use to frame the decisions that they have to take (Economist 2009b). Macroeconomic policymakers' models largely ignored the financial system and assumed that asset-price bubbles would either end benignly or could be cleaned up quickly once they had burst (see Chapter 1). Further, these models severely underestimated the impact that the crisis would have upon the real economy, and this, together with ongoing price pressures, especially in commodity markets, may have contributed to policy decisions to refrain from using interest rate reductions as aggressively as had been the case in response to past financial crises (see Chapter 3).

What is needed is a more complete model of the economy that captures the interaction between policy, the financial system and the real economy so that one has a better understanding of the link between policy on the one hand and output, employment and prices on the other. In this more complex world, one policy instrument may not be enough. Interest rate policy may need to be supplemented – not only under credit easing in a zero interest rate environment but in normal times as well – with other policy tools that impact directly on the financial system, if output, employment and prices are to attain and stay within the target range set by (or for) policymakers.

This will be difficult work to do, and theorists are only starting to do such work. However, it is already clear that the principal requirements for such models are to determine what causes the financial system to veer to the extremes of asset-price bubbles during a boom and to debt-deflation during a crash. Liquidity is the primary candidate – both funding liquidity and market liquidity – and this suggests that central bank actions with respect to liquidity will be particularly important (Adrian and Shin 2008b, Brunnermeier 2009; Brunnermeier and Pedersen 2009).

Two approaches to monetary policy

Monetary policy operates through setting the short-term interest rate. Central banks accomplish this through increasing or reducing its own assets, a process known as open market operations. Broadly speaking, there are two approaches to open market operations. The first restricts asset purchases and sales to government bonds and refrains from lending to banks. The second excludes government bonds from asset purchases and sales made by the central bank and executes monetary policy principally through refinancing banks' assets (either through repurchase agreements or collateralised loans). From the standpoint of monetary policy each is an equally valid and effective means to determine the short-term interest rate. The Federal Reserve (prior to the introduction of 'credit easing') and the Bank of England are prominent proponents of the first method; the European Central Bank, of the second (indeed the EU Treaty forces the ECB to use the second, as it contains a prohibition against the central bank's providing monetary financing to member states).

Under the first method – restricting open market operations to government bonds – central banks typically frown on banks' borrowing from the central bank (Akerlof and Shiller 2009: 74–9; Dornbusch, Fischer and Startz 2004: 418). Under this regime, a bank has to apply for credit each time it wishes to draw funds from the central bank, and the central bank reserves the right to refuse the bank credit, if the central bank considers that the institution is not viable (BoE 2008). Even if the bank has previously pledged adequate amounts of eligible collateral with the central bank, the central bank still reserves the right to say no to the bank applying for the loan or repurchase agreement.

The presumption that the bank and its supervisor must make is that the central bank could say no. The bank has the right to request credit, but no right to expect that it will receive it. Borrowing from the central bank is a privilege, not a right, and a privilege that the central bank may or may not award at its sole discretion. For this reason, banks that actually do approach the central bank for credit run the risk of being stigmatised in the market (Goodhart 2002: 232). The mere request for credit is taken by the market as evidence that the bank may be in trouble. For example, Barclays had to counter the rumours that it was in difficulty following its borrowing from the Bank of England's overnight facility in August 2007.

Under the second approach – executing open market operations through repurchase agreements and loans secured by banks' assets – central banks are lending to banks all the time. Borrowing from the central bank may still be a privilege, but it is a privilege that the bank can expect the central bank to grant to the extent that the bank is successful at the auction and the bank has pledged to the central bank or can furnish to the central bank adequate security for the loan in the form of eligible assets.

The central bank protects itself primarily through the quality and amount of the collateral. It does not necessarily conduct a review of the borrowing bank's viability each time the bank bids to refinance its assets. The central bank can remove a bank from the list of eligible participants in the auction on the grounds of prudence, but generally the central bank relies on the assessment of the bank's supervisor to assure that the bank meets minimum prudential requirements (ECB 2008). There is no stigma attached to borrowing from the central bank, for banks borrow from the central bank all the time, and the positive response of the central bank is practically automatic. Indeed, in the case of the ECB a debit at the end of the day in the bank's reserve account with the national central bank is treated as a request for recourse to the ECB's marginal lending facility (ECB 2008:20).[1]

The potential use of lending policy as a macroeconomic tool

If the central bank uses lending to financial institutions as part of its tool kit to implement monetary policy, there are several levers that the central bank may employ to influence the financial system more broadly. These may be particularly useful in terms of designing and implementing the more comprehensive approach to macroeconomic policy that is now required in light of the crisis. They may also be helpful in designing tools that central banks could use to deflate bubbles without raising the overall level of interest rates.

In addition to the interest rate, the policy levers available to the central bank would include determining what assets are eligible to be pledged as collateral, what haircuts should be placed on the value of such collateral and how long the term of any such lending should be. Variations in these terms and conditions can potentially be quite effective in changing conditions in financial markets, particularly for firms that mark their assets to market and finance themselves predominantly through secured borrowings.

If central banks do wish to use variations in conditions as a macroeconomic tool, eligibility for borrowing should be broad based and access to borrowing should readily and regularly be granted. Eligibility would have to convey an expectation that the bank could in fact borrow, if it is able to pledge the appropriate amount of eligible collateral, subject to any auction and allocation procedures that the central bank might apply. Hence, if the central bank wishes to use variations in lending conditions as a macroeconomic tool, all banks meeting threshold conditions should be able to obtain lending from the central bank. Central banks may also wish to have the option to extend this to non-bank firms at least on a temporary basis in order to preserve financial stability, but this may convey the impression that such firms would also be protected under the same safety net that applies to banks, so any such extension should be treated with caution (see "Eligible counterparties for central bank lending" below).

Assets eligible as collateral

For central banking the dividing line between eligible and non-eligible assets is critical (see Figure 6.1). Lending on the basis of eligible collateral constitutes normal central banking activity and may be the principal means by which the central bank executes monetary policy. Lending on the basis of ineligible collateral or without collateral at all effectively means that the central bank is acting as a lender of last resort (see "Lender of last resort" below). The question is whether this boundary line should remain fixed, or whether it should be varied in a counter-cyclical fashion as a tool of macro-prudential policy.

The criteria for eligible collateral are some combination of product category and credit rating. Generally speaking, central banks will always take as collateral, government bonds of the country or countries which issue the currency of the central bank as well as government bonds

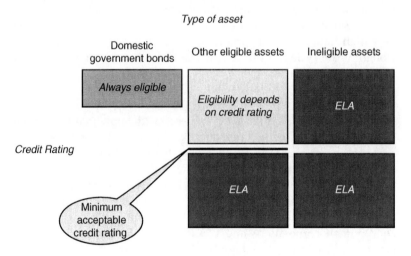

Figure 6.1   Eligibility criteria for bank borrowing from the central bank

considered equivalent to domestic government bonds (such as domestic government agency obligations or the government bonds of similarly rated governments issued in convertible currencies and traded in liquid markets). Central banks also take a range of other collateral, subject to some minimum quality standard or credit rating.[2]

If the central bank allows the use of such broader collateral in the general refinancing facility (rather than restricting its use to a discount window facility with a discrete viability test prior to draw-down), the central bank has the option to use the credit cut-off for such collateral as a macroeconomic tool. Any credit cut-off criterion creates a cliff effect. If an eligible asset becomes ineligible, the bank will either have to replace the newly ineligible asset with a higher quality asset or it will have to repay the facility from the central bank. As a boom progresses, raising the credit cut-off for eligibility will constrict the ability of banks to use lower quality assets as collateral for borrowing from the central bank. This may cool off overheating market positions, and at any rate will send a signal that the central bank is becoming concerned that the market is overheating. Conversely, as a recession deepens, the central bank may choose to reduce the credit cut-off point. This would prevent a cliff effect from occurring as previously eligible assets were downgraded and avoid compounding the recession by withdrawing banks' ability to refinance their assets just at the point in time when it is critical for the economy that banks be able to sustain lending.

The eligibility of illiquid assets, including loans, as collateral or routine borrowing from the central bank is especially important. Allowing institutions to borrow against such collateral – even under very high haircuts – will enhance overall liquidity particularly at the trough of the cycle. This in turn will help sustain the supply of credit to the economy overall.

Haircuts

Note that the credit cut-off does not necessarily imply that the central bank would be taking more credit risk. Haircuts, or excess collateral, are the principal means by which central banks can and should protect themselves against credit risk in lending to banks and/or other eligible counterparties. Conservative and continuously updated valuation of collateral pledged to the central bank is the basis for this protection. Such collateral valuations also allow the central bank to evaluate the condition of corporations and consumers in the real economy and gauge whether policy stimulus or policy constraint is needed. The base level of the haircut be should be set at a level that is related to the riskiness of the asset and sufficient to protect the central bank from loss if default were to occur during the anticipated life of the loan and the central bank had to sell the asset.

From a macroeconomic perspective, one could think of imposing a surcharge on this base level of haircut that would rise as a boom proceeded (again under the assumption that the central bank chooses to implement monetary policy through refinancing banks). Such a surcharge would reinforce the possible change in the credit cut-off point outlined above. For example, suppose the base haircut for a highly rated corporate bond was 15%. As the boom progressed, it might make sense to impose a surcharge of an additional 10 or 15 percentage points. This effectively reduces the advance rate against such collateral, raising the effective cost of financing and reducing the profitability of arbitrage operations that may be contributing to overheating in the market.

In any event, the imposition of the surcharge would give the central bank an opportunity to send a strong signal to the market with respect to its view on market conditions, without the need to raise the overall level of interest rates.[3] For example, as a boom develops, such a haircut surcharge could provide central banks with a powerful tool to indicate to markets those assets which they considered to be overpriced. By raising the haircut on specific assets the central bank could signal that it felt the risk of such assets had increased and/or make financing those assets more expensive. This could effectively provide the central bank with a 'big stick' to go along with the 'bully pulpit' that central banks have. In an extreme case the central bank could raise the haircut on an asset to 100%, effectively making the asset ineligible for discount, at least for a time.

Lending term

Varying the term of lending from the central bank can also be an effective macroeconomic tool (again under the presumption that the central bank chooses to implement monetary policy partially or wholly through the extension of credit to the banking system). By selecting the term on which funds will be made available to banks, the central bank can strongly influence the maturity of banks' liabilities and the degree of liquidity risk in the banking system. Clearly, in the recession the opportunity to borrow at longer term from the central bank is an effective means of allowing banks to extend the maturity profile of their liabilities. This underpins the ability of banks to lend and to sustain economic activity. Conversely, during the boom progressive shortening of the term on which central banks are ready to lend to banks (along with the maintenance of strict liquidity requirements on the banks themselves [see Chapter 9]) would tend to dampen the boom. So would limits on roll-overs of outstanding credit.

Pricing

Finally, a word on pricing as a macroeconomic tool. For central banks that operate monetary policy through lending to banks, the refinancing rate is the policy rate. Varying the refinancing rate is in fact the primary instrument of monetary policy.

For central banks that operate monetary policy through buying and selling government securities, the discount rate is a penalty rate designed to discourage borrowing from the central bank. Varying the discount rate (the rate which the central bank charges banks to borrow) primarily had a signalling function (as there is little or no borrowing at the discount rate). Raising the discount rate signalled that the central bank intended to raise rates at some point in the future. Conversely, lowering the discount rate is a signal that the central bank is considering reducing rates at some point in the future.

Interaction between monetary policy, resolution, regulation and supervision

The choices made by central banks with respect to monetary policy and its execution have very significant implications for regulation, supervision and resolution. Choices about the level of interest rates have a significant impact on the real economy, on credit and market conditions and on the degree of stress to which banks may be exposed and for which they must prepare. Choices about the way in which monetary policy is executed (through buying and selling government securities or through refinancing banks) have significant implications for the degree to which liquidity might be available to banks, either routinely or in emergency situations. In particular, the choice of the range of eligible assets and the determination of the credit cut-off for eligible assets creates the dividing line between normal funding and emergency liquidity assistance or lender of last resort facilities.

Economic stress

Had the real economy performed in line with the forecasts that policymakers made at the end of 2007 (see Chapter 3) it is safe to say that the crisis would not have been as severe. Better economic conditions would have meant lower arrears, lower impairments and lower losses.

The debt-deflation spiral would have been arrested at an early stage or even stanched at the start.

That was not the case. The feedback loop from finance to the real economy greatly aggravated the downturn in the real economy. This needs to be modelled better, and work has started in this direction (see "Toward a new macroeconomics" above).

The major question for regulation is the degree of economic stress to which banks and the financial system should be required to prepare themselves. Should banks be required to be prepared to bear any degree of stress that might arise? Or should there be some type of 'social compact', whereby policymakers would put a floor under the stress that might arise – simply because policymakers will never allow the economy to deteriorate to such an abysmal level?

Today, banks are being subjected to stress tests that envision a very severe downturn. In the United Kingdom this has been labelled as a 'U' scenario, one where the economy stabilises at the depressed level reached in the first half of 2009 but stays there for some time, before reviving at a modest rate. Such a scenario is an extraordinary departure from the pattern of 'V'-shaped recoveries from recession typically experienced in the post-war era, but the 'U'-shaped recovery is arguably not as severe as the decade of stagnation (an 'L'-shape scenario) that Japan experienced following the puncturing of its asset-price bubble (see Figure 6.2).

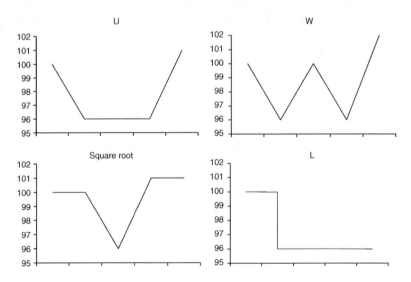

Figure 6.2   Economic scenarios

Should banks be required on an ongoing basis to prepare for stress equivalent to the 'U' scenario, some worse scenario (such as the 'L' scenario) or allowed to gauge their capital and liquidity requirements to one of the more favourable scenarios about how the crisis might end and the recovery develop (such as the square root ($\sqrt{\ }$) or 'W' scenarios)? The more severe the scenario, the greater will be the capital and liquidity that banks will require to survive under such a scenario, but at some point the capital and/or liquidity requirements would be so great as to reduce the ability of the banks to function effectively. This could slow growth and/or promote a shift of activity to less-regulated sectors.

Lender of last resort

As indicated above, the dividing line between eligible and ineligible assets and the cut-off for minimum credit quality for eligible assets sets the dividing line between normal central bank facilities and lender of last resort facilities. Setting a broad range for eligible assets and setting a relatively low credit cut-off will mean that more lending can be accommodated within normal facilities. Setting a narrow range for eligible assets and a relatively high credit cut-off will constrain lending under normal conditions. If lending does occur, it is likely to be characterised as emergency liquidity assistance (ELA) or lender of last resort (LoLR).

The allocation rules for auctions under normal facilities can also direct liquidity to the firms that need it the most.[4] Broad auctions open to all under a variable rate tender allow banks with the greatest liquidity need to bid aggressively for and usually to receive liquidity from the central bank. Banks that bid the highest rate can meet their entire liquidity demand without recourse to extraordinary facilities. Market participants assess that this has been an effective and efficient means for the ECB to pass liquidity to banks most in need of support during the crisis.

In contrast, fixed rate tenders allocate the available liquidity to all bidders on a pro rata basis. Rather than allocate purely on a pro rata basis, consideration might be given to allocating fixed rate tenders on the basis of some other variable, such as quality of collateral (fill demand in order of the quality of collateral with banks offering the highest quality of collateral being filled first) or the leverage ratios of the banks submitting bids (fill demand in the order of leverage with banks having the lowest leverage being filled first). Such supplemental allocation methods might be particularly effective at the top of the boom in curtailing arbitrage and tempering demand.

If lending does take place on the basis of ineligible assets or on an uncollateralised basis, this constitutes emergency liquidity assistance. It necessarily raises the question of whether the bank continues to meet threshold conditions and whether or not the bank should be put into resolution (see Chapter 7).

Eligible counterparties for central bank lending

Finally, there is the question of which institutions should be eligible to borrow from the central bank. Traditionally, access to the central bank has been limited to banks. Non-bank financial institutions and non-financial corporations have not had direct access to the central bank. To the extent that such institutions needed liquidity, they were expected to get it from banks. If banks needed liquidity, they could potentially come to the central bank.

During the crisis, central banks, particularly the US Federal Reserve, substantially expanded access to the central bank. Non-bank broker-dealers were granted access to the discount window facility and the Fed made a LoLR facility available to AIG. In addition, the Fed announced commercial paper purchase facilities that amounted to granting the right to borrow from the central bank to non-financial corporations, or at least to the finance company subsidiaries of such corporations (see Part II).

This has amounted to a considerable broadening of the so-called safety net beyond banks to what might be called a fuller set of systemically important institutions. It represents a very significant departure of policy from the bank-centric view that deposits are special, and that banks, and banks alone, merit a safety net and the regulation and special resolution regime that goes with that safety net. So the US proposal that a much broader set of institutions than banks be subject to a special resolution regime (UST 2009) is consistent with the view that this broader set of institutions should have some type of access to the central bank. So is the conclusion of the G-20 summit in April 2009 that all systemically relevant institutions should be subject to official supervision.

However, broadening out access to the central bank to non-bank financial intermediaries and possibly even to non-financial corporations may also imply a movement towards more universal protection. Broadening out access to the central bank beyond banks undermines the rationale for placing a differentially harsher system of regulation on banks. If banks are not to be accorded a higher degree of protection (i.e., if banks are no longer special), why should banks have a special regulatory regime?

In contrast, restricting access to the central bank to banks recognises the central role that deposits play in financial markets and the economy at large. It avoids extending the safety net and justifies the differentially harsher regulatory regime that applies to banks. The question, however, is how to put the genie back in the bottle, at least in the United States. Once the Fed has indicated that it will come to the support of non-banks, is there any credible mechanism that can convince the market that it will not do so in the future?

7
Better Resolution

Wretched resolution compounded the crisis (see Chapter 4), and reforming resolution holds the key to preventing future crises. Resolution policy determines what governments will protect, and what losses creditors of financial institutions, such as depositors and insurance policyholders, can expect, if a financial firm gets into difficulty. Resolution policy also determines when governments will intervene, and this intervention point effectively determines the minimum prudential standards for capital and/or liquidity. Formulating and adhering to a policy that is politically and economically consistent over time is crucial, if future crises are to be avoided.

To see why this is the case, take a step back to look at the risk that an investor takes when s/he extends credit to a financial institution. This risk compounds two factors: (1) the probability that the institution will require resolution, and (2) the loss given resolution. If the government provides a resolution regime that assures that all losses (beyond the equity that shareholders have put into the institution) will be for the account of the taxpayer, there will be little or no incentive for the creditors of the institution (e.g. a bank's depositors) to monitor the condition of the institution. That in turn raises the probability that the institution will require resolution in the first place, a phenomenon known as 'moral hazard'. To counteract this, the government would have to limit the risk that institutions could take and/or enact very rigorous capital and liquidity requirements.[1]

The letter of the law in most countries restricts protection to retail obligations of financial institutions, such as deposits, insurance policies or client money at broker–dealers. Other than such formal guarantees, there is no explicit assurance that governments will protect liability holders of financial institutions (see Figure 7.1).

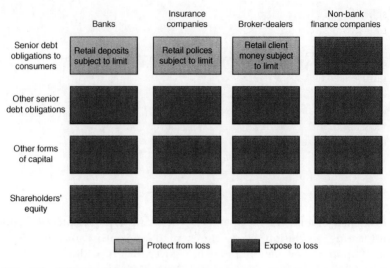

Figure 7.1   Official resolution policy

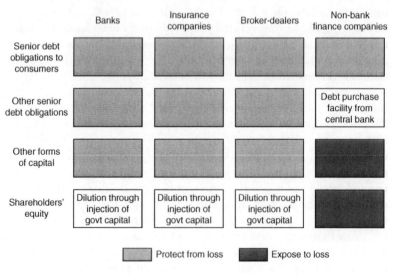

Figure 7.2   Resolution in practice

In practice, governments have not adhered to this 'protect only consumers' policy. In many cases they have protected far more than the retail obligations that they have committed to protect under law. Where banks have failed, governments have protected all retail deposits, not just deposits up to the limit under the deposit guarantee scheme. Where financial institutions have been very large, and/or have had strong interconnections to the rest of the financial system, governments have generally taken steps to provide open-institution assistance in the form of capital and/or liquidity support to prevent any failure (see Figure 7.2). Governments took these decisions in the belief that broader protection would promote financial stability, at least immediately. So there has arisen a "rule" that some institutions are "too big to fail". Lehmans was the exception to this rule, and Lehmans has come to be seen by many as the exception that that proved the wisdom of the rule.

Setting the right expectations

Expectations matter in finance, especially with respect to resolution policy. The risk of loss associated with extending credit to a financial institution, making a deposit in a bank or taking out an insurance policy, depends on the probability that the financial institution will require resolution as well as on the loss given resolution. The first factor (probability of resolution) involves not only a judgement about the risks that the financial institution assumes but also a judgement about the effectiveness of supervision in identifying those risks and getting the firm to mitigate them. The second (loss given resolution) is inherently difficult to predict. It involves forecasting whether the trigger for resolution is pulled promptly and appropriately as well as forecasting the decision that the government will make regarding the support that it may decide to give to a particular institution or to specific obligations of the institution at the point in time when that particular institution requires resolution. That decision depends on the government's assessment of the systemic risk at the time the institution in question might require resolution as well as the government's ability to provide the support that it may wish to give.

As the contrast between Bear Stearns and Lehmans demonstrates, loss given resolution can either be zero (if the authorities decide to protect the liability) or some very large amount (if the authorities decide to expose the liability to loss). With such a wide disparity of possible outcomes, market participants invest quite a bit of time and effort into developing predictions as to what the authorities would do, if they were confronted with the decision on how to resolve a troubled institution. This is part and parcel of the risk assessment of any credit exposure to a financial institution, just as the forecast of loss given default is part and parcel of any risk assessment of the credit to a non-financial corporation. In making this assessment, market participants try to mimic the decision process that the authorities would use and predict the conclusions that the authorities would reach.

Two factors predominate: the willingness of the authorities to provide support and their ability to do so. Market participants recognise that governments conceptually balance the cost of providing support against the reduction in collateral damage (e.g. direct loss of wealth, adverse knock-on effects on other financial institutions, possible damage to the payments and settlements systems) that could be achieved through that support. Market participants also recognise that the collateral damage/ adverse systemic effects are likely to be larger for a larger institution, especially one that has large numbers of retail clients and/or broad and deep interconnections to other financial institutions. Accordingly, market participants had formed a view that some institutions are 'too big to fail' and/or that the authorities would regard the failure of large, cross-border financial institutions as 'too complex to contemplate' (Herring and Carmassi 2010). Market participants reckon that the authorities would be more likely to be willing to support such institutions, if such institutions were to require resolution.

Whether the authorities would be able to save such an institution is another matter. As Iceland demonstrated in 2008 (see Chapter 4), some countries may be 'too small to save' the banks headquartered in their jurisdiction. If the country were forced to bear completely the entire bill for the bank's rescue, the country's government might have to default on its sovereign obligations and/or adopt severe cuts in public expenditure on critical services. In such instances, it is doubtful that the country could fulfil the implicit or explicit guarantees that it had provided to its banks.

Setting policy for resolution involves managing expectations of the market about what policymakers will do, if resolution is required. The market looks not just at what the law says, but more importantly at what the authorities decide to do with respect to troubled institutions. In forming an expectation, market participants appear to give consideration to three things: the legal framework, the willingness to provide support and the ability to provide support.

Whatever resolution policy is put in place, it should be 'time-consistent'. In other words, the policy should be one that the authorities can be reasonably expected to adhere to over time.[2] The resolution policy has to work for the isolated failure of a single institution in the midst of a sanguine economic environment. But it also has to work in the midst of a recession. That is a much taller order, for failures are likely to be more common in a recession and may occur in batches rather than one-by-one. Finally, the formulation of resolution policy has to take into account the possibility that the market will interpret decisions taken with respect to the resolution of one institution as an precedent for how the authorities might act in the future. Such market expectations will affect the risk premium that must be paid by institutions that remain in operation.

The options for resolution policy

Broadly speaking, resolution policy has two aspects: (1) how and when to initiate resolution, and (2) what to protect under resolution. The two questions are related. In brief, the broader and more extensive the protection afforded in resolution to the liabilities of a financial institution, the earlier the authorities should have the right to intervene to limit the risk to the taxpayer.

How and when to initiate resolution

Determining the basis on which the authorities can intervene to force resolution effectively sets the minimum threshold conditions that a bank must maintain to remain in business. And, the entity that 'pulls the trigger' effectively makes the supervisory judgement as to whether the institution should remain in operation or be resolved. For these reasons the UK Banking Act 2009 designated the point at which resolution could be initiated as the point where the bank's supervisor, the Financial Services Authority, determined that the institution failed to meet its threshold conditions or was likely to fail to meet those conditions.

Note that it is always possible for the government to initiate 'very early intervention' to support a financial institution without recourse to formal resolution proceedings, particularly if there is an element of voluntarism in the arrangement. Indeed, the recapitalisations of banks in the United States, United Kingdom, Germany, France, Italy, Switzerland and other countries in the fourth quarter of 2008 are examples of this as are the asset-protection schemes and 'bad bank' proposals advanced in early 2009 (see Chapter 5).

However, it should not be possible for governments to force resolution on financial institutions that are meeting their threshold conditions (in particular, minimum capital and liquidity requirements). If shareholders consider that the government could at any time take over the bank or at any time force the bank to issue more shares to the government at a price of the government's choosing, the threat of expropriation or massive dilution will depress bank equity prices and make it difficult, if not impossible, for banks to raise equity capital in the first place. If banks are to remain private enterprises, governments must offer shareholders some assurance that they will not be subject to unreasonable or arbitrary confiscation or dilution of their property rights. So the intervention point should be not too early and not too late, and there should be some type of rule assuring shareholders that this will be the case.

In practice, institutions that rely on the market for funding usually run out of liquidity long before they run out of capital. So the call as to whether the institution does or does not meet its threshold conditions is frequently bound up with the willingness of the central bank to extend credit to the troubled institution as well as with the terms and conditions on which it is willing to do so. The dividing line between normal liquidity provision, emergency liquidity assistance and resolution can be quite fine in the case of a troubled institution, and how central banks execute these responsibilities has a critical bearing on resolution policy and financial stability (see Chapter 6).

The policy of the central bank also affects the ability of the supervisor to exercise forbearance. Forbearance is extremely difficult for a supervisor to do on its own for any appreciable amount of time. The supervisor cannot keep open a bank that the market refuses to fund, unless the bank relies completely on insured deposits, and/or the bank has access to liquidity on an ongoing basis by virtue of a government guarantee of some or all of its liabilities or access to liquidity from a non-market source, such as the central bank. In the case of the United States, where there are large numbers of banks that finance themselves exclusively, or almost exclusively, through insured deposits, the law requires the regulator to step in to resolve a bank when the bank's capital falls below 2% of its US GAAP assets. Although labelled 'prompt corrective action', the requirement for the regulator to initiate resolution is really a measure to limit forbearance and limit risk to the deposit guarantee fund.

What to protect under resolution

As indicated in the introduction to Part II, resolution policy concerns far more than banks. Indeed, some of the key resolution decisions during this crisis have involved non-bank investment firms (Bear Stearns, Lehmans), insurance companies (AIG) or money market mutual funds. In the United States, at least, authorities have *de facto* moved away from a bank-centric approach to resolution and financial stability. In that respect, banks are no longer special.

This progression of protection from banks to non-banks may be a product of the regulation that the authorities deemed necessary to impose on banks as a result of the special protection that banks were deemed to have had. Business moved from the banking to the non-banking sectors, where other institutions extended credit and engaged in maturity transformation (see Chapter 2). When these non-bank institutions ran into trouble it was deemed in some cases (Bear Stearns, AIG, money market funds) but not others (Lehmans) to provide protection to their creditors and/or investors. So the framework for resolution policy has to encompass all financial institutions, not just banks.

Broadly speaking, there appear to be three options for what resolution policy should seek to protect:

1. *Universal protection.* No bank, and possibly no financial institution, will be allowed to fail. All liabilities (except stockholders' equity) will be protected.
2. *Consumer-only protection.* Troubled institutions will be allowed to fail, unless they can secure the capital and liquidity in the market to survive. Consumers will be protected up to a clearly defined limit from the consequences of failure via government guarantee schemes such as deposit insurance.
3. *'Constructive ambiguity'.* The authorities would decide on a case-by-case basis what should or should not be protected. This is essentially a continuation of the current mixture of action and policy.

Universal protection.   Under a regime of universal protection, all liabilities of banks, and possibly those of non-bank financial intermediaries as well, would be protected in the event of failure. There are three drawbacks to this approach. The first as mentioned above limits the incentive for credit providers to exercise market discipline. Universal protection could raise the likelihood that resolution will be required in the first place. The second drawback is that the absence of market discipline may mean that regulation and supervision have to so severely limit the risk that a financial institution can take that the very risk-intermediation function of financial institutions would be undermined.

The third drawback is a practical and probably determinative one. In all likelihood, universal protection won't work, because the market will quickly come to the conclusion that the government is too small to save the financial institutions that it has promised to support. Rather than discipline institutions on the basis of the risk that the institutions take, the market will look at the ability of the sovereign to meet its commitments to support its financial institutions, given the probability that the institution will require support. The market is likely to be especially critical of the ability of small countries to support large, internationally active financial institutions, especially if resolution continues to be carried out under the 'home country pays' principle.

Consumer-only protection.   Theoretically, this option has great appeal. It restricts government intervention to the minimum necessary to assure financial stability. This decision rule (or its first cousin, to resolve bank failures in the manner that causes the least cost to the deposit guarantee fund) biases resolution away from providing open bank assistance and towards a solution that imposes losses on the bank's creditors, including possibly uninsured depositors (as was the case in the resolution of Washington Mutual [see Chapter 4]).

However, there are two problems with this approach. The first is a practical one. The guarantee scheme actually has to be able to do what it says on the tin: perform in a timely fashion on the guarantee as promised. Not all schemes can do this, especially in Europe, and reform is urgently needed, if reliance on consumer guarantees is to be part of the resolution regime (see Chapter 8).

The second problem with the consumer-only approach is a political one. Governments have never in the past restricted themselves to protecting consumers only. They have always wished at least to have the option to protect a broader set of liabilities such as all retail deposits, all deposits or even all liabilities. Attempts to limit governments' discretion have been tried but have not been entirely successful, either because governments have found a way to avoid the rule (e.g. Bear Stearns and AIG) or because following the rule has had severely adverse consequences. For example, in the United States, there is a requirement that resolution of a failed bank be conducted in a manner that is likely to result in the least cost to the deposit insurance fund. There is a so-called systemic risk exemption to this general rule but this requires several levels of approval (two-thirds majority of the Board of Directors of the FDIC as well as two-thirds majority of the Board of Governors of the Federal Reserve System as well as the approval of the Secretary of the Treasury 'in consultation with the President'). The proposed Citigroup acquisition of Wachovia was the first time that this systemic risk exemption was invoked, and even then it was quickly reversed when Wells Fargo made a better offer (see Chapter 4). The decision to let Lehmans fail also followed the least-cost/consumer-only principle.

As shown above (see Chapter 4), this policy had disastrous consequences, and the United States shifted under TARP to a policy of 'very early intervention' that recapitalised major US banking organisations and/or provided asset guarantees (see Chapter 5). The United States also accelerated the conversion of Morgan Stanley and Goldman Sachs into bank holding companies so that they could benefit from injections of capital under TARP as well as from greater access to central bank discount window facilities. And, the United States elected to protect AIG so that its failure would not cause systemic havoc.

As the US experience demonstrates, it is extremely unlikely that a 'consumer-only' resolution policy would be 'time consistent'. At some stage, governments will want to exercise the option to protect more than just liabilities to consumers.

Constructive ambiguity.   This option essentially amounts to a continuation of the status quo. A firm's liabilities to consumers are the only liabilities that must be protected, but the authorities have the option, on a case-by-case basis, to extend protection to other liabilities or to offer assistance that will keep the firm open and its creditors whole. In the case of a failing bank the authorities would make a choice among four methods of resolution (see Table 7.1):

1. *Liquidation/insured deposit pay-off.*   Under this method the failed bank is liquidated much the way an insolvent non-bank financial corporation would be liquidated. Receivers would be appointed and they would liquidate the assets of the bank, paying out proceeds to the liability holders in strict order of seniority. The deposit guarantee scheme would pay out insured deposits to eligible depositors and step into their claim against the estate of the failed bank. As a result, insured depositors suffer no loss. In contrast, all other liability holders of the bank are at risk, including depositors who are not eligible for coverage. Deposits held by eligible depositors that are above the ceiling on the deposit guarantee scheme are also at risk.

Note that for this method to be feasible, the deposit guarantee scheme must be able to pay out the claims of eligible depositors promptly. Failure to do so would undermine the credibility of the deposit guarantee scheme and provoke the very panic that deposit guarantees are intended to prevent.

2. *Deposit transfer.*   This method has similar effects on the risk faced by liability holders. The only difference is that the insured deposits are transferred to a third party rather than having the deposit guarantee scheme pay off the insured deposits.

Table 7.1 Loss given resolution for various bank liabilities under different resolution methods to implement 'constructive ambiguity'

| Type of liability | Resolution method | | | |
	Liquidation/ insured deposit pay-off	Deposit transfer	Bridge bank	Open bank assistance including TPO
Insured deposits	No loss	No loss	No loss	No loss
Other deposits	Possible loss	Possible loss	Possible loss	No loss
Secured borrowings	No loss if collateral is sufficient	No loss if collateral is sufficient	No loss if collateral is sufficient	No loss
Subordinated debt (Tier 2 capital)	Possible loss	Possible loss	Possible loss	Unlikely to have a loss
Hybrid Tier 1 capital	Possible loss	Possible loss	Possible loss	May have coupons deferred
Preferred stock	Likely to incur a loss	Likely to incur a loss	Likely to incur a loss	May have coupons cancelled

In countries where there is depositor preference, uninsured deposits enjoying that preference are likely to be transferred with the insured deposits to a third party. The preference accorded to deposits makes it extremely unlikely that the uninsured depositors will suffer a loss. The preference accorded to deposits also makes it easier to transfer the good assets of the bank along with the deposits, so that there is a lower need for the deposit guarantee scheme/government to lend to the estate of the failed bank so that the insured deposits can be made whole.

3. *Bridge bank.*   In the bridge bank method, the resolution authority effectively splits the failed bank into a 'good bank' and a 'bad bank'. The good bank continues to operate as normal and meets its obligations, if necessary with the assistance of the resolution authority itself, the central bank or the government. Liabilities transferred into the good bank are paid in full; no loss is suffered. In contrast, liabilities left behind in the bad bank could suffer a loss. The bad bank is generally

subject to liquidation or run-off, and losses can be expected on the assets in the bad bank.

In countries where there is depositor preference all deposits would generally be assigned to the good bank and the best assets can be cherry picked from the failed bank to go into the good bank. In countries such as the United Kingdom where there is no depositor preference, safeguards have been established so that liabilities relegated to the bad bank suffer a loss that is no greater than would have been incurred had the failed bank been liquidated (HMT 2008b).

4. *Open bank assistance,* including temporary public ownership (TPO). Open bank assistance can take many forms, including the transfer of the failed bank into TPO. Under this method, only management and shareholders of the failed bank suffer a loss. Management generally loses their jobs and some or all of their accrued benefits. Common shareholders suffer at a minimum massive dilution and possibly the loss of their entire investment (this could be the case under TPO). In contrast, depositors suffer no loss. Nor do holders of the bank's senior debt. Although holders of capital instruments (subordinated debt, hybrid Tier 1 capital and preferred stock) might suffer the deferral (in the case of hybrid Tier 1 capital) or cancellation (in the case of preferred stock) of the coupons on such instruments and/or a loss of market value, open bank assistance has generally stopped short of requiring a write-down of the principal value of such instruments. Contractually, such instruments bear loss only if the concern becomes a 'gone' concern. The whole purpose of open bank assistance is to keep the bank as a going concern.[3]

In theory, 'constructive ambiguity' is a very attractive option. It creates a doubt about what the authorities may do in any specific case. Uninsured creditors of the bank, as well as shareholders and hybrid capital providers, are at risk of suffering a loss given resolution and so have the incentive to monitor and discipline the bank's risk-taking. But the authorities retain the option to protect more than just the insured depositor, should this seem appropriate at the time to preserve financial stability.

Although 'constructive ambiguity' is better than either universal protection or consumer-only protection, 'constructive ambiguity' does not necessarily meet the 'time-consistent' test. To work, 'constructive ambiguity' must in fact leave the market guessing as to what the authorities would decide to do in any specific case. What they did in the last case should have no bearing on what the market expects the authorities might decide in the next. Each decision should be independent, much like the outcome from the toss of a coin.

That is not the case. The authorities have generally followed a pattern that suggests that the larger and more interconnected the institution is with the market as a whole, the more likely it is that the authorities will intervene in a manner that protects the entire institution, not just consumers. Lehmans was the exception to this rule, but in the eyes of many, it is the exception that very much proves the merit of the rule.

If the rule has merit, there are limits to how effective 'constructive ambiguity' can be. Very small institutions can be reckoned to be liquidated, and protection will be restricted to the amount provided under consumer guarantee programmes. Very large institutions, especially those that are complex and/or cross-border, can be expected to receive (provided it is consistent with the home country's willingness and ability to pay) capital and/or liquidity assistance so that the troubled institution remains a going concern. Only for institutions in the middle would there be genuine doubt as to the scope and amount of protection that the institution would receive, if it were to become troubled.

This situation is deeply unsatisfactory for a number of reasons. First, it creates competitive distortions. Firms reckoned by the market to be too big to fail are firms that may not be effectively disciplined by the market. Over time, there may be a tendency for business to flow to such firms. Smaller firms may be at a competitive disadvantage, as will be firms that are headquartered in countries that are either less willing or less able to support their financial institutions. Within the European Union it could imply that some Member States would be more equal than others, despite the best efforts of the Commission to assure that national rescue plans for financial institutions are consistent with state aid rules.

Although burden-sharing and/or a move to a more federal system could correct some of the competitive distortions among Member States, it would do nothing to counter what might be called an avalanche effect. If 'constructive ambiguity' results in the bigger being rescued, over time the big will become bigger. If the market cannot discipline the bigger survivors, the burden falls much more fully on regulation and supervision to provide that discipline. So each crisis may provoke an upward ratchet in regulation. Too much regulation runs the risk of undermining the efficiency of financial intermediation and the spur to growth that it should provide. Too little regulation and/or too lax supervision runs the risk of permitting the seeds of the next crisis to be sown.

For 'constructive ambiguity' to be the basis of resolution policy, two things are required. First, the consumer guarantee schemes must be in a position to deliver promptly on their promise to pay consumers in the event that a firm defaults (see Chapter 8). If the guarantee schemes are not capable of doing so, the authorities are constrained in their choice of resolution methods and may not be able to achieve least-cost resolution. If a call is made to the deposit guarantee system to perform, it must do so promptly. If it does not, widespread panic could result.

The second prerequisite for 'constructive ambiguity' is a law that will provide the authorities with the ability to intervene early and decisively in the case of a troubled financial institution. This can facilitate prompt resolution and maintain significant value. In the absence of such a law, the shareholders and/or management of the troubled institution may have the opportunity to utilise temporary capital and/or liquidity support to 'play for redemption' by taking greater risks in the hopes of obtaining sufficient capital to keep their institution alive.

The UK Banking Act 2009 is an example of such a law. This permits the authorities to put a troubled bank into resolution upon determination by the bank's supervisor, the Financial Services Authority, that the bank does not meet or is likely to fail to meet, its 'threshold conditions' or minimum requirements. The Bank of England chooses the resolution method to be deployed, subject to the approval of the Treasury if the resolution method involves the use of public funds (Tripartite 2007, 2008a,b,c). The United States has a similar law (FDICIA) that creates a special resolution regime for banks. But not every country has a special resolution regime for banks. Several EU Member States lack such laws, although the Commission is considering introducing measures at Community level to rectify this (COM 2009c).

Even if all countries had a special resolution regime for banks, this would not completely pave the way to implement a 'constructive-ambiguity' principle of resolution. Practically no country has a law that permits the special resolution of non-bank financial firms such as investment firms and insurance companies. In the absence of such a law there is no alternative to either open-institution assistance (effectively the protection of all liabilities and the preservation of at least some stockholders' equity) or letting the firm enter a disorderly and lengthy bankruptcy proceeding. The United States has proposed a law that would allow the federal authorities to resolve non-bank financial firms as well as banks (US Treasury 2009: 76–8).

Even if all countries had the requisite national laws in place, there would have to be convergence and coordination on an international scale if constructive ambiguity is to be consistently applied to even the largest financial institutions. As the example of Lehmans demonstrates, large, complex financial institutions may be global in life, but they are national in death. Unless some way is found to handle a cross-border resolution smoothly,[4] constructive ambiguity for the largest financial institutions may be a prohibitively expensive option.

Restructuring resolution

This suggests that resolution itself needs restructuring. Rather than wait until the institution becomes troubled to decide on how it would be resolved, it may make sense for regulation to force each financial institution to plan more fully for its own resolution ahead of time, whilst the institution is still in sound condition. Essentially, this would amount to a 'pre-pack' resolution, so that shareholders and liability holders would know in advance how they would be treated in the event that the institution required resolution. This would move the financial system away from constructive ambiguity towards constructive certainty, but in a manner that will not imply either universal protection or a return to the consumer-only approach. The conclusion of this volume suggests a way in which this could be done.

8
Better Deposit Guarantee Schemes

No resolution policy can be successful without assuring that consumers' deposits are fully protected, at least up to certain limit. So a robust deposit guarantee scheme, capable of paying out insured deposits promptly in the event of a bank failure, is a critical component of the framework for a sounder financial system.

A credible and reliable deposit guarantee scheme requires that the scheme

a. provide adequate coverage to consumers;
b. be able to pay out insured deposits promptly, if called upon to do so; and
c. have an appropriate funding scheme for bearing the ultimate loss incurred under the scheme.

In addition, steps should be taken either by the deposit guarantee fund itself or via regulation of banks to assure that consumers are aware of the extent as well as the limitations of deposit guarantee protection. Finally, consideration has to be given to the scope of deposit guarantees:

• Should more than one deposit guarantee scheme be permitted to operate within a single country?
• Should guarantees cover only bank deposits, or should protection extend to deposit-like products such as money market mutual funds?

Determining the eligibility for coverage

The key choice in designing a deposit guarantee scheme is eligibility for coverage. Who should be eligible for deposit guarantees? Just consumers or any depositor? Most countries elect to limit deposit guarantees to natural persons or to natural persons plus small- to medium-sized business enterprises. This is appropriate. Deposits are effectively a loan to the bank, and consumers generally do not have either the knowledge or time to conduct a credit analysis of the bank in which they place their money. Without deposit guarantees, consumers could conclude that if one bank failed, all banks would be in trouble. This failure of one bank could lead to runs on others. Effective deposit guarantees put a stop to such contagion.

Determining the limit

The next design question is what should the limit be? Generally, countries opt to impose a legal limit on the amount of guaranteed deposits that a person can hold in any one bank. This is about one to three years' average family income for the country in question. Again, this is appropriate, for above a certain amount, it can be reckoned that the person is either sophisticated enough to carry out a credit analysis or wealthy enough to diversify his investments across a number of banks. Proposals to impose limits per account or limits per brand are really arguments that there should be no limits at all, at least for individuals. It should be emphasised that the deposit guarantee limit is the limit per person per bank. There is nothing to prohibit a person from having accounts at more than one bank, and from benefiting from insurance or guarantees on each of those accounts. So the total amount of deposit guarantees available to each person is the number of banks in the country times the deposit guarantee scheme limit. In the United Kingdom, this would yield potential deposit guarantee coverage of at least £10 million per person, and in the United States – where the limit is higher and there are many more banks – a sum of $2 billion (see Table 8.1). Certainly, this should be more than ample coverage for any

Table 8.1 Total deposit guarantees available to each person, selected countries, June 2009

	Limit per individual depositor per bank	Number of banks in the country (approximate)	Total deposit guarantee coverage available to each individual
UK	£50,000	200	£10,000,000
Germany	€50,000	2000	€100,000,000
USA	$250,000	8000	$2,000,000,000

individual, and with modern technology and deposit brokerage, there is no reason why even the truly wealthy could not completely cover all of the wealth that they choose to keep in deposits.[1]

Should co-insurance be required, or permitted?

In most insurance contracts, the insurance company requires the policyholder to take a deductible or first loss before the insurance company is liable to pay a claim. Some deposit guarantee schemes (including until very recently the UK) contain a similar feature. They envision that the depositor (as the holder of a deposit insurance policy) would bear a certain portion of the loss that could arise from the failure of the bank. As far as deposit guarantee schemes are concerned, such co-insurance requirements are completely counterproductive. Coverage should be for 100% of whatever headline limit is established. Although consumers may be aware that their deposits are guaranteed, they are only aware of the headline limit. Only when a bank gets into trouble do people become aware, indeed very quickly aware, of the fine print that says that they may be responsible for some portion of the loss for amounts below the headline limit. Certainly that was the experience in the United Kingdom in the case of Northern Rock, where websites, blogs and the personal finance columnists all made depositors aware that although the headline limit was £35,000, 100% insurance only applied to the first £2,000. Rather than calming depositors' fears, the deposit guarantee scheme added to the run on the bank as its details became more widely known. Shortly afterwards (1 October 2007), the FSA removed co-insurance from the UK deposit guarantee scheme, increasing the coverage to 100% of the £35,000 limit in force at the time.

Speed of payout

The next key design element in deposit guarantee schemes is to determine the speed of payout. Should this be rapid, or is it acceptable to pay out depositors over a longer period? The quicker the payout, the better deposit guarantees are. People are used to being able to access their current accounts and much of their savings on demand. The slower the payout, the less effective deposit guarantees are. Indeed, the threat of losing access to one's funds for an extended period is ample reason in and of itself to run on a bank in trouble, even if the deposit is fully guaranteed. People want to retain access to their money, and will take steps to do so, including, if need be, running on the bank. The lines of people in front of Indy Mac branches in the United States prior to its closure by the FDIC are ample testimony to this.

For this reason, both the United Kingdom and the European Union are adopting measures to curtail the interval between the date the bank fails and the date that eligible depositors receive payments from the deposit guarantee scheme. In the United Kingdom, the FSA has proposed that the FSCS be able to pay out guaranteed deposits within seven days of the failure of a bank (FSA 2009a, 2009f), and the EU Deposit Guarantee Schemes Directive envisions that Member States' schemes would be able to pay out deposits within 20 days of the failure of a bank.

To be capable of paying out depositors quickly in the event of a bank failure, the deposit guarantee scheme has to

- be able to calculate promptly the amount due to insured depositors of a failed bank;[2] and
- have access, if required, to the funds needed to pay out insured depositors immediately upon the insolvency of a bank.

Calculating the amount due to an eligible depositor in a failed bank

Conducting a payout starts with the very basic question of 'how much, to whom'? The deposit guarantee scheme must have information on which accounts in the failed bank are or are not guaranteed, and how much is in each of the guaranteed accounts on the day the bank fails. Since limits are per person per bank, the deposit guarantee scheme must also have a means to aggregate the deposits that a person may have in several accounts at the same bank to arrive at a 'single customer view' of the total balances that the person has in all accounts in the same institution. This total can then be compared with the limit for deposit guarantee coverage to arrive at the amount that the deposit guarantee scheme would pay the depositor. All this needs to be done very quickly indeed, if payout is to occur within a time frame that depositors would find acceptable. However, the only way that the deposit guarantee scheme will be able to make such rapid calculations of the amount due to depositors is by drawing on the information and systems of the failed bank itself. To do so requires that each bank – even those in robust good health – keep its data up to date and in a shape that would permit the authorities to make a rapid determination of how much the deposit guarantee scheme owes to each insured depositor. This involves setting a flag on each account to classify it as eligible or ineligible for coverage under the deposit guarantee scheme.[3] Determining the amount in the account is fairly straightforward, provided the deposit guarantee scheme's rules allow it to pay claims for deposits on a gross basis, ignoring any set-off that might otherwise exist between the deposit and any loan owed by the same individual to the failed institution.[4] Aggregating the accounts of a single individual across the bank is more difficult and more costly, but this needs to be done, if the per person per bank system of limits is to be retained. Although much has been made of the fact that this is somewhat simpler to do on a per brand basis, as that is the way banks' systems currently operate, the fact is that much of the expense of forming a single customer view would be required to form a single customer view per brand. The additional expense of forming a single customer view per bank is relatively small. And, the utility of a single customer view is not restricted to paying out depositors in the event of the bank's own failure. Indeed, some banks have implemented a single customer view for their own marketing and business purposes.[5]

Deposit guarantee schemes are implementing rules that require banks to keep their data in a manner that would facilitate the rapid calculation of the amount owing to eligible depositors, if the bank were to fail (FSA 2009a: 22–26; FDIC 2008). In addition, countries are working to assure that deposit guarantee schemes have access to banks that are in danger of failing in advance of the possible failure date, so that the deposit guarantee scheme can more promptly execute payout if required to do so. The FDIC has been particularly active and effective in this regard.

Obtaining access to funding for prompt payouts

Being able to calculate rapidly how much to pay and to whom is essential. But to actually execute the payout, the deposit guarantee scheme must have immediate access to the funding required. That implies some access to government funding, even if there is pre-funding (see below) of the deposit guarantee scheme. This access to government funding is needed to sustain the credibility of the deposit guarantee scheme in the eyes of the public. Limiting deposit guarantees to the amount in the deposit guarantee fund (if there is one) makes no sense whatsoever. Once the government has reassured the public through the introduction of a deposit guarantee scheme, the government must assure that the scheme is in a position to fulfil that promise if called upon to do so. In effect, the government has to act as a backstop to the deposit guarantee scheme and provide the scheme with funds, if necessary, to enable the fund to meet its obligations to insured depositors in a prompt manner. The recourse to funding can be quite large, given that the payout will be for the gross amount of the guaranteed deposits rather than the smaller loss amount after recoveries for which the deposit guarantee scheme will ultimately be responsible. For this reason, governments in the United States, the United Kingdom and other countries have granted their deposit guarantee schemes access to funding lines sufficient to enable the schemes to meet obligations to depositors as they fall due.

Setting an appropriate funding scheme for deposit guarantees

Funding is the next element in the design of deposit guarantee schemes. There is a general agreement that the banks whose deposits are covered by the scheme should bear the costs of the scheme, that is the losses attributable to the covered deposits in the estate of the failed bank.[6] Effectively, the deposit guarantee scheme stands in the shoes of these depositors as a creditor against the estate of the failed bank. Often the deposit guarantee scheme is the largest creditor of the failed bank, and this can provide the deposit guarantee scheme with the ability to influence greatly the course that the administrator/receiver will take with respect to the failed bank. Indeed, in the United States, the FDIC generally acts as the receiver of failed banks.[7]

Broadly speaking there are two ways to fund deposit guarantee schemes: ex post and ex ante. The former is a 'survivor pays' model. Usually levies are *pro rata* relative to the assessment base. Such a system can be pro-cyclical in the sense that losses from bank failures and deposit guarantee levies to pay for those losses are likely to loom largest when the economy is at or near its nadir. The increase in assessments to pay for the losses incurred by others can have an adverse knock-on effect and may make it more difficult for some other banks to avoid failure themselves. The recent experience of the UK deposit guarantee scheme is a case in point. Although the UK government advanced the FSCS the funds necessary to effect the fulfilment of deposit guarantees in connection with the failures of various UK banks pending the recoveries from the estates of those failed banks, the FSCS levy necessary to pay the interest cost on these loans will represent an appreciable share of the anticipated profit of some depository institutions. In insurance terms ex post levies amount to a 'reverse tontine' where the last bank standing pays for the failures of those who exit early.

Under a system of ex ante funding each bank pays each year for the protection provided by the guarantee scheme to its deposits. So the bank that fails has in effect paid up front for the protection that its depositors receive. Success is not punished through higher assessments or premiums, as it is under the ex post or 'survivor pays' plan. Ex ante premiums can either be at a flat rate proportional to the assessment base, or a risk-based levy, based on an assessment that the bank may fail. If the latter, the assessment of risk for the purpose of assigning a premium has to be aligned with and/or grounded in the supervisory judgement of the bank's risk. If risk-based levies are not so coordinated, the imposition of risk-based levies will amount to a second and parallel system of supervision (see Chapter 10). Note that the imposition of ex ante premiums does not imply that they will necessarily be accumulated in a fund, pending disbursement in the event of a failure. Ex ante premiums could simply be paid to a credible guarantor, such as the government, who would meet any claims on the fund as they fell due. Indeed, as discussed above, it would be counterproductive to imply that deposit guarantees were limited by the size of the deposit guarantee fund. What a fund does do is create a separation between the government, as the ultimate guarantor, and the banks protected under the deposit guarantee scheme. Without a fund, governments might be tempted to treat ex ante premiums as just another source of tax revenue similar to excise tax on spirits or tobacco. With a fund, there is an earmarking of revenues from the premiums or assessments on deposits that is reserved for protecting deposits, with a commitment that the government will extend credit to the fund, if need be, to enable the deposit guarantee scheme to meet its obligations in full and on time.

Finally, in deciding a funding regime for the deposit guarantee scheme, one has to determine the assessment base. This should be set in line with what is being protected. The most logical choice is to have the assessment base equal the amount of covered deposits. This aligns protection and premiums. It is particularly appropriate, if protection is in fact strictly limited to insured deposits. But insured deposits are by no means the only choice possible for the assessment base. In the United States, the assessment base is all domestic deposits rather than just insured deposits. In the United Kingdom, the assessment base for deposit guarantees is the amount of insured deposits, but there are also levies for the other products, such as insurance, which banks provide to customers, and a system that envisages that the assessment pool for another industry (e.g. insurance) could be tapped, if the annual cap on contributions from the deposit pool were exhausted (FSA 2007b).

Hence, setting the assessment more broadly than just insured deposits can either be construed as a tax on the larger banks or an implicit recognition that the government may decide under 'constructive ambiguity' to protect liabilities in addition to insured deposits.

Assuring appropriate consumer awareness of deposit guarantees

Deposit guarantee schemes will not promote financial stability unless consumers are aware that their deposits are protected. Accordingly, banks should be required to take steps to assure that consumers are aware of the extent, as well as the limitations, of protection afforded by the deposit guarantee scheme to their deposits. In particular, banks should inform their customers

- whether or not the account is protected under the scheme, and
- about the amount of coverage offered by the scheme.

Although publications by banks routinely refer to the existence of a deposit guarantee scheme, such references should be reinforced by measures such as printing on account statements whether or not the account is covered under the scheme. Once banks have a single customer view in place, consideration should be given to forcing banks to provide information to consumers on their aggregate balances at the bank and what portion of those balances are actually covered under the deposit guarantee scheme. This would give governments more of an option to back away from the implicit guarantee that they have given to all retail deposits during this crisis.

Should more than one deposit guarantee scheme be permitted to operate within a single country?

For EU Member States, an additional issue arises – whether there should be more than one deposit guarantee scheme in a country. Under the single market, each EU credit institution has the right to establish a branch in each of the other Member States and to accept deposits from retail customers. These deposits are currently covered under the home country scheme up to the limit of that scheme.[8] This means that there can be up to 30 deposit guarantee schemes in operation in any one Member State (one for each of the 27 Member States plus one for each of the three EEA countries [Iceland, Norway and Liechtenstein]).

For such a policy to be effective, Member States would have to require banks to state clearly and continuously the deposit guarantee scheme under which the deposit is covered. In the case of branches of EEA banks, the Member States would also have to assure that consumers were aware that, in the event such a bank were to fail, the consumer had no claim on the deposit guarantee scheme of the host Member State and that the consumer would have to go to the deposit guarantee scheme of the home Member State to secure compensation.

Effectively this system imposes on the consumers in host countries the burden of analysing whether or not the home country scheme will pay out insured deposits promptly. That requires the host country consumer to assess whether the home country's scheme is operationally robust and financially sound. It further requires the consumer in the host country to assess whether the home Member State is fiscally robust enough to stand behind the deposit guarantees that the home country scheme has given to the bank's depositors, including those depositors in branches in other EEA countries. Finally, it requires the host country consumer to assess whether the home Member State would actually have the political ability to push through the taxes on home country banks and/or taxpayers that would be necessary to enable the home country to meet the obligations of the home country deposit guarantee scheme to depositors in the failed bank's branches in EEA countries.

The regime also implies that host country governments will be content, when faced with the complaints of hundreds of thousands or more depositors (and voters) that the home country scheme has failed to pay out promptly, to simply tell those depositors (and voters) that they should have read the fine print, that they should have realised that they were covered under the deposit guarantee scheme of the bank's home country, that they should get in contact with the scheme of the bank's home country and that they should stop pestering their own government about their troubles.

If all schemes are actually able to pay out and do pay out within the 20 days as envisaged under the revised Directive, then such problems may not arise. But we are far from that state of affairs now, and we may remain so even after the amendments to the Directive have been implemented, for they do not assure that all schemes will have adequate funding and that all Member States will always be in the position to fulfil the guarantees that attach to the deposits of banks headquartered in their Member State.

All this is potentially confusing to consumers and at odds with the tendency of governments to wish to protect the interests of their own citizens (and voters). Consequently, the question arises as to whether we should have 'more Europe or less Europe' as far as cross-border retail banking is concerned (Turner 2009: 100–104). "Less Europe would imply either a tendency to conduct retail banking through subsidiaries and/or provision for the host country to take a greater role in supervision – a development that would be at odds with the single market and contrary to the principle of home country responsibility for prudential supervision. More Europe would imply a shift to a funded pan-European deposit guarantee scheme – but that would demand an agreement among Member States on the burden-sharing that would be required to back up such a pan-European scheme.

However, a middle way would be possible, if deposit guarantee schemes were to be pre-funded and premiums were based on risk. This middle way is to make deposit guarantees a host country responsibility. This would work as follows. Deposits would be guaranteed under the scheme of the jurisdiction in which they are booked. Subsidiaries would be handled just as they are today – the bank will be supervised by the host country supervisor and will be subject to the host country resolution regime. For branches, the host country scheme would provide the guarantee to the host country depositor. The host country would charge the branch a risk-based premium relative to the deposits covered under the host country scheme based on the risk of the whole bank.

Under this approach the depositor in the host country would have a claim on the scheme that is ultimately under control of and benefits from the support of the host country government. The depositor need not grapple with the home country scheme. The host country would not supervise the bank with branches, but it would be entitled to set a premium on the deposits that the branch insured under the host country scheme. To set this premium the host country scheme would have to have access to information about the consolidated position of the bank. This would be provided either by the bank directly to the host country scheme or by the home country supervisor.

Should guarantees cover only bank deposits?

Banks conduct a far wider range of businesses with consumers than merely taking deposits, and the failure of a bank can have wider consequences for consumers than the loss of availability or principal of the deposit that the consumer has with the bank. In particular, consumers may have investments or insurance policies with the bank and/or its affiliates, and these are likely to be adversely affected if the bank were to fail.

From the standpoint of financial stability, these non-deposit activities of banks have traditionally been considered less critical and to require less protection and/or less immediate settlement. In today's day and age, however, that may be questioned. Certainly, consumers would be adversely affected by the failure of an institution that holds an appreciable amount of client money in investment accounts. The prompt return of client assets to clients is essential, if the consumer is not to be exposed involuntarily to loss due to market movements in the price of securities held in his/her account pending the resolution of the failure of the firm holding the client's money. Similarly, consumers would be adversely affected, if the insurance companies that had issued the policies insuring their pensions, lives, homes, cars and/or health were to fail.

Many countries have therefore instituted protection for client money as well as for insurance policies. In some countries (e.g. the United States), there are separate schemes for each of these areas; in others (e.g. the United Kingdom), there is a unified compensation scheme. This has proved effective in coordinating all the different claims that can arise from the failure of a financial institution. However, whether these undoubted economies of administration justify the creation of cross-funding from one sub scheme to another is more controversial.

Summary

In sum, better deposit guarantee schemes are a critical component of the cure for crises. They underpin and are a precondition for better resolution policy. Deposit guarantees must be able to do what it says on the tin: to pay out promptly the insured amount to the rightful owner. This requires changes to the operations of the schemes themselves as well as to the way that banks organise the data on deposit accounts. It also requires access to funding and a back stop from the government to assure that the guarantee will be met. Without such operational and financial follow through, one runs the risk that the deposit guarantee scheme itself will fail – and such a failure would indeed be a recipe for panic. If one is to have deposit guarantees, one should have robust ones.

9
Better Regulation

This crisis has exposed fault lines in regulation. The previous system allowed the build-up in the so-called shadow banking system as well as on-balance sheet leverage in financial firms, particularly the systemically relevant firms at the heart of the financial system. This contributed to the financial crisis. And, when the crisis struck, the capital and liquidity demanded by the previous system proved insufficient. This magnified the financial crisis.

Fixing regulation therefore carries high priority. Indeed, in the G-7 (2008) and G-20 (2008, 2009) summits convened since the crisis began, heads of states have provided strong mandates to the Financial Stability Forum (FSF 2008, 2009c) and various international bodies, such as the IMF (2009b), the Basel Committee (BCBS 2009b,c), IOSCO (2008, 2009) and the IASB (2009) to accelerate the development of policies to reform regulation so that the financial system would be spared another crash of the magnitude of 2007–2009. These international efforts have been supplemented by EU initiatives (de Larosière 2009; COM 2009a) and national initiatives in the United States (UST 2009), the United Kingdom (Turner 2009; FSA 2009d; HMT 2009), Germany (Steinbrück 2009) and various other countries. In addition, the private sector has not only commented on official proposals but also made recommendations of its own (IIF 2008, 2009b; CRMPG 2008).

The focus of regulatory reforms has to be on condition and conduct. Regulation should require firms to remain in good condition and give regulators the power to put firms into resolution, if they do not meet threshold conditions. Regulation should also require that firms and markets conduct themselves appropriately and give regulators the power to discipline firms and/or markets that do not.

Broadly speaking, regulation seeks to assure that firms engage in 'good' conduct and that they remain in 'good' condition. Effectively regulation sets the framework in which financial firms must choose and implement their strategy (see Figure 9.1). Conduct of business regulation rules out certain strategies, such as market abuse, that could be quite profitable, but which are simply unacceptable. Firms have to operate in a manner that is fair to the market and fair to their customers. When they do not conduct themselves appropriately, as various players in the chain of mortgage brokerage and origination during the boom did not, severe harm can result, not only to consumers immediately involved but also to the financial system and to the economy as a whole.

Prudential regulation, especially the regulation of capital and liquidity, constrains the risk that a firm can assume so that the firm will remain safe and sound. Prudential regulation is akin to a set of covenants that a commercial lender would impose, if such a lender were to serve as a liquidity backstop to the firm and/or guarantor of a firm's liabilities (Dewatripont and Tirole 1994: 31–2, 87–92). Prudential regulation forces the firm's shareholders to limit the risks that the firm takes and to put shareholders' money between the firm and the taxpayer or deposit guarantee fund.

The two objectives of good conduct and good condition go hand in hand. Firms that engage in 'bad' conduct may undermine their own risk criteria (as was the case with respect to mortgage origination in some firms during the boom) or become subject to fines and/or orders banning them from continuing in business. In extreme cases, this can turn a firm in 'good' financial condition into one that requires resolution.[1] Supervision of the condition of the firm must take into

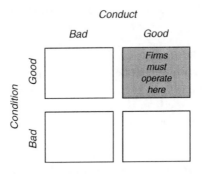

Figure 9.1   Regulation sets the stage for strategy at financial firms

account the results of supervision of its conduct. Conversely, regulation of conduct must also take condition of the firm into account. Firms in poor condition may be more tempted to cut corners on conduct to make ends meet. But those who develop conduct regulation must also keep it realistic, so that the cost of compliance does not remove the incentive for firms to provide the service in the first place.

Although good condition and good conduct are the outcomes that regulation seeks to achieve, experience has shown that certain methods are more likely to achieve the right results than others. Hence, it makes sense to regulate the controls (governance, risk management and remuneration) to ensure that firms have the right persons, processes, policies and practices needed to assure that they will maintain themselves in good condition and conduct themselves appropriately.

Regulating the condition of firms

At the top of the reform agenda are regulations to assure that firms, particularly banks, remain in good condition. In this crisis, banks have run out of capital and liquidity. They have had to turn to the state for new capital, to the central banks for liquidity and to governments for funding guarantees. That was not supposed to happen. How do we prevent it from happening again? Some portion of the answer is better regulation of capital and liquidity.

Capital regulation

The basic tenets of capital regulation are that capital should be available to absorb loss and that capital should be sufficient to absorb the losses that are likely to arise. These basic tenets remain valid. What has to change is the way in which they are put into practice. Regulation of the quality of capital has to change, as does regulation of the quantity of capital.

The quality of capital

The key function and characteristic of capital is its ability to absorb loss, and the key question for capital regulation is whether the capital absorbs loss whilst the firm is a going concern, or only after the firm has become a 'gone' concern, that is gone into resolution, restructuring, insolvency or liquidation.

This crisis has clearly demonstrated that not all forms of capital absorb losses whilst the firm is a going concern and that capital which is truly loss-absorbing was in many cases insufficient to bear all of the losses that had occurred or were considered likely to occur. The crisis further demonstrated that governments were unwilling to impose the losses on society that would have resulted from letting certain institutions become 'gone' concerns – these institutions were deemed 'too big to fail'. Finally, the crisis demonstrated that only governments were willing and able to supply truly loss-absorbing capital in the amount and in the time frame required to stabilise the banking system (see Part II). Capital that absorbed loss, if and only if the firm became a 'gone' concern, did not contribute significantly to containment of the crisis.

This experience calls into question the current complex classification of capital as embodied in the Basel Accord and the EU Capital Requirements Directive (see Figure 9.2). Under the current system, total capital must equal 8% of the bank's risk-weighted assets. Total capital consists of Tier II and Tier I capital. Tier II capital can be counted towards total capital, but only to the extent that the bank has Tier I capital (hence Tier II capital can only account for 50% of total capital). Tier I capital must be at least 4% of the bank's risk-weighted assets. Tier I capital consists of hybrid capital and core Tier I capital. Hybrid capital can be counted towards Tier I capital, but at most to the extent that the bank has core Tier I capital.

Hence, core Tier I capital forms the base of the entire capital structure. If the amount of core Tier I capital falls, the amount of non-core Tier I

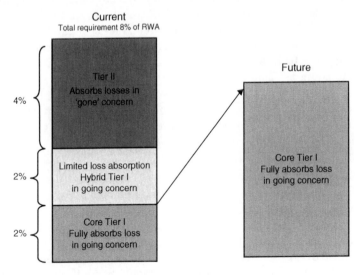

Figure 9.2 The quality of capital has to improve

capital that the firm may count towards its minimum requirements falls by an equivalent amount, and the amount of Tier II capital that the firm may count towards its minimum requirements falls by twice the amount of the fall in core Tier I capital. So losses that reduce a bank's core Tier I capital have a multiplier effect throughout the capital structure.

Therefore the dominant questions with respect to the quality of capital pertain to the degree to which one should rely on anything other than core Tier I capital, and what actually constitutes core Tier I capital.

Tier II capital. The most significant question must be raised in connection with Tier II capital. This only absorbs losses, if the bank becomes a 'gone' concern. In resolution, Tier II capital can and should absorb loss after shareholders' equity and any mezzanine capital instruments (such as preferred stock) have been fully written down. This has actually been the case in a number of resolutions during the crisis, and the market (as evidenced by the prices of such issues in the secondary market and the significant spreads on the limited number of new issues) now fully recognises that such instruments do in fact bear some appreciable risk of loss.

As long as one contemplates the possibility that any bank could become a gone concern, Tier II capital can continue to have a role in the capital structure for regulatory purposes. It is junior to deposits in resolution or liquidation and therefore provides protection to depositors and the deposit guarantee scheme (and the taxpayer to the extent that the government has provided any guarantees over and above the amount of covered deposits). However, if one does not contemplate allowing the bank to become a gone concern, banks should only be able to count as capital those instruments that absorb loss whilst the bank remains a going concern. That would exclude most, if not all, of the capital instruments currently classified as Tier II capital, unless such instruments were convertible into core Tier I capital whilst the bank remained a going concern (see "Contingent capital" below).

Hybrid capital. Similar questions arise with respect to hybrid capital (e.g. preferred shares), but the answer is not so clear-cut. To qualify as hybrid capital an instrument must have many of the features of shareholders' equity: loss absorbency, permanence and flexibility. Hybrid capital has to be fully issued and paid up, and it should be able to absorb loss whilst the firm is a going concern. The instrument should be undated. If the instrument has a call date, it should be at least five years after the issuance date, and there should be limits on the incentives of the issuer to redeem the instrument at the call date. Finally, the instrument should be flexible, in the sense that the issuer has the right to cancel any scheduled dividend or distribution at its sole discretion (and must do so if ordered by the regulator) without such a step triggering the insolvency, restructuring or administration of the issuer (CEBS 2008a).

However, hybrid capital is less loss absorbent than shareholders' equity whilst the issuer is a going concern. Hybrid capital generally only absorbs losses to the extent that scheduled dividends or interest payments are cancelled. Generally, the principal amount of hybrid capital does not absorb losses whilst the firm is a going concern. The principal amount of the hybrid capital instrument generally remains intact, unless the firm goes into resolution or insolvency. Then, the principal of the hybrid instrument may be used to absorb loss, but only after the shareholders' equity has been completely exhausted.

This is fine as long as one contemplates the possibility that any bank could become a gone concern. It is deeply dissatisfactory, however, for those banks where one wishes to preclude the possibility that they could become a gone concern. At any point in time, the amount of loss that could be absorbed is limited to the amount of coupon that can be cancelled. One cannot write down the principal, and one cannot use the principal to absorb loss. So the immediate loss absorbency might be on the order of 10% of the principal amount of the hybrid capital instrument. This is hardly a sufficient basis to count the entire amount of the instrument as capital.

Core Tier I capital. In contrast, shareholders' equity unequivocally absorbs loss whilst the firm is a going concern; indeed, it absorbs first loss. It is permanent in the sense that it does not have to be repaid at any time. It is also flexible, in the sense that there is no obligation to pay dividends or to effect distributions to shareholders. The failure to pay a dividend is not an event of default and cannot give rise to insolvency or bankruptcy proceedings – a stark contrast to debt finance where the failure to make an interest payment could be an event of default and may ultimately be grounds for a bankruptcy proceeding or winding up order. For this reason, shareholders' equity and instruments that can be demonstrated to be equivalent to shareholders' equity (such as the reserves of a mutual building society) are deemed to be Core Tier I capital.

However, shareholders' equity is just the difference between the value of the firm's assets and the value of its liabilities, and the exhaustion of shareholders' equity formally marks the boundary between solvency and insolvency of a firm. Hence, calculating shareholders' equity inevitably involves accounting issues and what adjustments or filters regulators deem appropriate to place on shareholders' equity as calculated under generally accepted accounting rules such as US GAAP or IFRS to arrive at the amount of money that is truly available to absorb future losses. These adjustments and filters will be harmonised and deductions will be made from core Tier I capital on a schedule to be agreed by the Basel Committee (BCBS 2009c). This will result in a considerable strengthening of capital.

In sum, the current classification of capital for regulatory requirements only makes sense, on the premise that banks could become 'gone' concerns. If governments are willing to allow banks to become 'gone' concerns, Tier II capital and the full amount of hybrid capital provides protection to depositors. If governments are not willing to allow banks to become 'gone' concerns, Tier II capital and anything but the immediately payable coupons on most forms of hybrid capital provide no capacity to absorb loss, and no capacity to maintain the bank as a going concern. Therefore, if one wishes to maintain banks as going concerns, much greater emphasis has to be placed on core Tier I capital, or capital that can absorb losses whilst the bank remains a going concern.

Assessing the risk against which capital should be held

The quantity of capital should be the amount required to assure that the bank can absorb losses whilst remaining a going concern. The term 'going concern' should be understood in both the audit sense of the words as well as in the market sense of the words – does the bank have enough capital to convince funds providers that they should continue to lend money to or place deposits with the bank. There is no uniform answer to this question. It is bank-specific and situation-specific.

However, most importantly it depends on the assessment of risk. For example, a loan currently on the books may go into default, and the bank may suffer a loss a result. Or a bond currently held in the portfolio may decline in value. The riskier is the loan or bond, the higher is the possible loss that the bank could incur, and the greater is the amount of capital that the bank should hold to offset that possible loss.

What regulation (as embodied in the Basel Framework and the EU Capital Requirements Directive [CRD]) attempts to do is set a framework under which banks calculate the possible future losses that may arise from their current portfolio. This framework essentially divides the bank into two parts: a trading book (based on mark-to-market accounting) and a banking book (based on accrual accounting). Banks could either use the standard approach set out in the Framework/CRD, or they could employ their own models (subject to regulatory approval) to estimate the risk weights that should apply to the assets in their portfolio.

The crisis has exposed flaws in the design of capital requirements for the trading book. The crisis has also demonstrated that current capital requirements are pro-cyclical: they potentially aggravate boom and bust. Efforts are under way to correct each of these flaws.

Trading book risks. The broad assumption underlying the Basel Capital Accord – that regulators around the world could rely on firms' own risk models as the basis for capital requirements – has not turned out to be correct, at least for the trading book. Losses in trading books have been several orders of magnitude larger than the capital which the models said had to be held against those risks, and these losses set in motion the overall contraction in banks' capital that contributed to the crisis.

Banks' models have worked well for the highly liquid instruments such as on-the-run US government securities, investment grade corporate bonds and foreign exchange contracts. These products trade frequently so that a market price can be readily established, valuations can be made at fair market value and positions can genuinely be marked to market because there is a market.

Banks' models did not work for structured finance products or complex derivatives. By and large, banks' models ignored liquidity – both market liquidity (the ability to sell the instrument readily within a narrow bid-offer spread) and funding liquidity (the need to be able to fund the position). Banks focused solely on credit risk, and many appear to have believed that the AAA-ratings on the super-senior tranches of asset-backed securities made them immune not only from default but also from a major decline in price. Nor did the standard approach to capital requirements for the trading book envision the possibility that the trading book could contain products that were essentially illiquid and did not trade frequently. The standard approach would have assigned a specific risk weight of 20% (and hence a capital requirement of 1.6%) to the senior- and super-senior tranches of asset-backed securities, solely based on their rating. In contrast, if those same positions were held in the banking book, the risk weighting would have been 100% and the capital charge would have been a full 8%. Consequently, firms had a considerable incentive to place the highly rated senior- and super-senior ABS tranches into their trading books, even though the instruments by and large did not trade.

The Basel Committee (BCBS 2009a) has already proposed measures that will eliminate this flaw in trading book capital requirements. Securitised products will, with limited exceptions, be subject to the same charges as they would carry in the banking book. Non-securitised credit products will be subject to an incremental risk charge and the entire trading book will be subject to an additional stressed value at risk requirement. These changes will in effect equalise the capital treatment for illiquid assets in the trading book and the banking book. This will remove the regulatory arbitrage that contributed to the crisis. The net result of the changes will be a two to three fold increase in capital requirements for risks in the trading book.

Pro-cyclicality. The second flaw in the current approach to capital requirements is that the requirements themselves may be pro-cyclical. In other words, the requirements may aggravate the amplitude of the business cycle. They may induce banks to expand too much during the upturn and to contract too much during the downturn. That could turn the upturn into a boom, and the downturn into a bust (see Figure 9.3).

Pro-cyclicality arises because requirements are linked to risk, and estimates of risk are linked to the stage of the business cycle. As the business expands during the upturn, the immediate point-in-time estimate of the risk of a loan or bond should decline. If capital requirements are based on the risk which might arise over the short term (as they are under the Basel Framework and the CRD), then requirements will fall as the upturn proceeds. Conversely, the requirement will rise, as the downturn gathers steam, and this can aggravate the downturn. Unless banks have built up a buffer of capital during the upturn, they

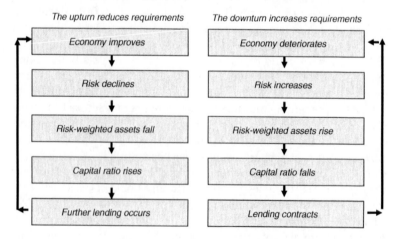

Figure 9.3   Pro-cyclicality

will have to raise new capital and/or restrict lending in the downturn to meet their capital requirements. If all banks have to do this, it could aggravate the downturn (Greenlaw et al. 2008).

One cure for pro-cyclicality is to remove the link between capital requirements and risk. But that would be akin to throwing out the baby with the bathwater. Reinstating (or keeping in the case of the United States) a uniform charge for capital across all the loans in the bank's portfolio would create different problems. If capital charges were set at a level sufficient to offset the losses that could arise from the average loan, they will be too high for lower risk loans and too low for higher risk loans. This will drive lower risk loans outside the banking system and induce banks to hold riskier loans – a phenomenon observed under Basel I. That does not make sense. What should be done is to assure that banks build up a buffer to offset the migration of risk ratings that occurs during the business cycle, that is, that they build up this buffer during the boom so that they can draw it down during the downturn.

There are various ways to do this. Perhaps the simplest is to require that banks move away from a point-in-time estimate of risk and that they move to estimating probability of default and loss given default across the business cycle or even at the trough of the business cycle. If banks had to base their capital requirements on the amount of losses that could occur at the trough of the business cycle, they would have in place at all times the buffer that they would require if the business cycle did take an adverse turn. But that buffer would be hidden. Capital for a loan would remain the same throughout the cycle. It would be enough to offset losses at the trough of the cycle, and 'too much' for the losses that might occur at the peak of the cycle.

Alternatively, one can retain the point-in-time method of estimating the risk in a bank's portfolio and force banks to build buffers against the possibility that the business cycle will turn and risk will increase. Again, there are various methods proposed to do this, including dynamic provisioning, building non-distributable reserves and/or creating a counter-cyclical buffer (FSA 2009d).

Pro-cyclicality also occurred in the trading book (see Chapter 3). During the boom volatility, or the expected variability in future prices, declined markedly. This reduced risk as calculated in the value at risk (VaR) models that both banks and regulators use to calculate capital requirements under the Basel Framework and the CRD. This reduced risk resulted in lower capital requirements, allowing greater positions to be held for any given amount of capital. In the downturn, the opposite occurred. Volatility surged, and so did the estimated risk of holding trading book positions. This resulted in higher capital charges, forcing banks to reduce their positions and/or raise additional capital.

The interaction of accounting and capital further aggravated pro-cyclicality in the trading book (Adrian and Shin 2008a; Greenlaw et al. 2008). Positions in the trading book are subject to mark-to-market accounting. This required the banks to mark up the value of instruments in the trading book as risk premiums declined. This mark up was immediately taken into profit, and the resulting increase in capital could serve as the basis for further leverage and further acquisitions of trading book positions (which in turn may have further increased prices or values of the positions, allowing the process to be repeated). Conversely, in the downturn the increase in risk resulted in a reduction in the market value of the positions in the trading book. This had to be immediately deducted from capital, just at the time when capital requirements were increasing, so that banks had to raise additional capital and/or reduce their overall positions (which in turn may have further reduced prices or values of the positions, forcing the process to be repeated).

Leverage ratio. Although the incremental risk charge may limit the presence of illiquid instruments in the trading book, pro-cyclicality is likely to remain. To limit this may require imposing on banks a supplemental non-risk based capital ratio, such as a leverage ratio.

Basing capital requirements solely on risk creates the possibility that banks may amass very large amounts of assets relative to very small absolute levels of capital. High risk-weighted capital ratios are consistent with very low overall capital ratios. If the system of risk-weighted requirements is prone to error, the losses that go against the very small absolute amount of core Tier I capital could bring the institution into a liquidity crisis and lead to the failure of the institution. Such risk-based requirements may also be prone to pro-cyclicality (see above). For these reasons, the risk-based system of capital requirements could be supplemented with a leverage ratio that would limit the amount of assets that a bank could have relative to its capital.

Conceptually this makes sense. The leverage ratio (ratio of capital to assets) sets limit on the amount of assets that can be supported by a given amount of capital as well as a limit on the amount of assets that need to be funded from sources other than capital. The higher this ratio, the riskier the bank tends to be.

Practically, however, implementation of a leverage ratio (in particular, setting a level for the ratio) depends on the resolution of two issues: what should go into the numerator, and what should go into the denominator. The numerator should be the amount of capital that the bank holds. Logically, this should be the same loss-absorbing capital that counts as core Tier I (see discussion above). The denominator should be the bank's total assets. Ideally, total assets would simply be the number stated on the bank's balance sheet, but there are two issues standing in the way of implementing this simple approach: the treatment of off-balance sheet vehicles, such as conduits and SIVs, and the valuation of derivative contracts.

The first problem undermined the usefulness of the leverage ratio that the United States had imposed on its bank holding companies. Under US GAAP, conduits and SIVs were not consolidated onto the balance sheet. They were therefore outside the total assets against which capital needed to be held, even though the bank had sponsored the vehicle, managed the vehicle and given implicit (and in some cases explicit) funding commitments to support the vehicle. This was less of an issue under IFRS where conduits had tended to be consolidated onto the balance sheet of the sponsoring bank. To implement a sensible leverage ratio, banks have to consolidate, for the purposes of the leverage ratio, the vehicles for which they have effective economic responsibility (in terms of assuming losses incurred in the vehicle and/or in terms of assuring the funding of the vehicle). The standards for consolidation with respect to the leverage ratio may therefore differ from the accounting standard that the bank employs.

The valuation of derivative contracts also poses an issue for the leverage ratio. If the leverage ratio is to make sense, derivatives have to be valued on the same basis as they are valued for the purposes of calculating risk-based capital requirements. This may differ from the accounting standard that the bank employs. Under IFRS, the balance sheet reflects the gross amount of derivative contracts outstanding. This vastly overstates the obligations of the bank, inflating both the asset and liability sides of the balance sheet. In contrast, under US GAAP, derivatives are valued at their net economic value. This is a truer reflection of the possible losses as well as of the possible funding requirements that could face the bank.

Finally, there is the question of whether the leverage ratio should be a hard limit or merely a risk indicator that supervisors may use as part of their overall assessment of whether or not firms have adequate capital. Imposing the leverage ratio as a hard limit has the potential advantage of constraining asset growth during the boom phase of the business cycle. A hard limit may also be linked to resolution and can serve to restrict the forbearance that supervisors might otherwise be tempted to exercise, particularly with respect to banks that fund themselves exclusively through insured deposits. Further in this vein a hard limit would constrict the size of banks that might be considered 'too big to fail' – the leverage ratio effectively demands that equity holders proportionately put more and more 'skin in the game' as they expand their business.

The leverage ratio as a hard limit may work well across the board in a boom, and it may work well with respect to individual institutions. However, the hard limit may serve to aggravate the downturn, if it leads banks generally to contract lending and assets more aggressively than they otherwise would do – just at the time when banks are likely to be called upon to make up for the shortfalls in lending that arise from the constriction of the securities markets during the downturn. This suggests that the leverage ratio might be used as an indicator, perhaps with the option, if macro-prudential supervision is initiated (see Chapter 10), for the macro-prudential supervisor to switch this into a hard limit during the boom much the way the highway authorities can temporarily impose a special speed limit on certain sections of the highway if the traffic gets too heavy.

The minimum capital ratio

The ultimate question, however, is not how to remove pro-cyclicality or how to introduce counter-cyclicality into capital requirements. The ultimate question is 'what is the level of capital that banks require in order to operate smoothly at the trough of a recession?' How can we assure that banks have enough capital to survive under stress?

Current capital requirements are essentially a snapshot of the capital that would be needed to absorb loss in the current portfolio. Certainly, capital needs to be sufficient to do that. But capital should also be sufficient to absorb losses over time as the bank's portfolio changes in response to the implementation of its strategy, even if the economic environment deteriorates. This suggests framing the capital ratio requirement in both forward looking as well as current terms.

If one takes as the ultimate basis for capital requirements the amount of capital that one would wish the bank to have under a stress scenario, one can work backward to the amount of capital that banks should hold in conditions that are more normal. Roughly speaking, this ratio should be the one that enables the bank to continue to conduct its business in a normal way and to continue to be able to attract unsecured wholesale funds in the markets (so that the bank is not exposed to an idiosyncratic liquidity shock [see below]).

Under current capital regulations the minimum amount of core Tier I capital that banks must hold under the Basel Framework/CRD is only 2% of risk-weighted assets. This is plainly insufficient. Long before banks get to that low point, banks come under pressure in the funding markets. Debt providers simply do not consider a core Tier I ratio of 2% of risk-weighted assets as sufficient protection. If the minimum capital ratio is the point at which regulators can intervene to force a bank into resolution, leaving the core Tier I ratio at 2% of risk-weighted assets is leaving things too late.

Experience during this crisis suggests that banks would require a core Tier I ratio of at least 4% relative to risk-weighted assets to survive a severe stress scenario. This would suggest that such a ratio be established as the minimum capital that banks would have to maintain at all times, both on a current and forward-looking basis.

To assure that the bank will have at least 4% core Tier I capital after stress, the bank should be expected to maintain a buffer of capital above that minimum that could be run down, if stress develops. The level of the buffer should reflect the state of the economic cycle: it should be higher in good times, so that it can be drawn down as the economy deteriorates. The level of the buffer should also reflect the condition of the individual bank and its exposure to the stresses that are considered likely to develop. Finally, the level of the buffer should take into account the ease with which a bank might recapitalise itself, if it were to come under stress.

This forward-looking approach to capital requirements is already being employed in the United States, United Kingdom and other countries in connection with the asset-protection, credit-guarantee and recapitalisation schemes employed to contain the crisis (see Chapter 5). Moreover, this forward-looking approach is already contained in the Basel Framework/CRD, where banks are required to estimate their capital requirements under a stress test that assumes the economy undergoes a severe downturn. The results of this test are incorporated into the bank's capital requirements under Pillar 2 of the Basel Framework/CRD.

Future capital regulation needs to build on this foundation. In addition to assuring that the bank currently has enough capital, supervisors should be able to require the bank to have in place sufficient capital to survive future stress. Given the starting position of their current business plan and portfolio, banks should be required to demonstrate that they could maintain their capital above a certain threshold over the next three to five years, even if a severe macroeconomic stress were to develop. If the stress were to push banks below that threshold, are there credible actions that management could take to put the bank above that threshold? If not, the bank would have to undertake measures now to prepare itself for the stress that could materialise. Such measures might include obtaining tail-risk insurance against losses in the portfolio, raising capital, selling businesses or running down portfolios.

The degree of stress to which banks may become subject is a matter of judgement for banks and their supervisors. Plainly, the stress should involve a significant deterioration from the current forecast of future economic conditions, and the stress scenario would have to be adjusted, as the overall economy changes. Indeed, as the economy worsened in 2007, 2008 and 2009, it became apparent that the actual economic performance veered towards and beyond what was considered a stress scenario in mid-2007. The worst case became the base case, and a new stress scenario had to be developed. As and when the economy improves, the question will become whether the stress scenario should become less severe as well, or whether it should remain anchored at the low point reached during this cycle. At least for some time, it would seem prudent to leave it anchored at that low point.

The focus on maintaining a minimum core Tier I ratio of 4% after stress implies that banks will have to maintain a buffer above 4% during more normal conditions. This will allow them to run the buffer down as the stress develops and still keep above the minimum. Although supervisors should set this buffer for each individual bank, there is also some merit in assuring that banks generally maintain a sufficient buffer in normal conditions. For example, if the buffer were set at 2% of risk-weighted assets, this would suggest that banks would have to maintain a minimum core Tier I capital ratio of 6% of risk-weighted assets to remain 'well capitalised' (with possibly higher ratios for banks that are systemically relevant). Banks that did not maintain this buffer would face restrictions on the distributions to shareholders such as dividends and share buy-backs, and banks without the necessary buffer would be required to file plans on the management actions that they would take to assure that they could maintain core Tier I capital at the 4% minimum under stress.

The actual level of the buffer should be set in conjunction with other decisions with respect to capital – whether probability of default is estimated as a point in time or at the trough of the cycle (see above), whether dynamic provisioning is or is not required, whether a leverage ratio is introduced and whether banks are required to build up non-distributable reserves. Finally, the level of the buffer should depend on whether the bank can readily replace core Tier I capital, if this falls below a certain threshold. If it has a reliable back-up source of core Tier I capital, the buffer or core Tier I capital can be somewhat smaller.

Contingent capital

Contingent capital can serve as a back-up source of core Tier I capital. Such capital would convert into core Tier I capital at the discretion of the regulator if the bank's core Tier I ratio relative to risk-weighted assets fell below a certain threshold level (say 5% of risk-weighted assets). Upon conversion into core Tier I capital, the contingent capital would be fully available to absorb losses whilst the bank remained a going concern. Under this approach, banks would effectively have to arrange in advance for at least the first round of their own recapitalisation rather than turning to government for assistance once losses have been incurred. In this respect contingent capital is more effective at absorbing loss whilst the bank is a going concern than the current forms of hybrid Tier I and Tier II capital. Contingent capital effectively amounts to a 'pre-pack' recapitalisation, and the use of contingent capital might lower the buffer of core Tier I capital that might otherwise be required.

A further advantage of contingent capital is that there will be a class of investor in addition to the common shareholders who will monitor the bank's condition and impose market discipline.[2] This is a vital reinforcement to the scrutiny that supervision provides. In the absence of such a class of investors, the predominant and perhaps only discipline for large, systemically important banks (which could be considered 'too big to fail') could be the institution's own shareholders and the institution's supervisor. Given shareholders' asymmetric returns (unlimited upside, whilst limited liability constrains the downside), some doubt may be cast on the effectiveness of shareholders' disciplining risk-taking. Therefore, without the discipline that contingent capital could provide, discipline would fall predominantly, if not completely, on supervisors.

Summary: capital regulation

In sum, capital regulation requires reform. Although capital requirements should continue to be risk-based, the requirements for the trading book need to be revised, so that the risk of illiquid instruments is fully covered. Pro-cyclicality in the current requirements needs to be eliminated. The quality of capital needs to be improved. Greater emphasis needs to be placed on core Tier I capital, or capital that is convertible into core Tier I capital whilst the institution remains a going concern. Contingent capital has that property, and consideration should be given to instituting a separate requirement that banks (especially large, systemically relevant banks) issue contingent capital (see Conclusion). Finally, capital requirements should be more forward looking. In addition to assuring that banks have enough capital to meet losses in the current portfolio under current economic conditions, they should also assure that banks would have, or be able to obtain, enough capital to meet losses even if economic conditions deteriorate markedly over a three to five year horizon.

Liquidity regulation

If capital regulation requires reform, liquidity regulation requires resurrection. Relative to capital regulation – where the Basel Committee and national regulators have struggled for over two decades to come up with an international standard – liquidity regulation has been neglected, even though banks generally fail because they run out of liquidity. Although a start has been made (BCBS 2008; CEBS 2008b, 2009b; FSA 2007a, 2008d), much more needs to be done quickly.

This will be difficult, for liquidity is a difficult risk to measure, quantify and control. It is a contingent risk, dependent on market conditions as well as on the particular situation of the specific bank. So regulation of liquidity must take into account both market liquidity and funding liquidity. It must also be consistent with central bank policy with respect to the provision of liquidity through normal facilities or extraordinary liquidity assistance. Finally, liquidity regulation has to be flexible enough to allow institution-specific supervision and remediation.

The starting point for liquidity regulation is a definition of the liquidity stress that an institution should be able to withstand. It should certainly be on the order of the liquidity pressures experienced in this crisis. At a minimum, institutions would have to plan how they would deal with liquidity risks that could crystallise because of a name-specific stress, a market-wide stress and a combination of the two. At a minimum, the bank should be able to survive – without recourse to liquidity assistance from the central bank – a very severe name-specific stress for a period of two weeks or more as well as a coincident chronic market stress that would last three months or more (FSA 2008a).

Liquidity regulation and supervision needs to be tailored to the individual institution. It is envisaged that firms would provide the supervisor with an individual liquidity assessment which would form the basis for the individual liquidity guidance that the supervisor would provide to the firm.

To measure and assess its liquidity risk, the bank will need to set out the contractual maturities of assets and liabilities as well as setting out how these assets and liabilities can be expected to behave under various conditions. Particular attention needs to be paid to formal and implicit commitments of the bank to provide liquidity to its clients through committed but undrawn facilities such as revolving credit or stand-by/back-up lines for commercial paper. Any put options that the bank has granted to clients to allow them to sell securities and/or other instruments to the bank also need to be considered. In addition, account needs to be taken of the prepayment and/or extension options that are present in loan and/or bond agreements, and an estimate needs to be made of the likelihood that such arrangements will result in a delay in inflows to the bank or an acceleration of outflows.

From such a schedule, one can derive a cumulative liquidity profile for the bank. Such a schedule indicates the degree of liquidity risk that the bank runs. This would show the net outflows or inflows that the bank could be expected to experience over various time periods, starting with one day (overnight) and going out to one week, one month, three months and one year under the assumption that some or all of the bank's liabilities do not roll over on their scheduled or anticipated maturity dates. Particular attention should be paid to the bank's core funding ratio – the proportion of its funding that it can rely on keeping through thick and thin.

Liquidity risk may be further heightened if the bank is overly dependent on a particular source of funding or a particular group of funds providers. If the bank depends heavily on a particular product for its funding, and the market for that product closes, the bank will find it difficult, if not impossible, to replace the funds that it had expected to raise in the market that had closed (this was what ultimately led to the failure of Northern Rock [see Chapter 3]). If the bank depends heavily on a particular group of funds providers, the bank will find it difficult, if not impossible, to find new funds providers at short notice, if its traditional funds providers are unable or unwilling to continue to provide funding to the bank. Ideally, the bank would avoid such concentrations in funding. It would diversify both the markets and products in which it funded itself, and it would assure that it drew funds from a wide variety of funds providers. In addition, the bank would take steps to assure that it developed a strong relationship with both its secured and unsecured funds providers and disseminated them appropriately detailed information about the bank's strategy and performance on a timely and regular basis.

In addition to setting out a liquidity schedule, firms should also set out what might be called a collateral budget. This would outline the total unencumbered assets of the firm as well as the claims that might be made on such assets if a firm-specific stress were to develop. This would allow the firm and its supervisor to determine whether the firm had enough qualified collateral to meet the additional margin calls that might develop in the event that the firm's own credit rating was downgraded by one or more notches. Subtraction of such potential demands on collateral from the amount of unencumbered assets would result in an estimate of the liquidity buffer or net collateral available to meet a severe firm-specific and/or market-wide stress.

Finally, the individual liquidity assessment should include a contingency funding plan that the bank will implement if certain triggers are breached. This may include a reduction in assets through run-off and/or sale as well as tapping contingent funding lines. Such contingency funding plans should be tested operationally and practically. (Can the bank really raise as much money in a particular market with a particular instrument?)

Special care needs to be taken in contingent funding plans with respect to secured funding. To be effective, the bank will need to have established such secured funding lines well in advance of coming under liquidity pressure. There may be no time to establish such lines once the bank gets into trouble, and lenders may have no inclination to establish new lines with banks that are already in trouble. Having the collateral available is not enough; the bank must also have some assurance that it will be able to convert the collateral into cash at short notice without suffering ruinous losses.

This conversion into cash should take place without the assistance of the central bank. Central banks provide a back-up to the contingency plans of banks; they are not, and should not be, a primary source of liquidity to a bank. Even if the central bank chooses to implement monetary policy through refinancing banks (see Chapter 6), it will do so on a market-wide basis rather than a bilateral basis. There can be no assurance that a bank will win sufficient liquidity in the central bank's periodic auctions or that the auction will be conducted on precisely the date or in precisely the amount that the bank may require. Consequently, the individual bank must plan its own liquidity on the basis that it will need to fund itself in the market.

Supervisors need to review these individual liquidity assessments (liquidity profile, collateral budget and contingency funding plan) and provide the bank with individual liquidity guidance. The focus of the individual liquidity guidance is to assure that the bank has sufficient liquidity to withstand the possible stresses that it may encounter.

This guidance may entail recommendations that the bank reduce outright its liquidity risk by shortening the maturity of assets and/or lengthening the maturity of liabilities. The guidance may also order the bank to improve and/or test its contingency funding plan. Finally, the supervisor may order the bank to raise its liquidity buffer.

For supervisory purposes, the liquidity buffer will be narrower than the pool of unencumbered assets that the bank has at its disposal. The supervisor should set a range of admitted assets that will count towards the supervisory buffer for liquidity purposes. Ideally, the supervisory liquidity buffer would consist of securities that could be sold outright in the markets at little or no discount from the price at which the bank carries them on the books. On-the-run government securities are the best example of such instruments. These can generally be sold practically immediately at no discount in price. Other instruments are less liquid and provide a less effective secondary reserve, since their sale may require the bank to take a capital loss and thereby diminish the bank's creditworthiness. If such instruments are to be included in the assets admitted to the liquidity buffer, the supervisor should establish haircuts for such assets. Such haircuts should reflect the 'fire-sale' price that the seller would have to accept under a rapid sale as a forced seller of the instrument. In addition, the supervisor should set concentration limits on the assets within the buffer to the extent that it is not comprised entirely of on-the-run government securities.

Finally, supervisors and central banks should assure that the bank is prepared to access the central bank, if it were required to do so. This is not the bank's contingency funding plan, but the back up to that plan, so that the central bank can provide emergency assistance should such assistance be required and the central bank elect to provide such assistance. Such preparation includes documenting loan agreements and possibly pre-positioning of collateral with the central bank or making arrangements for the title to such assets to be transferred to the central bank in an extremely rapid manner. Banks should also periodically test their ability to borrow from the central bank from an operational perspective, so that such borrowing could proceed smoothly if the bank were required to draw upon the central bank to meet extraordinary short-term liquidity demands, such as might arise from a technology failure at the bank itself or in a payments or settlement system.

However, it should be stressed again that such 'back-ups to the contingency' are just that. The primary and secondary source of liquidity for an individual bank should be the market, not the central bank. Supervisors should challenge vigorously any bank's liquidity plan that involves early and/or extensive reliance on central bank facilities in times of stress. Indeed, such reliance should be taken as an indication that the bank in question needs to pare back its liquidity risk and/or bolster its own liquidity buffer.

Governance

Although capital and liquidity are the immediate lines of defense for a bank, the governance of the bank ultimately determines the bank's strategy, business model, risk management and controls (Walker 2009). Do banks have the right people in place, and do those people employ the right structures to assure that risks are properly managed and controlled? Current controls for banks are differentially greater than they are for non-financial companies, but do they need to be strengthened still further?

There has long been a requirement that the chief executive of a bank be 'fit and proper' – that is, that s/he has the requisite experience, expertise and managerial capability to run the bank. But this requirement is not enough. Many other individuals exercise 'significant influence' over the bank, and these people should be 'fit and proper' as well. For this reason, the approved persons regime in many countries covers not just the chief executive but others as well, including the chief risk officer, chief financial officer and non-executive directors as well as individuals, such as proprietary traders, who are likely to have a significant influence on the overall risk level of the firm (FSA 2008c, 2009e).

During the crisis, it became apparent that boards of directors of banks – particularly non-executive directors – could have potentially provided a better check on risk-taking. But such directors were not subject to the same fit-and-proper test that applied to executives, and many non-executive directors lacked the expertise and/or inclination to challenge the strategy, business model and risks that the executives of the bank recommended to the board. Nominally, there was governance, but it was not effective governance. The solution is to subject the non-executive directors of the board to a fit- and-proper requirement similar to that imposed on the chief executive. Such a test is particularly important for non-executive directors who chair the audit, risk or remuneration committees as they will exercise key control functions. These positions will require appropriate expertise as well as a considerable amount of time, if they are to be done well.[3]

Choosing the right people is only the first step towards effective governance. As important is the right structure. Not all of the Board's work can or should be taken in the main Board. Specialised committees to deal with audit, risk and remuneration are sensible divisions of labour, especially for a large, complex, internationally active bank. These should be adequately supported and have sufficient time to explore the issues thoroughly, and the effectiveness of these arrangements should be periodically reviewed by the board (in addition to the ongoing review of the effectiveness of the board that the supervisor will perform [see Chapter 10]).

Risk management

Risk is the raw material of financial intermediation. Banks make money by taking risk, so managing risk is central to everything that a bank does, and the governance of risk management is central to the control of a bank. Some elements of risk management are susceptible to rules; most, however, are more properly the purview of supervision (see Chapter 10).

The key rules applicable to risk management are that it should be independent from the executives taking the risks and that the bank should have in place appropriate systems to facilitate the control of the bank's risk. In terms of independence, the risk management function should be in the business but not of the business. It should have a separate reporting line, and a real voice in determining which business is done, or, perhaps even more importantly, which business is not done. In terms of systems and controls, the bank has to have in place adequate means to record transactions, value positions, set limits, control adherence to limits and run stress scenarios. These systems and controls have to work around the clock throughout the year, and they have to update the requisite information on practically a continuous basis.

The current crisis has underlined numerous areas where banks need to improve their risk management practices (Senior Supervisors Group 2008, 2009; IIF 2008). Four deserve special mention: the conduct of valuations, the management of concentration risk, the role of internal transfer pricing and the importance of stress testing.

Valuations.   Valuations are at the heart of risk management. Although accounting standards provide a broad framework in which valuations need to be struck, they do not always provide a unique answer to the question, 'what is this asset worth'? For example, assets booked in the trading book should be marked to market. This is fine for instruments such as spot foreign exchange and on-the-run US government securities that trade all the time in vast quantities and where no one institution holds a large share of the total outstanding volume of the instrument. A market price is readily available, and there is no doubt that the bank's position could be readily sold at that price.

However, not all instruments held in trading books conform to this ideal. They trade infrequently, if at all, and the question of how to value the instrument is important. Effectively recourse has to be made to models, and these models need to determine the underlying factors that could have a significant impact on the value of the instrument and/ or take into account the prices at which similar instruments actually transact in the marketplace. This yields a range of values for the instrument, each of which would be consistent with fair value accounting standards. Valuation at the top of the range generally presents the view most favourable to the trader but increases the probability that the bank would suffer a loss if the position had to be sold. Valuation at the bottom of the range is the most conservative view of the instrument's current value but increases the probability that the bank would realise a gain, if the instrument were to be sold. Effectively valuation at the bottom of the range creates what amounts to a valuation reserve.

The task of risk management is to assure that this valuation process is robust (FSA 2008f). That involves controlling the models to assure that they incorporate the drivers of value of the instrument, validating the models so that they are checked against the values that are actually realised when the instrument does trade in the marketplace, and, perhaps most importantly exercising judgement about where the value of an instrument should be pitched at any point in time.

However, the real litmus test for risk management is who gets the nod when there is a difference of opinion between the trader and risk management on the value of the instrument that the trader holds. If the trader's view is allowed to prevail, risk management is likely to be ineffective. The better course is to have the risk manager's view prevail, unless the trader can actually sell some portion of the position at a price higher than the value set by the risk manager.[4]

Concentration risk. Concentration risk requires greater scrutiny. Indeed, for some institutions concentration risk during this crisis proved their downfall. Some institutions (e.g. Northern Rock) had become overly dependent on a single source of funding. Changes to the regulation of liquidity risk should address this issue. Some institutions (e.g. Countrywide in sub-prime) were specialised in a line of business that collapsed. Capital regulation will have to build in charges for this type of concentration risk. Consideration will also need to be given on how to limit what might be called concentrated marketability risk. This involves taking positions in the trading book or in assets held for sale that are very large relative to the daily trading volume in those assets. Such positions pose significant risks with respect to market liquidity, as it is unlikely that the institution could sell those positions without adversely affecting the price of the instrument. If, in addition, the sum total of these marketability risks is large relative to the institution's overall capital (as was the case in Citi, Merrill Lynch and UBS), this poses significant risks to the overall soundness of the institution and needs to be controlled and limited.

Transfer pricing. Transfer pricing systems within institutions also require review. These set the terms and conditions on which divisional or business line profits and losses are determined, and the basis for remuneration decisions. As such, they are important drivers of behaviour, and they need to be consistent with sound overall risk management for the institution as a whole. That was not always the case during the boom. In particular, some institutions (e.g. UBS) failed to charge their trading businesses a market price for the funding that ultimately came from the retail and wealth management areas of the bank. This amounted to a cross-subsidy to the trading business and artificially inflated its profits during the boom. Many more institutions made their Treasury operations into profit centres. This not only diverted their attention from managing funding and liquidity but it also encouraged them to reach for yield and invest their secondary reserves in illiquid instruments such as asset-backed securities and CDOs.

Stress testing. Finally, risk management needs to include comprehensive stress testing. Capital regulation (see above) is already moving in the direction of requiring banks to maintain capital sufficient to withstand a severe stress in the economic environment or to have in place plans for credible management actions that would assure that the bank's capital remained above a threshold level. Liquidity regulation (see above) is also moving in the direction of requiring banks to manage their liquidity risks (either by limiting asset-liability mismatches or by holding a buffer of liquid assets) so that the bank can withstand idiosyncratic, specific market or generalised liquidity stresses.

In addition, banks will need to conduct reverse stress testing. This involves banks setting out the possible scenarios under which they could fail, making some assessment of the likelihood that such a scenario could occur and determining what actions to take in response. This can be effective with respect to mitigating the risks that would arise from the stresses that are identified, but it should be noted that the method is far from fool-proof. Indeed, it is singularly prone to errors of omission (leaving off the list of stresses the one that will result in the failure of the institution) as well as errors in estimation (underestimate of the probability that the stress scenario will occur and/or underestimate of the impact of the stress on the market and/or firm).

Remuneration

Remuneration policies at banks also require reform, for faulty remuneration practices contributed to the crisis (FSF 2009b; IIF 2009a; UBS 2008). Henceforth, remuneration policies, practices and procedures have to be consistent with and promote effective risk management (FSF 2009; FSA 2009c, g).

Remuneration policies can undermine the incentives for firms to institute and maintain effective risk management. If remuneration consists predominantly of cash bonuses that are paid out immediately without any deferral or claw back mechanism based on a formula that links bonuses to current year revenues rather than risk-adjusted profit, there are strong incentives for managers to compromise effective risk management. Such remuneration policies may encourage managers to shy away from conservative valuation policies, ignore concentration risks, jigger the internal transfer pricing system in their favour and/or ignore factors that could place the institution under stress at some point in the future.

Regulation of remuneration has to reinforce sound risk management practices. To this end, the Financial Stability Board developed a set of recommendations (FSF 2009b) on the regulation of compensation that regulators around the world are now in the process of implementing (FSB 2009). In the United Kingdom, for example, the FSA (2009g) introduced a general rule stating that 'A firm must establish, implement and maintain remuneration policies, procedures and practices that are consistent with and promote effective risk management.' The FSA has further established eight provisions outlining how firms should comply with the general rule. These deal with the governance of the remuneration process, the basis on which firms calculate compensation and the structure of remuneration, especially variable compensation such as bonuses. Other countries, including France, Switzerland, Germany and the United States, have adopted or are considering adopting similar measures.

Bonus should come after the shareholders have earned a risk-adjusted return on their capital, not before (see Figure 9.4). This implies that

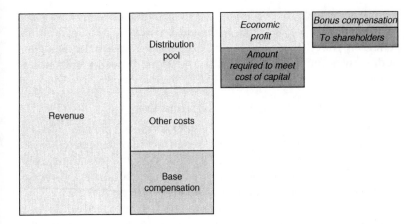

Figure 9.4 Good remuneration practice: bonus comes after profit, not before

the pound of revenue first goes to meet normal costs and generates an operating profit. This goes first to paying the shareholders a minimum risk-adjusted return. Anything above this minimum can then be divided between management and the shareholders according to a formula to be agreed between them. In addition, that formula would call for management to keep some skin in the game by deferring some of the bonus payment and requiring the management to keep stock in the company. This would align the interests of management with the long-term interest of the company and its shareholders.

Conduct regulation

As outlined at the start of this chapter, conduct of business regulation sets the framework within which businesses can develop a strategy. Financial firms must treat customers fairly and this requires that they do not abuse conflicts of interest, that they do not mis-sell products, that they do not mis-inform customers and that they segregate client assets appropriately. Firms must also treat investors fairly. They cannot engage in market abuse, and they cannot mislead investors about their own condition.

These regulations are ideally market-wide regulations. Banks should be subject to the same conduct regulations as other market participants. There are and should be no special requirements for banks to behave better than other market participants. Nor should there be any tolerance for banks behaving in a manner that does not meet minimum requirements for market conduct. Although conduct issues have paled in this crisis in comparison with issues pertaining to institutions' condition, the crisis has highlighted necessary reforms to the regulation of disclosure and diligence as well as the segregation and protection of client assets.

Disclosure, diligence and the rating agencies

Disclosure and diligence are the cornerstones of effective markets. Assuring adequate disclosure and requiring rigorous due diligence are the key to restoring the effectiveness of the capital markets, especially securitisation and structured finance. But issuers, investors, intermediaries and rating agencies will all need to do their part.

Constraints on disclosure of information to prospective investors need to be lifted and disclosure requirements for banks and other intermediaries need to be strengthened so that prospective investors can evaluate the risks they face. For many securitisation issues, regulations in the United States limited the ability of the issuer to disclose information about the performance of the assets underlying the structure to investors who did not already hold the security. This restricted the ability of investors to analyse the cash flows underlying the securities and induced investors to rely on the rating agencies for analysing the instruments. Such constraints on the disclosure of information need to be removed.

However, even where investors could have had access to the information about the underlying cash flows, institutional investors were not always diligent in analysing this information and conducting their own credit analyses. Far too often they simply relied on the rating agencies' assessment of the credit risk of the security. It may be questioned whether investors managing assets on behalf of others, such as money market mutual funds, unit trusts and pension funds, were fully complying with their fiduciary duty towards their end investors. It may also be questioned whether banks and insurance companies were fully complying with requirements for effective risk management, if their sole criterion for investment was the rating given to the security by the rating agencies.

As to the rating agencies themselves, either much more or much less regulation is required. Under the current regulatory framework, rating agencies have a privileged position. A limited number of authorised rating agencies are allowed, even expected, to receive confidential, non-public information from issuers both prior to the original issue and whilst the obligation remains outstanding so that they can reach a conclusion about the credit risk of the issuer's obligations and transmit this opinion to investors. As the issuer generally pays for the rating, ratings agencies have a conflict of interest, particularly where the issuer accounts for a large portion of the revenues and/or profits of the rating agency.

Such conflicts were particularly rife in the rating of securitisation issues. Although there were thousands of securitisation issues, they were predominantly arranged by a small handful of large investment banks. Ratings fees for securitisation issues made up a large portion of the total revenues and profits of the rating agencies. The success of the securitisation issue depended critically on the senior tranche obtaining a AAA rating – without such a rating the issue would not have succeeded, as many investors were only able to buy securities that had a rating. Ratings agencies and investment banks therefore had an incentive to engage in a close dialogue with each other to understand the criteria that the ratings agencies would use, and how the securitisation issue in question could meet those criteria. The integrity of the ratings process depends critically on the ratings agency's not abusing this conflict of interest, and that is what the proposals for further regulation of rating agencies aim to prevent (IOSCO 2008).

However, preventing the abuse of conflicts of interest will not necessarily make ratings more accurate. Nor will it prevent deterioration in the rating of an issuer, if the fundamental factors affecting the credit change for the worse. Regulation of ratings agencies will not and cannot endow the ratings agencies with better foresight. The question is therefore whether regulation should continue to place such reliance on ratings, and whether ratings agencies should continue to have privileged access to non-public, confidential information.

Certainly for banks and insurance companies it is reasonable to expect that they should be able to assess the creditworthiness of the institutions to which they have credit exposure. That is part of their business. The same should be true for institutional investors such as money market mutual funds, unit trusts and pension funds. Provided issuers must disclose, investors should be able to exercise diligence, and measures should be taken to reduce the reliance on ratings in the regulation of banks and insurance companies.

Consideration should also be given to greater disclosure to all, not just privileged disclosure to the ratings agencies. Certainly barriers to the disclosure of the performance of assets underlying securitisation structures should be removed, so that all investors, current and prospective, have access to the information required to analyse cash flows and calculate the probability of default and the loss given default.

In sum, measures to reduce reliance on ratings and to promote disclosure to and diligence by investors will provide a useful complement to the regulation of ratings agencies.

Client assets

One of the basic principles of financial regulation is the requirement that firms protect the assets that clients entrust to them. During the crisis it became apparent that several firms failed to do so in spectacular fashion. The Madoff and Stanford cases were examples of fraud on a massive scale. In each, the entity concerned self-administered the funds under management. There was no third-part custodian and no checking whether the fund actually had the assets that it claimed to have. Nor did all fund of funds managers exercise sufficient diligence over the Madoff fund – some were persuaded to put money of their end investors into the Madoff fund despite the fund not having an independent custodian and despite the fund not having an accountant of the size and sophistication that would ordinarily be associated with a fund of that size.

The failure of Lehmans raised different issues with respect to client assets. These have been tied up in the bankruptcy of the firm, and it has been difficult, if not impossible, for investors to recover these assets promptly. This is particularly the case where the client pro-vided collateral to Lehmans in connection with loans that Lehmans had made to the client and the client's loan agreement with Lehmans allowed Lehmans to re-hypothecate the client's collateral as security for Lehmans' own borrowings from third parties. In such cases, the client has become an unsecured general creditor of Lehmans for the amount by which its collateral exceeded the amount of the loan from Lehmans to the client.

Although some of these shortcomings are more matters for enforce-ment than reform of regulation, consideration should nonetheless be given to reform in the regulation of the protection of client assets as well as to reform of the resolution procedures for non-bank financial firms (see Chapter 6). Reform of the rules pertaining to client assets might include requirements that asset managers demonstrate that they have independent versification of the value and existence of client assets (e.g. through third-party custodians and/or administrators) as well as greater assurance that end investors are aware (or requirement that end investors approve) that the asset manager may allow lenders to re-hypothecate the investors' assets.

Regulation of market infrastructures, clearing and settlement

Finally, reforms are required with respect to the regulation of market infrastructures, clearing and settlement, particularly with respect to derivatives, to assure that they remain robust.

Regulators have been long concerned about the structure of the derivatives market, especially that for credit derivatives. Although the ISDA contract succeeded in standardising the documentation of such trades and in creating a sound legal basis for close-out netting, significant structural issues remained. These included the growth in unauthorised assignments, the growing backlog of unconfirmed transactions, the settlement procedures in the event of a default by a reference entity and the lack of transparency with respect to the volume of derivatives outstanding either with respect to a single reference entity or by a counterparty to the market as a whole.

Such shortcomings posed significant systemic risk, and regulators moved as early as September 2005 to counteract this. At a meeting at the Federal Reserve Bank of New York, the leading regulators confronted the leading derivative dealers and told the dealers to eliminate unauthorised assignments and to work down the backlog in unconfirmed transactions (see Chapter 2). By the time the crisis erupted in August 2007, dealers had accomplished the first task and made significant progress on the second. They had also established a data warehouse with the intent that it would record all OTC derivative trades, but this was not yet fully operational. In addition, ISDA established a protocol that streamlined the settlement process for dealing with the default of a reference entity so that claims for protection could be settled quickly.

Although these measures considerably strengthened the infrastructure of the derivatives market, certain gaps remained and the crisis laid these bare. The most important was the lack of oversight and/or control over the amount of derivatives that a single counterparty could write. In contrast, payments systems have in place a net debit sender cap which limits the amount that any one bank can owe to all other banks in the payment system.

The failure of AIG (see Chapter 4) illustrated the need for such oversight and control. Based on its AAA rating, AIG had written credit protection contracts with many of the world's leading banks as counterparties on numerous reference entities including ABS and CDOs amounting to hundreds of billions of dollars. Each of the counterparties knew its exposure to AIG, and took some comfort in AIG's credit rating as well as in the requirement that AIG would collateralise its exposure if AIG's credit rating slipped below AAA. But few or none of the counterparties knew the full extent of AIG's contracts as a whole and therefore few or none of the counterparties could reckon how adversely affected AIG would be, if it did in fact get downgraded. Prevention of contagion to AIG's counterparties was one of the reasons that the Fed stepped in to rescue AIG, and the prompt payment to AIG's counterparties of the mark-to-market value of their bilateral derivative contracts succeeded in mitigating this threat to financial stability.

To prevent such risk from recurring, it is proposed that all standardised derivatives contracts be executed through a central counterparty (UST 2009; COM 2009). This would allow better oversight over the total number and value of transactions outstanding as well as the net exposure of dealers with respect to the failure of a specific reference entity (many of the dealers' trades with each other cancel out, so that the net exposure of a dealer or the market as a whole to the default of a reference entity may be quite small). More importantly, the introduction of a central counterparty would bring with it risk-control mechanisms for the market as a whole. In particular, the central counterparty would act, as the name implies, as the counterparty for each of the trades that a dealer might make so that the net exposure of the dealer to the central counterparty would effectively be the net of all the positions that the dealer had previously had with the other counterparties in the market. In addition, risk controls at the central counterparty will limit the exposure that the central counterparty could have to any particular counterparty and provide for members to furnish a separate pool of collateral that could be liquidated to pay for the obligations of any defaulting counterparty to the central fund. That will make the infrastructure robust. Anything less will mean that the infrastructure itself poses a significant systemic risk.

The scope of prudential regulation

In sum, extensive reforms to the regulation of banks need to be made. Capital regulation needs to be strengthened, with respect to both the quality of capital and the quantity of capital. Liquidity regulation needs to be introduced. Governance needs to be reformed, risk management to be made more rigorous and remuneration needs to reinforce risk management.

All of the above constitutes a massive reform agenda. The question is whether it strikes the right balance. Should these reforms stop at banks, or should they also be extended to other financial institutions? Prior to the crisis, regulation was based on the premise that deposits were special and so were the banks that issued them (Corrigan 1987). Deposits formed the principal component of consumers' liquid wealth. Debits and credits to deposit accounts were the essence of the payments system. Banks therefore required special protection (access to the safety net of deposit insurance and to the central bank as liquidity provider) and a special system of regulation. This encompassed not only capital but also restrictions on the activities in which banks could engage, either directly or through affiliates. Banks would be subject to a special resolution regime, but the safety net would be restricted to banks, and other financial firms could be settled through normal bankruptcy proceedings.

The trouble with such an approach is that it induces a shift in activity away from the more-heavily regulated sector towards less-regulated channels that fulfil the same economic functions. Although regulation can make banks much, much safer, it may also make them much, much smaller as a proportion of total economic activity. During a boom, activity can be diverted from the bank market to the non-bank and/ or securities markets – markets that are perhaps even more sensitive to changes in the business cycle than banks. In a downturn, the securities and non-bank markets have evaporated more quickly than the bank market, leaving the bank market (from the standpoint of economic stability) with a nearly insurmountable burden to attempt to bear.

The US experience following the S&L crisis illustrates this. Capital requirements and other regulations (e.g. Community Reinvestment Act obligations) impacted banks differentially more than other forms of finance, so that business flowed to less-regulated channels. For example, money market mutual funds arose alongside deposits. The former offered investors the equivalent of an interest-bearing demand deposit. Funds had a fixed unit value (equal to $1) and offered very competitive rates compared to demand deposits at a bank. Effectively, money market mutual funds engaged in the same type of maturity transformation as banks, but were not subject to capital requirements. This was on the theory that an investment in a money market mutual fund was an equity investment, and that the investor in a money market mutual fund put his entire investment at risk. That conformed to the fine print of the offering prospectus but not necessarily to the marketing literature of the funds that positioned money market mutual funds as alternatives to deposits and fixed income investments. Similarly, insurance companies issued guaranteed investment contracts that were economically similar to long-term time deposits at banks.

The crisis demonstrated that failures at non-bank financial intermediaries, such as broker-dealers (Bear Stearns, Lehman Brothers), insurance groups (AIG), non-bank finance companies and money market mutual funds, could also have significant adverse effects on financial stability. The Fed consequently extended the discount window to such firms and the government has in some cases provided guarantees to enable non-bank entities to continue as going concerns (see Part II). So banks, at least in the United States, may no longer be as special as they were once considered to be.

The G-20 concluded in its April 2009 summit that all financial intermediaries should be subject to official supervision and therefore to some sort of regulation. There should be no gaps in the system of regulatory oversight. This implies extending the scope of regulation to entities, such as hedge funds and non-bank finance companies, which are significant actors in financial markets but had not previously been subject to official supervision. It also implies that all activities of banking and insurance groups should be subject to official supervision. The United States has gone further to suggest that all systemically important firms should be subject to resolution by the authorities. This implies setting some type of minimum prudential standards for all such firms as the basis for determining when the authorities would have the power to force resolution (see Chapter 7).

What should those prudential standards be, and should they be the same for banks and non-banks? The safety net and regulation need to be in alignment. What will potentially sow the seeds of the next crisis is a middle course, one that tightens the regulation of banks, but leaves in place the extension of the safety net to non-bank entities such as non-bank investment firms, non-bank finance companies, insurance companies and money market mutual funds. If the safety net extends broadly, so should the system of regulation, and this should be uniform across different types of institutions. If the safety net is restricted to banks, the issuance of deposits and deposit-like instruments should be restricted to banks.

Either one has to move to extend bank-like regulation and supervision to a much broader spectrum of the financial sector, or one has to move to reserve key activities, such as maturity transformation, to banks and to restrict the issuance of deposit-like contracts to banks. If one chooses the latter course, it would imply measures such as prohibiting money market mutual funds from having a fixed unit value (so there would be no buck to break) and prohibiting insurance companies from offering guaranteed investment contracts. Firms that engage in bank-like activities should be regulated and supervised as banks and subject to the same capital requirements. This will help assure financial stability.

10
Better Supervision

The fifth and final element in effecting a cure for crises is better supervision. This has two aspects: micro-supervision, or the supervision of individual institutions, and macro-supervision, or the supervision of the financial system as a whole, including its interaction with macroeconomic policy, especially monetary policy.

Both types of supervision demand judgement. Indeed, micro-supervision involves making 'judgements on judgements' (Sants 2009). Supervisory judgements must be based not only on a thorough analysis of the current facts but also on a forecast of how those facts may develop, if stresses were to occur either at the specific institution or in markets or the economy as a whole. But judgement is just the start. Supervision also requires a willingness and ability to act on that judgement.

Supervisors have to focus on risk. The very essence of financial intermediation is the assumption and management of risk. Financial intermediaries have to be allowed to take risks, if they are to contribute to economic growth and development. At the micro, or firm-specific, level supervision has to assure that financial intermediaries have adequate capital, liquidity, systems, controls and people to bear the risks that they assume without recourse to the taxpayer. At the macro level, supervision has to assure that the sum of what individual financial intermediaries do is consistent with financial stability. In addition, supervision at the micro level may need to send signals to macroeconomic policymakers concerning what economic policy is required, given the state of the financial system, to assure price and output stability.

Micro-supervision

The core responsibility of supervision concerns the condition and conduct of individual institutions. With respect to condition, the supervisor needs to determine whether a bank will be able to survive in the future even if the economic environment deteriorates. If that does not appear to be the case, the supervisor has to get the bank to take the steps that will be required for it to survive, whilst taking at the same time the necessary steps to prepare for the resolution of the bank, should the bank fail to recover. With respect to conduct, the supervisor needs to assure that firms conduct themselves appropriately and to sanction those who do not. For supervision to be effective, it should be risk-based, proactive and, if need be, intrusive.

The key supervisory decisions are about entry and exit. With respect to entry, it is critical to keep out persons who are not fit and proper. They should not be allowed to assume a position of significant influence and, if a person exercising such a position should fail to remain fit and proper, s/he should be banned. With respect to exit, the supervisor has to determine when the firm no longer meets threshold conditions and the supervisor has to pull the trigger for resolution in a timely fashion.

Supervision starts with an assessment of the persons running the authorised firm. Are they fit and proper, will they act with integrity, will they exercise due skill, care and diligence and will they be open with the regulator about what might be wrong at the firm? In particular, taking deposits is a public trust, and the public needs to be sure that the bankers who take deposits will act responsibly and honestly. Letting the wrong person own or manage a financial institution is the first step towards problems. Essentially, supervisors have to make a judgement about the character and about the competence of persons who will exert significant influence over financial institutions, especially banks, as owners, directors or executives. How the people in charge of a bank actually govern the bank and manage its risk sets the frame for the condition the bank will have as well as for how the bank will conduct itself in markets and vis-à-vis customers. The supervisor must judge whether the governance of the bank is set up to provide adequate controls and whether the business model is consistent with the maintenance of sound condition and good conduct.

With respect to governance, the supervisor must review not only structure but also more importantly substance. This starts with the board of directors. The review of persons who exert significant influence over the bank should help assure that the bank has the right persons on the board. However, the right structure and the right activity are also essential, if the board is to function properly. Does the board have audit, remuneration and risk committees? This is relatively easy for the supervisor to determine. It is more difficult to determine how effective the boards and their committees are in providing reviews and challenge to the executive team, but this is an essential judgement for the supervisor to make, for without strong and effective governance at the board level, a bank is more likely to have problems with either condition or conduct.

The supervisor should pay special attention to audit, risk and remuneration. These are the real litmus tests as to whether a bank has effective governance. Is the audit plan of the bank comprehensive in terms of covering businesses and functions, and does the audit schedule prioritise work according to risk? Are the findings of the audit teams accurate, and does the audit team set rigorous yet realistic targets for corrective action by management? As importantly, what is the attitude of senior management towards audit failures? Does failing an audit merit no more than the equivalent of a parking fine, or does failing an audit put a manager in serious difficulty, with respect to bonus and/or future career prospects?

Effective risk management is central to banking. Risk is the raw material of banking. To make money it is necessary to take risk, and to fulfil its function as a financial intermediary it is necessary for a bank to take risks. The supervisor has to judge whether the bank is managing that risk effectively so that the bank can achieve the required outcomes of sound condition and good conduct. This starts with some basic questions (see box), and the supervisor not only needs to know the answers to them but also needs to get banks to correct promptly any wrong answers.

Remuneration policies, procedures and practices have to be consistent with and promote effective risk management. The supervisor needs to make a judgement as to whether this is the case. This starts again with the business model. Does the bank run itself on what might be called the 'pay first' principle in which everyone, including shareholders, is subordinated to the compensation of the employees (especially senior management)? Or does the bank assure that compensation is put in context so that management will only earn a superior return if the shareholders receive an adequate risk-adjusted return on the capital that they have invested in the bank? Do remuneration structures with respect to deferral, clawback and division between cash and stock awards promote or hinder effective risk management? If the latter, the supervisor needs to intervene.

Assuring that banks have the right persons in positions of significant influence and assuring that banks have the right governance in place

---

Five Key Questions for Risk Management

1. *Is there a separate risk committee of the board of directors?* Is risk management separate from the line business? Does the bank have a Chief Risk Officer and does s/he have a direct line to the risk committee of the board (similar to the arrangement for internal audit to report to the audit committee of the board)?
2. *What is the relationship of risk management to the line business?* Does risk management merely provide recommendations to line management, or is there dual control, so that transactions are done only with the approval of both line management and risk management? Whose view prevails with respect to valuation – the trader's or the financial controller's? What is the practice of dealing with breaches of limits? Do risk and line management explore how businesses with extraordinarily good results achieved such outcomes, or are these merely put down to superior management ability?
3. *What is the overall risk appetite of the bank?* Under what circumstances does the board envisage that the bank would suffer a loss? What is the target credit rating of the bank and can the bank sustain this rating even under stress to one or more of its principal lines of business and/or in a severe economic downturn? What is the bank's target rate of return on equity, and what type of risk does this target rate of return imply? Are the target rates of return on equity and target credit rating consistent with one another, especially in a stressed environment, or does a high target rate of return on equity imply that the bank cannot sustain its credit rating in a downturn?
4. *Does the bank's business model accurately capture and price the key risks that the bank takes?* In particular, how does the model deal with concentration risk and liquidity risk? Does the bank's internal price transfer mechanism accurately reflect risk, or does it subsidise risk-taking in a particular unit?
5. *Does the bank regard the treasury unit as a profit centre in its own right?* Or is its function restricted to overall firm-wide tasks such as managing funding and liquidity and assuring that the internal transfer pricing system is an accurate reflection of risk?

---

is only the start of effective supervision. Supervisors also have to assure that banks achieve the right outcomes, that they remain in sound condition and that they engage in good conduct. The supervision of a bank's condition should be akin to the monitoring that a lender would impose on a borrower and to the actions that a lender might take if the borrower breaches its covenants.

Indeed, as shown in Chapter 9, regulations are similar to the covenants that a lender would impose of borrower. The supervisor has to assess the likelihood that the bank will come close to breaching its covenants/regulations. This involves making an ongoing judgement about the bank's management, its business model and strategy and its capability to execute that strategy as well as an assessment of its systems and controls, capital, liquidity and portfolio quality.

Importantly, supervision requires judgement about how the institution will fare under stress. The supervisor must form a judgement about whether the firm has an accurate view of the stresses to which it may become subject, and whether it is adequately prepared to withstand such stresses. If the supervisor judges that the firm is ignoring a possible stress that could significantly adversely affect the firm, the supervisor must call this to the firm's attention and get the firm to explicitly consider such a scenario and take corrective action if needed.

As outlined in Chapter 9, both capital and liquidity regulations are and should be moving in the direction of assessing the capital and liquidity that a bank would need to maintain if stress were to develop. In the case of capital regulation, this involves setting the requirement that a bank maintain core Tier I capital greater than or equal to some threshold amount (e.g. 4% of risk-weighted assets) even in the stressed environment. To implement this regulation the supervisor must set, in conjunction with the central bank or other macro-prudential supervisor, the stress scenario that the banks would have to withstand. In addition, the supervisor must make a judgement on whether the bank can in fact succeed in maintaining its ratio above the threshold level in the stressed environment. This involves not only a detailed review of the results of the bank's own stress tests (FSA 2008b) but also independent verification of the impact of the stress scenario on the bank's portfolio, given the bank's business model. Where the result of such an exercise reveals that the bank would have insufficient capital to withstand the possible stress environment, the supervisor has to judge whether the bank has in place plans to take credible management actions to bring the capital ratio up to the required level within the period required. If the supervisor judges that the bank will not have adequate capital to withstand the stress and that the bank does not have credible plans to enable it to correct that deficiency should the stress develop, then the supervisor must induce the bank to take corrective action immediately. This may involve raising capital, restricting asset growth or changing the bank's business model so that it is less exposed to stress.

Assuring resiliency in the face of stress lies at the heart of liquidity regulation (see Chapter 9). To implement liquidity regulation the supervisor must form a view of how the bank would fare under a variety of stresses, such as a firm-specific deterioration in credit ratings and/ or the closure of one or more funding markets for an extended period.

This involves the supervisor reviewing the bank's asset and liability maturity profile on both a contractual and behaviour-adjusted basis and reaching a judgement on the amount of liquid assets that the bank should hold as a buffer against the liquidity risk that results from the asset-liability profile.

These judgements about a bank's capital and liquidity must be kept up to date as economic conditions change and as the bank's situation changes. The supervisor has to keep an eye on the horizon of how the bank might develop over the next three to five years and assure that the bank takes timely and appropriate measures to maintain adequate capital and liquidity even if stress does develop.

Perhaps the most important decision the supervisor has to take is the decision to 'pull the trigger', that is the decision that the bank no longer meets threshold conditions and must be put into resolution. It should be emphasised that this is the key supervisory decision, and the entity that makes this decision is in fact the supervisor. In my view that argues for a single finger on the trigger, although the entity pulling the trigger should be required to consult with those responsible for executing the resolution and those responsible for paying for the resolution before actually pulling the trigger. Sending a bank into resolution demands that the resolution be executed promptly and efficiently, so that those with claims on the failed bank know where they stand, and so that consistent signals are sent more broadly to all those who have claims on banks as to how they would fare, if the bank on which they held a claim were to be put into resolution (see Chapter 7).

With respect to conduct, the supervisor needs not only to act as an umpire or referee to sanction bad conduct when it occurs but it also needs to assure that banks' business models and governance arrangements are set up to promote good conduct. To act as a referee, the supervisor must be on the field. It has to engage in extensive testing of how products are sold in the marketplace to assure that firms are treating customers fairly. The supervisor also has to engage in extensive surveillance of markets to control for market abuse and price manipulation. When breaches do occur, the supervisor has to enforce promptly, proportionately and publicly (see below) so that the good conduct called for in regulation does not become a dead letter.

However, there is more to the supervision of conduct than acting as an umpire on the field. Good conduct cannot be left to chance. Good conduct must be a basis for any firm's business model, and firms must put in place the policies and procedures necessary to assure that good conduct is the norm. The business model must be based on the proposition that the firm will treat customers fairly, and the firm needs to apply this principle in the design of its products, services and communications with clients. In particular, the firm needs to take steps to assure that products and advice are suitable for clients and that information is provided to clients clearly and fairly and in a manner that is not misleading. If the client has entrusted his own assets to the firm, the firm must have in place adequate measures to protect those assets from harm, including the harm that could result, if the firm itself were to become insolvent. In addition, the firm must have in place adequate polices, procedures and practices to control conflicts of interest both between itself and its clients and between one customer and another client. Finally, the firm must put in place adequate systems and controls to assure that the firm is observing at all times the proper standards of market conduct.

All this amounts to a large supervisory agenda. To accomplish this, the supervisor will need the right people, the right methods and the right powers, especially with respect to enforcement. To make the judgements that a supervisory authority is required to make, the supervisory authority itself have, or have access to, professionals capable of making such judgements and acting on them. To monitor the firms, the supervisor will need specialists to look at particular risks as well as generalists to pull the overall picture together. Supervisory decisions are inevitably ones about priorities – which risks are most likely to impact the firm in a significantly adverse fashion, which risks are not being adequately mitigated by the firm itself and which actions should the supervisor induce the firm to take to correct the deficiencies identified by the supervisor? To make these judgements and take these decisions about the firms the supervisor will need persons with a blend of regulatory and business experience, but above all persons who are able and willing to make difficult decisions quickly and, if need be, on the basis of imperfect information, having due regard not only for the impact of the decision on the firm in question but also for the impact that the decision may have on similarly situated firms and/or the economy at large.

The right people are necessary but not sufficient for the supervisory authority to be effective. It must also employ the right methods. This starts with a thorough understanding and evaluation of the firm's business model and strategy and continues through an assessment of the principal risks facing the firm to arrive at an overall assessment of the firm and development of a risk mitigation programme that the firm must follow. In making its assessment the supervisor will need to balance firm-specific work with cross-firm or thematic work that will allow peer analysis and the identification of outliers. High-level discussions of strategy must be supplemented by 'deep dives' that analyse specific risks or portfolios so that the supervisor can test the strength of the firm's systems and controls and draw its own conclusion about the condition and conduct of the firm as well as what the firm needs to do to mitigate its risk.

Finally, the supervisor requires the right powers. The supervisor must be able to enforce the decisions that it takes. With respect to regulations concerning conduct and condition, the supervisor has to have the authority to impose conditions on the bank that will reduce the risk that the bank will breach the requirement. If a breach does occur, the supervisor should have ability to impose sanctions on the firm, to assure that the firm corrects the breach and to limit the possibility that the breach would recur. Such sanctions include the ability to require that the bank conduct a so-called skilled persons' review and require the bank to implement the recommendations of that review, to impose cease-and-desist orders or to vary the permissions that the bank enjoys, to impose incremental capital and/or liquidity requirements and to impose fines. If the breach is so severe and/or incapable of correction, the supervisor must have the possibility of placing the firm into resolution. In addition, the supervisor must have the ability to remove persons from positions of significant influence in a bank, if those persons are no longer fit and proper or fail to act with due skill, care and diligence. Finally, the supervisor should publicise widely the outcomes of its enforcement actions. That will enhance the supervisor's ability to use enforcement to create a credible deterrence.

With such enforcement tools in its arsenal, the supervisory authority may well find itself able to induce the bank to take steps to mitigate risks without recourse to formal orders. Indeed, the most effective supervision can take place without recourse to formal orders on the basis that the supervisor is making 'recommendations' that are proportionate and risk-based. Knowing that the regulator could publicise and ultimately enforce its decisions, the bank is usually inclined to follow the recommendations of the supervisor. Without such enforcement tools, the supervisory authority might be powerless to persuade the bank to follow the regulation as required.

In sum, micro-supervision, or the supervision of individual firms, is a critical component of the cure against future crises. It should identify problems early, especially at systemically relevant institutions, and induce the firm to correct those problems quickly, before they endanger the firm itself and its depositors. If the problems cannot be corrected, the supervisor may have to resort to more formal enforcement tools or even place the firm into resolution. This calls for judgement and the willingness to act on that judgement. And, for internationally active firms supervisors need to coordinate their activity through colleges and cross-border stability groups.

Macro-supervision

However, micro-supervision is only part of better supervision. Macro-supervision is also required. This means two things: first, supervision of the system as a whole to assure that individually rational decisions do not collectively constitute a threat to financial stability, and second, an assessment of the risks to the financial system posed by monetary and fiscal policy so that harmful feedback loops can be avoided.

Macro-prudential supervision is not new. Indeed, it was practised during the boom with some success. Supervisors assessed whether hedge funds posed a risk to the financial system (see Chapter 2). Supervisors also outlined a means to control that risk – namely, indirectly, through tight control over the lending policies that major investment firms and banks exercised. This review assured that prime brokers monitored the risks of the hedge funds to which they had extended credit and main-tained adequate collateral against such exposures. In addition, official scrutiny led hedge funds themselves to propose and move towards implementing a code of practice with respect to risk management (HFWG 2008). Supervisors conducted a similar review for private equity (FSA 2006a) and induced private equity firms to adopt a code of practice to control their risks (Walker 2007). These steps mitigated the systemic risks that hedge funds and private equity posed.

Supervisors also identified the risks posed by the credit derivatives market to financial stability and they initiated changes in that market to eliminate those risks (see Chapter 2). In particular, regulators identified unauthorised assignments as a clear and present danger to the financial system, and they put a stop to the practice. Supervisors identified that backlogs of unconfirmed transactions had risen to dangerous levels, and they forced dealers to work down these backlogs and take measures to prevent new backlogs from developing. Supervisors noticed that there was no standard procedure for calculating and settling the payments due to protection buyers upon the default of a reference entity, and they forced the dealers to develop and implement one. Finally, supervisors recognised that the introduction of a central counterparty (CCP) can, provided the CCP has the right risk controls, reduce systemic risk, and supervisors pushed banks to clear their credit derivative trades through central counterparties.

These exercises exhibit the strength of macro-supervision. Where the authorities did identify a risk to financial stability, they generally undertook action to limit that risk and/or reduce the impact of such a risk if it were to materialise. In the cases mentioned above (hedge funds and credit derivatives), macro-supervision had some measure of success. The failure of hundreds of hedge funds during the crisis did not bring down the financial system with it. The elimination of unauthorised assignments made the credit derivative markets and financial system more robust, as did the reduction in backlogs of unconfirmed transactions and the establishment of settlement procedures for the default of reference entities.

However, there are limits to macro-supervision. The authorities may identify a risk to financial stability, but underestimate the probability that it will occur or the impact of failing to mitigate the risk. Such was the case with asset-price bubbles. Chairman Greenspan clearly identified an asset-price bubble as a risk to financial stability, but pointedly declined to do anything about it on two grounds. First, he thought the only way to puncture the bubble was to raise interest rates to the point where a recession would start, and second, he thought that it would cost relatively little to clear up the mess from the bubble after it had burst (see Chapter 1). This policy proved to be a mistake.

The other limit to macro-supervision is that it will fail to detect risks that will prove to be systemic. Some are inherently difficult to spot, much like finding a needle in the haystack until the sunlight heats the needle to the point where it emits the spark that sets the haystack afire. Then of course it may be too late to take mitigating action. Such arguably was the risk to the financial system posed by sub-prime securities. Initially, the structuring and ratings agency review process provided strong protection to investors. However, when the ratings agencies changed their procedures without too much fanfare or warning, risk rose. This only became transparent as the relaxed underwriting standards collided with rising interest rates to produce faster acceleration in arrears (see Chapter 2). By then it was too late to eliminate the risk that sub-prime ABS would pose to the financial system and ultimately to the real economy.

Therefore, we should embark on the road to macro-supervision with a clear idea of its limitations. Macro-supervision can identify possible risks and stimulate action to mitigate the risks that it does identify.

Macro-supervision can do nothing about the risks that it does not find, and these 'unknown unknowns' are ultimately the risks that may pose a threat to financial and economic stability in the future.

Despite these limits, we should embark on the road to macro-supervision. This type of supervision should focus on two things: first, the resiliency of the financial infrastructure, and second, the financial sector as the transmission mechanism between macroeconomic policy and the real economy.

Collectively, the financial system is a critically important infrastructure that must continue to operate if the modern economy is to function at all. At the heart of this infrastructure are a set of payments, clearing and settlement systems over which practically all financial transactions occur and without which the economy would grind to a halt. Therefore, the first broad task for macro-supervision is to assure that the financial infrastructure remains resilient in both an operational and a financial sense.

Assuring operational resilience involves contingency planning to assure that the infrastructure and the firms using that infrastructure can continue to operate, even if there is a technological failure, a terrorist attack, a pandemic or some other shock. Such contingency plans need to be tested periodically in both an institution-specific and market-wide context, and macro-supervision needs to assure that institutions make the necessary investments in people, systems and controls necessary to maintain the financial infrastructure. This macro-supervision is necessary since each of the participants would otherwise have the tendency to free ride on the investments of others, and collectively this would result in underinvestment in the development and maintenance of vital systems.

Macro-supervision must also assure that payment, clearing and settlement systems are financially as well as operationally robust. Such systems are in effect a single point of failure; if a payment, clearing or settlement system were to fail, it could have severely adverse repercussions on all the firms who use the system and/or who might have exposures to it. Such payments, clearing and settlement systems must be robust.

In particular, they have to be able to withstand the failure of their largest member and still keep functioning. That requires the development and implementation of strict risk controls, collection and management of up to date (generally real time) information, and the establishment of collateral pools and collateral management systems that can be used to offset any risk that might materialise from the failure of one or more of the system's members.

There is already a rich tradition of such macro-supervision of infrastructures. This has materially reduced risk in payments (CPSS 1997, 2001a), foreign exchange (CLS), securities settlement (Group of Thirty 1989, 2003, 2005; CPSS 2001b, 2002, 2004) and derivatives (see above). Private initiatives have complemented these official actions, including the three CRMPG reports chaired by Jerry Corrigan over the years. Collectively, these efforts have substantially reduced systemic risk, but macro-supervision needs to continue this effort, not just with respect to credit derivatives, but more broadly (see Table 10.1).

In addition to assuring the resiliency of the financial infrastructure, macro-supervision needs to identify systemic risks in the financial system, especially those that would destabilise the financial system's role as transmission mechanism between macroeconomic policy and the real economy (see Chapter 6). Such macro-supervision requires a

Table 10.1   Macro-supervision of financial infrastructures

Type of system	Risk mitigation measures
Payments	➤ Real time gross settlement ➤ Sender, receiver and settlement finality for net payment systems
Foreign exchange	➤ Continuous linked settlement
Securities clearing and settlement	➤ Dematerialisation ➤ Automation and acceleration of trade matching and confirmation ➤ Reduction in interval between trade date and settlement date ➤ Delivery versus payment ➤ Introduction of a central counterparty (CCP)
Derivatives	➤ Netting via standard ISDA contract ➤ Elimination of unauthorised assignments ➤ Reduction in backlogs of unconfirmed transaction ➤ Protocol for calculation and settlement of payments to buyers of protection in the event of default by reference entity ➤ Introduction of data warehouse ➤ Introduction of central counterparty (CCP)

Source: Huertas 2006a.

much deeper understanding of how monetary and fiscal policy affects asset prices and market liquidity as well as how changes to these variables affect consumer and corporate decisions to spend and invest. Already, it is apparent that price stability and strong economic growth can give rise to asset-price bubbles that can in turn, thanks to mark-to-market accounting and bank capital rules, give rise to pro-cyclical expansions of credit.

Therefore, it may make sense for macro-supervision to have a set of tools that it can use to dampen the business cycle. These might include the imposition of gross leverage limits as a 'speed limit', the introduction of a countercyclical buffer[1] of core Tier I capital that banks should hold relative to risk-weighted assets, or variations on the terms (haircuts, eligibility requirements and/or rates) at which central banks extend liquidity to banks or variations in the haircuts on and in the range of assets admitted to the supervisory liquidity buffer (see Table 10.2). Singly or in combination, these tools could be used to induce banks to

Table 10.2 Possible macro-prudential policy tools

Tool	Description
Gross leverage limit	Sets a limit on ratio of core Tier 1 equity to total assets (not adjusted for risk)
Counter-cyclical capital buffer	Sets a target buffer of capital above the minimum that banks should build up during a boom as a precaution against an economic downturn (such a buffer would be released in the downturn)
Terms of central bank lending to banks	Vary the range of assets that are eligible as collateral for borrowing from the central bank
	Vary the advance rate against eligible collateral
	Vary the rate of interest at which banks may borrow on collateralised basis from the central bank
Assets admitted to supervisory liquidity buffer	Vary the range of assets that are eligible for inclusion in the supervisory liquidity buffer
	Vary the haircut applied to assets included in the supervisory liquidity buffer
Lending commitments	Arranges for each bank to commit to new lending to reduce/eliminate the collection action problem

temper their risk appetite so that the boom can be flattened out and stretched out rather than spike and then crash.

In addition, it will certainly make sense for macro-supervision to look at changes in the structure of financial markets and shifts in the share of products and providers, to ask whether business flows to new products or new sectors are consistent with the maintenance of financial stability and to take steps – as the authorities did in the case of hedge funds and credit derivatives – to mitigate the risks that macro-supervision identifies.

Finally, it will make sense for macro-supervision to engage in a two-way dialogue with micro-supervision. Micro should provide to macro a sense of how the financial system will transmit the policy impulses of the central bank and fiscal authorities to the real economy. This should yield better forecasts and help make policy decisions more accurate. Macro should feed to micro the economic scenarios that micro and the individual firms supervised under micro need to take into account in determining how the banks will fare under a base case or central forecast as well as how they would fare if a stress scenario were to develop. From this dialogue there should also develop a sense of the extent of the collective action problem that the economy may face, and what the authorities might undertake to counteract such a problem. An example is the collective contraction in credit (and therefore contraction in the economy) that would result, if each bank were to seek to conserve capital and/or liquidity by reining in credit. To counteract such a tendency, the macro supervisor could potentially induce all banks to sign a lending commitment so that no bank would contract credit unduly.

Conclusion

Crises recur with frightening frequency for a variety of causes (Reinhart and Rogoff 2009), and at the time of this writing (December 2009) it is not as yet safe to say that the crisis that began in August 2007 has completely run its course. Although recovery has begun, there is still a danger of relapse into recession.

Nevertheless, this book has attempted to outline the elements of a cure against future crises – or at least a cure against future banking crises. That cure should be a comprehensive one, encompassing better macroeconomic policy, better resolution, better deposit guarantee schemes, better regulation and better supervision. Although the outlines of the cure are clear, two important details remain to be finalised: how should society tackle the issue of 'too big to fail', and at what level should capital and liquidity requirements be set. The two questions are interconnected. To the extent that society can design a method whereby banks can be resolved in a manner that does not impose costs on the taxpayer, capital and liquidity requirements can be designed in a manner that will enhance the ability of banks to act as financial intermediaries and promote economic growth. If society cannot design such a method, society will face a far more difficult choice between restricting banks and restricting growth.

Too big to fail

The acid test for a cure to what ails the financial system is whether the cure will work with respect to financial institutions that are considered 'too big to fail' – the large complex, cross-border financial institutions (LCFIs) that are the principal players in financial markets, the principal users of payment, clearing and settlement systems and a major source of credit to consumers and corporations around the world.

These institutions want to live by the market. They want to retain the profits that success can generate and pay their people for their role in generating that success. But in this crisis society reached the conclusion that it could not afford to let these institutions die by the market (see Chapter 5). Society had tried this with Lehmans, and the financial system nearly went into meltdown (see Chapter 4). Only through massive monetary and fiscal stimulus were central banks and governments able to arrest the worst economic slide since the Great Depression (see Chapter 5). Total support to the financial system – direct loans, asset purchases, collateral swaps, guarantees, asset insurance and direct equity injections – amounted to over $13 trillion (see Introduction). By anyone's reckoning that is a lot of money.

'Heads the firm wins, tails the taxpayer loses', is not a game the public should allow financial institutions to play. Society needs to find a way that financial institutions, especially the LCFIs that are at the centre of the financial system, can either avoid failure altogether or fail in a controlled manner so that the impact on the financial system and society as a whole is reduced to manageable proportions.

The measures outlined in Part III – better macroeconomic policy, better resolution, better deposit guarantee schemes, better regulation and better supervision – are the basis on which a cure for crises can be found. But these measures do not represent a full solution to the problem posed by LCFIs.

Something extra is needed. Steps should be taken to assure that there is an extraordinarily low prospect that an LCFI will fail in the first place. Steps should also be taken to assure that, if an LCFI were to fail, the financial system would remain intact and costs would fall, not on taxpayers, but on shareholders, other capital providers and creditors whilst protecting deposits, especially retail deposits.

A first step is to assure that LCFIs are well supervised wherever they operate in the world. Colleges of supervisors with the strong leadership by the home country supervisor, reinforced by cross-border stability groups, are the path to this end (FSF 2009c). But more will be needed to assure that LCFIs do not pose excessive risk to the financial system.

Who are LCFIs and why are special measures needed for LCFIs?

There is no commonly agreed definition of an LCFI, but such a list would encompass institutions that are 'too big to fail' as well as institutions that are so interconnected that their failure would be 'too complex to contemplate'. Such a list would probably include the world's top 50 to 100 financial institutions in terms of the book value of their liabilities (deposits, insurance policies, securities and derivatives outstanding). Although small in number, these financial institutions account for the bulk of the financial system's assets, liabilities and transactions. They are at the centre of the world's financial markets and are heavily interconnected with one another. The failure of one of these institutions could have significant implications on the ability of the others to survive and on markets to continue to function.

Such a list is not static. It depends first of all on the efficacy of deposit guarantee schemes and resolution procedures. The more able deposit guarantee schemes are to assure depositors full and rapid access to the insured deposits that they hold at a bank that fails, the greater the use the authorities can make of resolution methods (bridge bank, deposit transfer and liquidation/deposit payoff) that reinforce market discipline and therefore make failure less likely in the first place. If retail depositors of a failed bank can promptly obtain their money, one of the principal knock-on effects of a bank failure is eliminated, and the need for open-bank assistance is much reduced, if not eliminated entirely.

Similarly, the more resilient are payment, clearing and settlement infrastructures to the failure of one their participants, the less reason there is to provide open institution assistance to allow any one participant to continue in operation. Over time, the authorities and industry have made considerable strides in making such infrastructures more robust. Indeed, the ability of the major infrastructures to withstand the failure of Lehmans underscores that progress, and further steps to clear OTC derivative trades through robust central counterparties will sustain that progress (see Chapter 10).

But significantly more progress needs to be made, before one could say that the failure of LCFIs should be resolved entirely by methods that do not involve open institution assistance. Insolvency and administration proceedings for large institutions are time and capital consuming, even if they are confined to a single jurisdiction. If the institution is a cross-border one, the administration proceedings are likely to be even more complex, for there are significant differences in the way that various jurisdictions regard the overall process. Although most countries take a unitary view of a bankruptcy and look to resolve the failure from a global point of view, one of the most important jurisdictions, the United States, looks to resolve each failure from its own national point of view (the US portion of the estate of the failed institution is resolved as if the US portion were a stand-alone company and the net difference is either credited [if positive] or presented as a claim [if negative] to the estate of the remaining institution). This difference in approach alone considerably complicates the resolution of cross-border institutions, and it is not likely that reform of national bankruptcy laws will lead any time soon to the necessary convergence and coordination of resolution procedures for LCFIs.

So the failure of one LCFI could still have significant impacts on others as well as the economy at large, and the authorities may therefore be reluctant to let an LCFI fail in the first place, particularly after Lehmans and its disastrous aftermath. Although the authorities may espouse the doctrine of 'constructive ambiguity', the market is likely to conclude that the authorities would in fact seek to preserve the LCFI as a going concern rather than incur the social costs that would result from tipping the LCFI into 'gone' concern status. Consequently, the market may doubt whether it would ever suffer loss given resolution, and consequently the market may not effectively discipline LCFIs. Hence, countervailing measures are needed.

What are the alternatives?

If normal market measures cannot discipline LCFIs, what can? Some proposals are on the surface quite simple: if a bank is too big to fail, make it smaller; if a bank is too complex to fail, make it simpler. That way any financial institution could fail without overly adverse consequences for the system as a whole.

If by too big to fail, one means that a bank would have to be small enough that the deposit guarantee fund could pay out promptly the insured deposits of the bank, banks will have to be very small indeed, until such time as the deposit guarantee funds are really in a position to pay out the deposits of any failed bank promptly. Even in the United States, where the FDIC has had decades of experience in dealing with failed banks, the deposit guarantee fund has trouble in resolving failed banks above a certain size. To resolve IndyMac, a bank with $19 billion in insured deposits, the FDIC had to send in hundreds of staff months in advance of the actual failure of the bank to prepare the bank's systems for the point at which the bank would fail and payments be made to insured depositors. Although measures are being undertaken in various countries to require banks to keep their data in a format that would strengthen the capability of the deposit guarantee fund to pay out insured deposits promptly in the event of the failure of a bank (see Chapter 8), these will take some time to implement, and even when they are in place it may not be practical to pay out promptly all the insured deposits of a very large bank, if that bank were to fail.

Even if a concerted break-up campaign were to succeed in creating a system of small financial institutions, it can be seriously questioned as to whether such a system of institutions would necessarily be safer, sounder or more efficient. Small banks are not necessarily safer banks (as the failure of hundreds of small banks demonstrates), and large financial institutions (Corrigan 2009; IIF 2009b) would contend that small institutions lack the scale and scope necessary to make markets or provide financial services to the largest corporations.

Those who maintain that LCFIs are too complex have a simple solution: make them less complex. The favourite solution is to split investment (or 'casino') banking from commercial (or 'utility') banking, and the implied assertion is that utility banking is safe banking, and that casino banks could simply be allowed to fail.

Both components of this assertion are open to doubt. So-called utility banks have ample opportunity to take risks. Just as real utilities operate nuclear power plants that can go into meltdown, so can so-called utility banks generate losses through making loans – as Countrywide, IndyMac, HBOS and numerous other banks have amply demonstrated during this crisis and as the US S&Ls demonstrated so thoroughly in the 1980s. Indeed, lending on the collateral of commercial real estate can be just as risky as engaging in proprietary trading. Utility banks can also run large liquidity risks, as Northern Rock demonstrated. And utility banks would presumably have the ability to make investments in highly rated securities, as IKB and Landesbank Sachsen did (in AAA-rated asset backed securities) prior to the onset of the crisis in 2007.[1]

Moreover, complexity would not be cured simply by splitting investment and commercial banking. Lehmans was a stand-alone investment bank, so recommendations to split commercial and investment banking would also have to encompass some type of limit on the activities in which an investment bank could engage, so that the investment bank would be simple enough to resolve, if it were to get into trouble. That might entail pushing investment banks into becoming advisory boutiques or back to the strict originate and distribute model of the 1950s – no lending (and therefore no prime brokerage), no derivatives, no foreign exchange trading, but simply cash trading in spot securities markets, underwriting new issues and distributing them fully to end investors with stringent limits on the underwriting exposures that the bank could have at any one point in time. Unless one tackles the limits on what stand-alone investment banks can do, and decides how a large complex, cross-border investment bank could be resolved without damaging the financial system, simply splitting commercial and investment banking will solve neither the too-big-to-fail nor the too-complex-to-contemplate problems.

Moreover, universal banking is not necessarily unsafe banking. It was not unsafe in the 1920s (Benston 1990), nor was universal banking uniformly unsafe in the first decade of the twenty-first century. Some universal banks (e.g. Citigroup) made poor risk decisions and had to be rescued. Others (e.g. J.P. Morgan Chase) managed their risk more prudently and were able to act as a source of strength to the financial system by acquiring institutions that had failed (Washington Mutual) or had to be rescued (Bear Stearns).

Contingent capital, contingency funding plans and 'living wills'

If changing the structure of LCFIs won't work, what will? There has to be a mechanism that will reduce the probability that an LCFI will fail, and reduce the scale and scope of an LCFI to manageable proportions, so that if it were to fail, it would not bring down the financial system with it.

The simplest way to accomplish the former is to place more stringent capital and liquidity requirements on LCFIs. This reduces the probability of failure. In addition, each LCFI should be required to demonstrate that it could survive the failure of its largest counterparty (in all likelihood another LCFI). That will limit the risk of contagion that LCFIs could pose to the financial system.

If stricter capital, stricter liquidity and 'contagion control' are not enough to arrest the deterioration in the condition of the LCFI, the LCFI should be forced to trigger a previously developed resolution and recovery plan or 'living will'. This would either enable the institution to recover, or it would shrink the risk and size of the institution whilst the institution remained a going concern so that if it were to fail, the consequences of its failure would be reduced to manageable proportions.

Stricter capital.   Although all banks will need to maintain more capital and all banks will need higher quality capital (see Chapter 9), it is particularly important that LCFIs have sufficient capital to avoid failure and the higher social costs that their failure would entail. For this reason, LCFIs should have a supplemental capital requirement, an extra margin of safety (see Figure C.1).

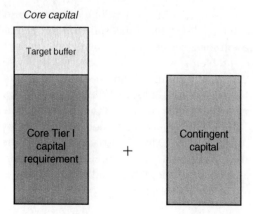

Figure C.1   Contingent capital can limit too big to fail and/or too complex to contemplate

This should, in my view, involve a redefinition of the regulatory capital structure. The primary or minimum requirement would be for the institution to hold core Tier I capital (shareholders' equity or its equivalent) equal to some proportion of its risk weighted assets. Risk weighted assets would fully reflect the changes to the trading book that the Basel Committee has ordained for end 2010 (see Chapter 9), and the core Tier I capital requirement would be the net figure after taking account of the deductions for prudential filters, as envisioned by the Basel Committee (see Chapter 9). This minimum requirement might be supplemented by a counter-cyclical buffer that firms would build up during the boom and be able to draw down during a recession.

The primary change to capital requirements for LCFIs would be to require that other elements of capital – hybrid Tier I (e.g. preferred shares) or Tier II capital – be convertible into core Tier I capital upon a finding by the regulator that the Core Tier 1 ratio of the bank fell below a certain threshold.[2] This would transform such instruments into contingent capital, or capital capable of bearing loss whilst the bank is a going concern. This would cure one of the glaring deficiencies in the current capital structure of banks (see Chapter 9).

Contingent capital would amount to a pre-pack recapitalisation from the private sector, not the taxpayer. Unlike current forms of Tier II capital and hybrid Tier I capital, contingent capital would be fully loss absorbent whilst the LCFI is a going concern. Pricing for the instrument should be in line with the risk that conversion will occur and the risk that subsequent losses would be incurred. To the common shareholder, the prospective conversion of contingent capital into common equity holds out the prospect of death by dilution, and it can be anticipated that shareholders would therefore task management to undertake the necessary measures to avoid dilution. That would limit the risk of the institution.

Conversion of contingent capital into core Tier I capital would imply that the institution was under some stress. For this reason it is important to assure that the institution has enough contingent capital available for conversion, so that the conversion would restore the core Tier I capital ratio to a healthy amount, well in excess of the minimum core Tier I capital requirement. It therefore makes sense to consider creating a separate requirement that banks hold contingent capital equal to the amount of core Tier I capital that the firm is required to hold. This would assure that the firm could replenish the minimum amount of core Tier I capital that it required through conversion of the contingent capital into core Tier I capital.

Effectively, this new requirement would amount to two things: a requirement that hybrid capital (non-core Tier I) and subordinated debt (Tier II) be convertible into core Tier I capital, and a requirement that the bank have a minimum amount of such instruments outstanding. The total capital requirement would therefore consist of a core Tier I capital requirement (plus a possible counter-cyclical buffer) and a separate requirement for contingent capital that would replace the current rules relating to non-core Tier I and Tier II capital.

Contingent capital holds the promise of providing real market discipline. It introduces a class of investor in addition to the common shareholders who will monitor the bank's condition.[3] This is a vital reinforcement to the scrutiny that supervision provides. In the absence of such a class of investors, the predominant and perhaps only discipline for an LCFI could be the institution's own shareholders and the institution's supervisor. Given shareholders' asymmetric returns (unlimited upside, whilst limited liability constrains the downside), some doubt may be cast on the effectiveness of shareholders' disciplining risk taking. Therefore, without the discipline that contingent capital could provide, discipline would fall predominantly, if not completely, on supervisors.

Contingent capital can also limit the size of banks. In effect, the imposition of a separate and distinct contingent capital requirement would allow LCFIs to grow to whatever size the market is willing to recapitalise immediately even under adverse conditions. If a bank cannot find investors who are sufficiently confident that conversion is remote, or sufficiently confident that the LCFI would have a robust long-term future even if it were to suffer a severe setback, the bank's size and/or activities would have to be scaled back to the point where investors would in fact have such confidence.

Should an LCFI have to convert its contingent capital into core Tier I capital, and should such a conversion bring the amount of contingent capital below the minimum requirement for contingent capital, the bank should have a limited period to replenish its contingent capital and restore this to the minimum, either by issuing new contingent capital or by shrinking its risk exposures. Should the bank not succeed in restoring its contingent capital to the required minimum within this time frame, the bank would have to implement its living will (see below).

Stricter liquidity.   In addition to stricter capital requirements, LCFIs should have stricter liquidity requirements. These can be set in the context of the individual liquidity guidance called for in the reform of liquidity regulation (see Chapter 9).

Particular emphasis should be placed on assuring that the LCFI has a robust, market-based contingency funding plan in place. Such a plan requires the LCFIs to establish beforehand back-up sources of liquidity from the market, such as long-term repurchase facilities, as well as having in place the requisite collateral to furnish into such facilities. The latter will require the LCFI to maintain a 'collateral budget' to assure that it will in fact have sufficient collateral to secure adequate funding, even if the LCFI itself is downgraded, and/or there is a contraction in the liquidity and/or pricing of the securities in the collateral pool.

Contagion control.   In addition to stricter capital and stricter liquidity requirements, LCFIs should be required to demonstrate more rigorous protection against large exposures. In particular, they should be required to demonstrate that they would be able to withstand the failure of the single largest counterparty (usually this will be another LCFI). This would include the ability to calculate on an ongoing basis the group-wide exposures to major counterparties as well as the operational ability to net and close out contracts, realise collateral, and so on.[4]

'Living will'.   Severely ill patients draw up so-called living wills that allow another person to take decisions for the patient whilst the patient is incapacitated, pending the patient's recovery (in which case the patient again resumes responsibility for his/her own affairs) or the patient's death (in which case the patient's last will and testament becomes effective). Something similar is needed for LCFIs, if the market-based

contingent capital and market-based contingent liquidity plans do not succeed in arresting the deterioration in the condition of the LCFI (see Figure C.2). LCFIs should be required to draw up such a recovery and resolution plan in advance so that it can be triggered if needed.

Under such a recovery and resolution plan (RRP), the LCFI's ability to conduct its own affairs would be severely restricted. Whilst the RRP is in operation the LCFI would not be able, without the prior approval of the regulator, to

- pay dividends or make distributions to shareholders;
- make capital investments above a certain threshold amount or acquire businesses;
- pledge assets to third parties (other than as envisaged under the contingency funding plan); and
- pay bonus or other discretionary compensation without the prior approval of the regulator.

The living will would contain a recovery capital plan, a recovery liquidity plan and a contingent resolution plan. The first two set out a path for the firm to recuperate. To support these two plans, the LCFI should have in place a risk reduction plan that would enable the LCFI to wind down or liquidate its trading book over a 30 to 60 day period.[5] In addition, the LCFI should have a sale or break-up plan that would sell

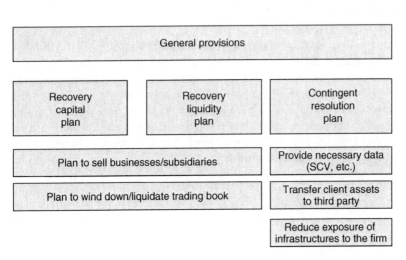

Figure C.2 Living wills

the institution as a whole to a third party or one or more businesses to a third party to reduce the scale and scope of the LCFI.[6]

As part of the recovery liquidity plan (and as a back-up to its market-based contingency funding plan) an LCFI should take measures to assure that it could access central bank facilities such as discount window facilities. In particular, the LCFI should conclude the necessary legal and operational agreements with the relevant central bank(s) as well as taken steps to preposition collateral with such central bank(s) for ordinary and emergency liquidity facilities. However, these precautions do not convey any right on the LCFI to borrow from the central bank. Instead, they provide the central bank with the opportunity to provide liquidity assistance rapidly, should the central bank come to the conclusion that it is economically important to do so.

Finally, the living will should contain a contingency resolution plan. The LCFI would have to take measures that would enable it to furnish data to the deposit guarantee funds so that they could undertake prompt pay out of the LCFI's insured deposits, if the LCFI were to fail. The LCFI would also be required to have a plan to transfer client assets to a third-party custodian so that clients would not be seriously adversely affected, if the LCFI were to fail. Finally, the LCFI would have to have a plan in place that would enable payment, clearing and settlement infrastructures to 'unplug' the LCFI from the infrastructure without damaging the rest of the financial system (e.g. this might require the LCFI to operate on all payments systems without incurring daylight overdrafts).

Trigger for living will and link to resolution.   As indicated above, the trigger for the living will would be a determination by the regulator that the LCFI did not meet its contingent capital requirements and the failure of the LCFI to rectify this breach within the designated cure period.[7] Another possible trigger for the living will would be the failure of the institution to repay within a very short period of time any emergency liquidity assistance that it may receive from the central bank.

What should trigger the end of the living will? If the LCFI recovers to the point where it again fulfils its supplemental capital, liquidity and contagion control requirements, the living will should be deactivated, and the constraints imposed on the firm removed.[8] If the condition of the LCFI deteriorates to the point where the LCFI fails to meet threshold conditions (e.g. the minimum core Tier I capital requirement for all banks), the LCFI should become subject to resolution according to the special resolution regime applicable to banks and/or other financial institutions (see Chapter 7).[9]

In sum, the supplemental capital, liquidity and contagion control requirements for LCFIs, together with living wills, provide a means to limit the risk that an LCFI would fail.[10] They also represent a method by which a troubled LCFI can either recover or be resolved in a manner that limits the impact of the institution's failure on the economy as a whole, the financial system and the taxpayer. In this respect, living wills (together with supplemental capital, liquidity and contagion control requirements) represent a method by which LCFIs can die by the market as well as live by the market.

Calibrating the new regime

Calibrating the new regime of capital and liquidity requirements is a complex and important task. Broadly speaking, it involves setting a risk-tolerance level for society as a whole vis-à-vis financial institutions. This level can be defined as the probability of that failures will occur times the impact that such failures would have. In this crisis the impact of bank failures has been very large indeed. If one counts the loss in output from the recession as entirely due to the crises, this would amount to at least 5 per cent of the GDP in advanced industrial economies. There may be further losses in connection with the equity investments, credit guarantees and asset protection that governments have accorded the banks. And, these losses will be compounded, if the recovery falters, and there is a relapse into recession. Total direct and indirect costs of the crisis are well in excess of $1 trillion.

How much is society willing to sacrifice to reduce the risk that such a calamity will recur? The simple view is that 'the banks should pay', but the facts are that increased capital and liquidity requirements are costs to the banks that they will pass on to their clients. Higher capital and liquidity requirements mean that banks must earn more to provide investors a return that is commensurate with the risk taken by the investor and competitive with the returns available from other investments with a similar risk profile. To earn more banks have to increase their margin. In other words, banks have to charge more for loans and/or services or banks have to pay less for deposits. This will increase the cost of bank credit. For those entities, such as small businesses, which are dependent on bank credit, costs may rise. This will reduce the ability of such firms to undertake new projects and create new jobs. That will slow economic growth.[11]

One has to strike a balance. Figure C.3 illustrates how this might be done conceptually. The left-hand panel of the figure sets the risk

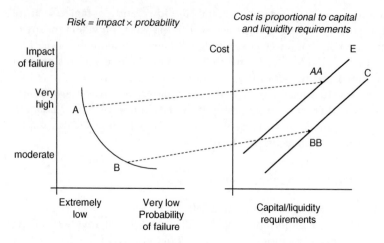

Figure C.3   Calibrating the new regime: impact, probability and cost

tolerance for society as a whole: what is the expected value of losses that would result from the failure of an LCFI? This is a product of two factors. The first is the impact that such a failure would have upon the economy at large (taking into account the direct losses to the firm's creditors as well as the indirect losses or knock-on effects from the failure of the firm). The second factor is the probability that the LCFI would fail. Any given aggregate risk to society is compatible with a variety of combinations of impact and probability. For example, in the figure, the same level of aggregate risk is present at point A (very high impact and extremely low probability of failure) and point B (moderate impact and very low probability of failure).

The right-hand panel of the figure describes the costs of reducing failure. Broadly speaking, reducing the probability of failure increases costs, for the reasons outlined above. So an extremely low probability of failure is likely to involve higher costs than a very low probability of failure. So each point along the impact/probability trade-off is associated with a point on the cost – probability chart. The actual point on the cost – probability chart depends on the form of capital and liquidity regulation that is employed. If all capital has to take the form of core Tier I capital (shareholders' equity) there will be a higher cost associated with any given probability of failure. This is depicted by curve E in the right-hand panel of Figure C.3. If some capital can take the form of debt, costs will be lower. This is depicted by curve C in the right-hand panel of Figure C.3.

The solution advocated here – moderate impact of failure (via living wills) and very low probability of failure (through stricter capital and liquidity requirements) – is represented by point B on the left-hand panel of Figure C.3. This is associated with point BB on the right hand panel of Figure C.3. This is on the lower cost curve C due to the fact that some portion of the capital requirement can come in the form of contingent capital.

Such a solution may be difficult to implement. Living wills are only in a pilot stage (FSA 2009i), and contingent capital has barely begun to be issued. So much work remains to be done to determine whether the solution advocated here can be made practical. The pilot should do that for living wills, and something may need to be done to jump start the market for contingent capital (see Box).

Without such a solution to the LCFI problem, society faces in my view unpalatable alternatives. Without living wills the impact of the failure of an LCFI could be very high indeed, as was the case with Lehmans. To offset that very high impact, society would have to move towards

---

Jump-starting the market for contingent capital

The issuance of Enhanced Capital Notes (ECNs) by Lloyds Banking Group in 2009 in exchange for various non-core Tier I and Tier II capital instruments represents the first significant issuance of contingent capital. To further develop the market for this instrument, it may make sense for the authorities to give banks the incentive to convert existing non-core Tier I and Tier II instruments into contingent capital. This might be done by measures such as restricting the ability of banks to call such existing instruments and would be consistent with recommendations that banks be encouraged to convert such instruments into ones that are capable of bearing loss whilst the bank is a going concern (Tucker 2009).

Another possibility is to allow banks to invest in a mutual fund that would in turn buy issues of contingent capital from the banks that participated. After an initial period (say two years), banks would have to deduct such an investment from their own capital. This would give banks the incentive to sell their shares in the mutual fund to third-party investors.

In addition, the fund itself would be encouraged to sell the individual issues of contingent capital that it had bought from the banks to third-party investors. Over time, the fund would increase the proportion of cash that it had in its portfolio. This would enable the fund to act as a back-up provider of liquidity to banks in exchange for a commitment fee. Such a fund would be available as a source of back-up funding for contingency funding plans. In this manner the industry (not the taxpayer) could build up a bank recovery fund (as called for by Tucker [2009]).[12]

forcing LCFIs to operate with an extremely low probability of failure (in other words move to point A on the left-hand panel of Figure C.3). That would in turn create very high costs, especially if all capital had to take the form of equity (that is depicted by the point AA on the right-hand panel of Figure C.3).

Doing nothing would be even worse. That would pose a very significant risk to society that the crisis of 2007 could become the precursor to the next and perhaps even bigger crisis. That cost is not something society can afford and that risk is not something society should allow banks to pose.

Notes

Introduction

1. According the Federal Reserve Board's Flow of Funds statistics (11 June 2009, Table B.100 (http://www.federalreserve.gov/releases/z1/Current/z1r-5.pdf) total assets of households and non-financial corporations amounted to $64.5 trillion at the end of the first quarter of 2009, a decline of $12.4 trillion from the year-end 2007 level of $76.9 trillion.

1 Rational Exuberance

1. See Economist (18 July 2009b). The general macroeconomic approach can be found in Blanchard (2009), Dornbusch, Fischer and Startz (2004) and Romer (2006). Tucker (2007) acknowledges that neither asset prices nor the financial system figure prominently in the macroeconomic models that the Bank of England used to implement its inflation targeting regime.
2. Source: IMF World Economic Data Base 22 April 2009 (available at http://www.imf.org/external/pubs/ft/weo/2009/01/weodata/index.aspx).
3. For a discussion of global imbalances see Wolf (2009) and Turner (2009).

2 Too Much of a Good Thing

1. For discussions of the cause of the crisis see Brunnermeier (2009), de Larosière (2009), IIF (2008), Sinn (2009) and Turner (2009).
2. For a general description and analysis of securitisation see Fabozzi (2001), Goldman and Fabozzi (2002) and Milne (2009).
3. The equity in the SPV does not actually bear loss. It remains in place so that the SPV remains a going concern and the losses can be allocated in line with strict seniority.
4. For a general discussion of credit derivatives see Caouette et al. (2008: 411–36).
5. For an overview of ratings agencies see Caouette et al. (2008: 81–102), IOSCO (2008).
6. In contrast, banks reporting under IFRS generally had to consolidate any conduits or structured investment vehicles that they created.

3 Conditional Containment

1. For details of the forecasts see Bank of England, *Inflation Report* (November 2007).
2. For a fuller discussion of Northern Rock see Shin (2009), Treasury Committee (2008), FSA (2008e).

3. JP Morgan Chase effectively had to complete the deal or it would have been left exposed to Bear Stearns under the terms of the hastily negotiated guarantee granted to Bear Stearns pending completion of the deal. For details see Cohan 2009.

4   Moving towards Meltdown

1. For details of the decisions reached in the United States during these weeks see Sorkin (2009).
2. Under re-hypothecation a broker that accepts collateral from a client is able to pledge the securities received from the client to a third party. Such re-hypothecation allows the broker to use the client's securities as collateral to secure funding that the broker obtains from the third party. Thus, re-hypothecation represents a way for brokers to lower their cost of funding, and prime brokers passed some of this cost reduction on to their investor clients in the form of lower rates on the loan that the investor had taken from the prime broker. However, this lower cost came with an increase in risk. If the broker fails, the lender to the broker liquidates the securities pledged by the broker to the lender to repay the loan to the lender. This effectively reduces or eliminates the ability of the broker to return to the investor the securities pledged by the investor to the broker, and the investor becomes a general creditor of the failed broker for the amount of the excess collateral. For further details see M. Huertas 2009.
3. Figures for assets and retail deposits are as of 30 August 2008.
4. Under EU law in force at the time the home country was responsible for the protection of the deposits in the host country branch up to the maximum amount of the home country coverage. In Iceland's case this was equivalent to €20,887. For amounts above this limit the branch had the option to top up the coverage by joining the host country scheme so that the depositor in the host country branch could get a total amount of coverage equal to what the host country scheme afforded to banks headquartered in the host country. In the case of the United Kingdom, the Icelandic banks had all taken such top-up coverage for their branches, so the UK compensation scheme provided cover for deposits between the Icelandic limit of €20,887 and the UK limit of £50,000.

   So when the UK government announced that it would protect all retail deposits, the Treasury assumed the liability of the Icelandic scheme to the UK depositors for the amount covered under the Icelandic scheme as well as for any amounts over the £50,000 UK limit.

5   Unconditional Containment

1. Fisher (1933) first put forth the idea of a debt deflation spiral and Bernanke (1983) further examined the effect of non-monetary factors in the Great Depression. Greenlaw et al. (2008) and Brunnermeier (2009) describe the debt-deflation spiral as it applies to this crisis.
2. For institutions that availed themselves of the Government's offer to subscribe to new capital, the Government imposed additional institution-specific

conditions relating to dividends, executive compensation, board represen-
tation, management and strategy (including commitments with respect to
lending to individuals and SMEs in the United Kingdom).
3. In grossly oversimplified terms, the debt-deflation theory posits that

$$Y^* = f(C^*)$$

where Y is GDP in nominal terms and C is the aggregate amount of credit supplied to resident households and corporations, and the superscript * denotes
percentage change.

Bank credit (C_B) is only a part of the credit extended to households and
corporations. Non-bank credit sources include trade credit, non-bank financial intermediaries and direct issuance of securities (collectively C_{NB}). So total
credit is

$$C = C_B + C_{NB}$$

The growth of total credit is therefore

$$C^* = b\, C_B^* + (1-b)\, C_{NB}^*$$

This implies that total credit to households and corporations could be
falling, even if bank credit is increasing. For total credit growth to remain at
levels required to sustain the economy, bank credit may have to increase at
very significant rates indeed. In effect, the growth in bank credit would have
to make up for the decline in non-bank credit.

A simple hypothetical example illustrates this effect. Suppose the pre-crisis
growth in credit was 10% pa, with bank credit and non-bank credit each
growing at 10% pa. If the rate of growth of non-bank credit falls to zero (i.e.,
non-bank credit remains constant), then the rate of growth of bank credit
may need to be considerably higher than 10%, if the total growth of credit is
to reach the level required to sustain economic activity. Indeed, the growth
in bank credit will have to be higher, the lower is the share of bank credit in
total credit and the higher is the rate of growth in the overall level of credit
required to sustain the economy ($C^\wedge$). The following table illustrates these
effects:

Rate of growth of bank credit required
to sustain economic activity

B (%)	$C^\wedge$ (%)		
	5	8	10
25	20.0	30.0	40.0
50	10.0	15.0	20.0
75	6.7	10.0	13.3
100	5.0	7.5	10.0

4. For example, the FSA (2005b) highlighted the importance of stress testing for
banks. Thematic work indicated that banks were not being tough enough in
their tests and the FSA pushed banks to increase, for the purpose of the test,
the severity of the stresses to which the bank might be exposed (FSA 2006b,
Huertas 2006b).
5. Quotes are from Geithner et al. (2009).
6. Sweden (Finansinspektionen 2009) published its results.

7. With respect to loans to individuals, governments in some countries have been more insistent that banks take steps to help consumers avoid default and foreclosure.

6   Better Macroeconomic Policy

1. Marginal lending facilities are administered by the national central banks under uniform conditions across the eurozone. There is a penalty rate for accessing this facility (at the end of July 2009 this was 75 basis points). With the exception of October and November 2008, this facility was rarely used, and even in these two crisis months total usage peaked at €12.7 billion.
2. The ECB (2008: 41) sets a standard equivalent to an 'A' rating (probability of default over a one-year horizon of 0.1%). The admission of an asset to the list of eligible assets for discounting with the central bank adds to the liquidity of the asset and has a favourable impact on its price.
3. This proposal should be differentiated from, but also compared to, the imposition of margin requirements on customer borrowing from banks and/ or broker-dealers. The proposal here effectively amounts to variations in margin requirements for borrowing from the central bank.
4. Confining open market operations to a group of primary dealers restricts central bank liquidity provision (via repurchase transactions) under normal facilities largely to those firms.

7   Better Resolution

1. There is an extensive literature linking the existence of the safety net (deposit guarantees and lender of last resort) to the need for regulation. For a summary of this see Dewatripont and Tirole as well as Chapter 9.
2. Rochet (2008: 22) characterises this as a 'fundamental commitment problem'.
3. However, institutions that have received open bank assistance have conducted liability management transactions to buy back non-equity capital instruments at a discount to par, with the difference between the par and price paid being booked to profit. In this sense non-equity capital instruments have born loss, but this has been a result of voluntary market transactions rather than a contractual feature of the instrument.
4. The Financial Stability Board has formed a group to attempt to do just that. It will seek to implement the FSF's Principles for Cross-border Cooperation in Crisis Management (FSF 2009a).

8   Better Deposit Guarantee Schemes

1. An exception to this rule might be foreseen in the case of temporary high balances that a consumer might need to keep in a single bank for a period. Such temporary high balances might arise, for example, from the proceeds of the sale of a house. If the bank were to fail soon after the seller received the proceeds, the seller could suffer a catastrophic loss. For this reason, it

has been suggested that a higher limit might be initiated for temporary high balances (FSA 2009b). However, such an exception for temporary high balances would be difficult to implement and could stand in the way of assuring fast payout.

2. In addition, procedural obstacles to rapid pay out need to be removed, such as the requirement that the depositor in the failed bank file a claim prior to receiving any payment, accept the offer of the deposit guarantee scheme in settlement of that claim and assign his rights with respect to the insured deposits to the deposit guarantee scheme with respect to recoveries from the estate of the failed bank. Such obstacles can add weeks or even months to the payout process.

3. This task is greatly simplified, if the eligibility criteria for coverage under the deposit guarantee scheme are broadly phrased, such as 'all natural persons' without exclusions for certain individuals, such as the family of executives and directors (see FSA 2009f: 9–11).

4. In addition, ignoring set off in calculating the amount due to consumers under deposit guarantee schemes also improves consumer liquidity. If the consumer had deposits of €25,000 and a mortgage of €50,000 using the deposit to offset the mortgage would potentially pose significant liquidity issues for the consumer and could pose refinancing costs to the consumer (e.g. if s/he had a fixed rate mortgage at below current rates).

5. If banks were to keep their data in such a format, it would also facilitate the collection of levies in a pre-funded scheme based on the amount of covered deposits (see below). Keeping the data in such a format would also facilitate the provision of information to consumers about the amount of deposits that are actually guaranteed under the scheme (see below).

6. The actual loss attributable to the deposit guarantee scheme depends, among other things, on the seniority of deposits relative to other liabilities, as well as whether the resolution arrangements allow others (e.g. government) to take priority in capturing recoveries. For example, in the United States, domestic deposits have a preference over other liabilities and in the United Kingdom members accounts at building societies are subordinate to other forms of funding.

7. This arrangement requires the FDIC to manage the conflict of interest between its role as receiver (where it has to act in the interests of all creditors) and its role as a claimant on behalf of the fund.

8. Under EU law the home country bank could also seek to 'top up' its deposit guarantee coverage, if the host country scheme had a limit higher than the home country scheme. The host country scheme would provide coverage for any amount up to the host country limit that exceeded the home country limit. For example, if the home country had a limit of €20,000 and the host country a limit of €50,000 a deposit of €35,000 in the host country branch of the home country bank would be covered for the first €20,000 by the home country scheme and for the remaining €15,000 by the host country scheme.

Top up will become irrelevant if the proposed amendments to the EU Deposit Guarantee Scheme Directive become effective. A single limit of €100,000 is to be introduced that will be effective across the EU (and EEA). Member States may not have a limit lower than or higher than this single EU limit.

9   Better Regulation

1. Drexel, Burnham, Lambert is an example of such a firm. The US Department of Justice subjected the firm to criminal indictment in 1990 based on the firm's conduct in the junk bond market.
2. In this respect the proposal for contingent or 'top-up' capital requirement is a more effective version of earlier proposals that market discipline be imposed on banks via a requirement that they issue subordinated debt (Benston et al. [1986] and White [1991]). Subordinated debt only absorbs loss in a gone concern scenario (as did other mechanisms such as double liability for share-holders). Tipping a bank into gone concern status is precisely what society seeks to avoid, if not eliminate entirely. This dictates that some method be found to force the shareholders to accept a recapitalisation well before the point at which it would become profitable for the shareholders to default and 'put' the bank's assets to the debt-holders (depositors). Contingent capital does this.
3. Compensation of non-executive directors may have to increase to attract appropriately qualified candidates who are able and willing to devote the time required to provide effective governance.
4. Valuation with respect to the banking or accrual book is also important. However, here the principal issue is how to estimate amount of provisions that may be required to absorb losses in the accrual book at some point in the future. This is closely connected to the implementation of stress testing.

10   Better Supervision

1. Such a counter-cyclical capital buffer might be imposed via rules or at the discretion of the authorities (see BoE 2009b).

Conclusion

1. Kay (2009) has suggested an extreme form of narrow banking where retail deposits would be backed by government securities and all other banking activity would be unregulated. Although this would protect retail deposits, it leaves open how the rest of the financial system would operate. Turner (2009b) outlines different variations on the theme of splitting 'utility' banking from investment banking as well as highlights the difficulty of and questions the rationale for doing so.
2. This threshold should be somewhat above the minimum required level or core Tier I capital so that the conversion occurs before the minimum is breached.
3. In this respect the proposal for contingent or 'top-up' capital requirement is a more effective version of earlier proposals that market discipline be imposed on banks via a requirement that they issue subordinated debt (Benston et al. [1986] and White [1991]). Subordinated debt only absorbs loss in a gone concern scenario (as did other mechanisms such as double liability for share-holders). The proposal made here is similar to that made in Flannery (2005). See also Kashyap et al. (2008).

4. This recommendation is similar to that contained in CRMPG 2008.
5. Trading book risks that could not be liquidated over this period should either not be in trading books at all or be subject to supplemental capital charges on an ongoing basis.
6. There is much discussion of corporate structures as a means to aid resolution (see Turner 2009b), but it should also be emphasised that separability is at least as important for recovery. Separately incorporated subsidiaries are much easier to sell than businesses that are embedded within a single legal vehicle. And selling a healthy subsidiary is likely to be a much more effective method of facilitating recovery or avoiding resolution than allowing a separately capitalised subsidiary to fail. If a LCFI were to walk away from subsidiary, this is very likely to have very adverse consequences for the group's ability to fund itself in the markets.
7. During the cure period, the LCFI would be expected to update and finalise (subject to the approval of the regulator) the terms of the recovery capital and recovery liquidity plans as well as populate the data room that would back up the sale and break up plan and begin to refine/execute the wind down/liquidation of the trading book.
8. Note that this restoration could occur either through the issuance of new contingent capital or through shrinkage of risk weighted assets in line with the risk reduction and/or sale/break-up plans.
9. Note that the period under which an LCFI could operate under a 'living will' could be quite long. However, there should be a limit on the amount of time that the LCFI is able to operate without having contingent capital in place. If the LCFI has failed to restore its supplemental capital ratio to the required level within a certain period of time (say three months) after the original breach occurred, the LCFI could be required to provide an option to the authorities to acquire new contingent capital in the LCFI sufficient to give the authorities control of the LCFI upon conversion of that contingent capital into core Tier I capital.

   Effectively, the authorities would have the option (but not the obligation) to act as a back-up underwriter of new contingent capital. If the LCFI could not persuade the market to subscribe to new contingent capital, the authorities should have the right (but not the obligation) to do so. In any such 'backstop' underwriting of contingent capital, it can be anticipated that the conversion price of the continent capital into core Tier 1 capital would occur at an extremely low price per common or ordinary share. For the common shareholder, such a conversion would effectively amount to death by dilution, so the LCFI should be given the right to redeem the contingent capital instrument issued to the authorities (prior to conversion into core Tier I capital) upon payment of a sizeable premium provided such redemption would not cause the LCFI to fall below the minimum supplemental capital requirement.
10. The combination of supplemental capital and liquidity requirements together with living wills greatly alleviates not only the problems of too big to fail and too complex to contemplate, but it can also be used to address the issue of 'too small to save' and/or burden sharing more generally.

    The issue of 'too small to save' arises under the current regime where resolution of financial institutions is conducted under the 'home country pays' principle. The authorities in the institution's home country make the decision about the form and amount of assistance that might be provided to a troubled institution and are generally expected to fund the entire amount of any assistance themselves. That raises the prospect that a 'small' country may be too small to save a large bank headquartered within its jurisdiction.

The problem is particularly acute within the European Union. Under freedom of establishment, a bank headquartered in one Member State may open a branch or subsidiary in any other Member State. This raises the possibility that a bank established in one Member State would have operations in many others, and that the home country state would be expected to pay for the resolution of the entire group. Although this unites the fiscal responsibility with the supervisory responsibility, it creates the prospect that Member States may be very unevenly able to bear the fiscal responsibility that may come with the incorporation of a large banking group within its jurisdiction. Accordingly, host Member States may be concerned about the ability, and possibly the willingness, of the home country to follow the home country pays principle, should resolution become necessary.

Contingent capital forces the private market to bear at least the first round of any recapitalisation of a LCFI, regardless of the country in which the LCFI is headquartered. Contingent capital therefore goes a long way towards neutralising the country of incorporation of the LCFI. Further steps can be taken through the operation of the living will and the prospect that the authorities would provide a backstop to a new issue of contingent capital for the LCFI. The requirement that the living will would contain a break-up plan would allow the authorities of other countries to express an interest in buying one or more of the LCFI's operations. The option for the authorities to provide a backstop to the contingent capital for the LCFI need not be exercised exclusively by the home country regulator. One could envision that the home country regulator would seek to syndicate – whilst the LCFI remained under the living will and remained a going concern – such a backstop among the relevant authorities in which the LCFI did business. Countries that participated in the syndication would have a voice in how the LCFI would ultimately be resolved, if it did not recover. Countries that did not participate would have to accept whatever decision the home country supervisor or those contributing to the syndicate made. Those that decided to share in the burden would have a voice in determining the resolution.

11. This cost may be reduced, if borrowers are able to bypass banks and raise credit directly in the securities markets. The increased cost of bank credit will induce borrowers to seek alternative forms of credit, such as trade credit or direct issuance of debt instruments to investors via the securities markets. The greater is the increase in the cost of bank credit, the more powerful are the incentives of borrowers to seek such alternative forms of credit.

That's fine as long as the economy stays on an even keel. All that happens is a shift from bank markets to securities markets. But there is no guarantee that the economy will remain on an even keel. Business cycles occur for many reasons, not just variations in the banking system. If an upturn were to develop, this would accelerate the shift from banking markets to securities markets. Such a shift could be quite rapid, especially if the market for securitisation were to revive. In such an environment it might be feasible for non-bank lenders to originate loans, package them into securities and sell them on to end investors. Borrowers would benefit because they would get a lower rate than the rate the bank would have to charge to break even. Investors would benefit because they would get a higher rate than what they could earn by placing funds on deposit with a bank. Again, that's fine as long as the upturn lasts. All that happens is a shift from bank markets to securities markets.

But what happens if the boom goes into reverse? New securities issuance dries up; indeed it can dry up completely. New credit becomes scarce, and total credit may contract. That could aggravate the downturn, unless banks are able to pick up the slack.

Banks' ability to do so depends on the total excess capital that banks have available going into the downturn. The release of the counter-cyclical buffer may provide some capital to banks to sustain lending, but this may not be enough to counteract the contraction in securities market credit that takes place in a downturn. If the shift to the securities market during the upturn allows banks to meet their capital ratio requirements with a constant or even reduced absolute amount of capital, banks will in the aggregate be too small to provide the credit that may be needed to support the economy during the downturn phase of the business cycle. If so, the higher capital and liquidity requirements would not necessarily produce a more stable economic environment.

12. The net effect of this proposal would be to build a significant investor base for contingent capital, and (upon the sale by the fund of the contingent capital instruments to third-party investors) create a lender of next to last resort that can provide financing to banks on commercial terms without recourse to the taxpayer or to central banks.

In outline, the fund could operate as follows:

1. Each participating bank would invest a certain proportion of its risk weighted assets into a specialised mutual fund. For example, each participating bank would invest 0.2 per cent of its risk weighted assets (or 5% of its core Tier I capital under the assumption of a core Tier I capital ratio of 4%) into the fund annually for a period of say five years.

2. This specialised mutual fund would initially invest each bank's subscription to the fund in a contingent capital instrument issued by that bank in an amount equal to the bank's subscription to the fund. The contingent capital instruments would have to meet minimum regulatory conditions, particularly with respect to the conversion trigger (trigger for conversion of the contingent capital into core Tier 1 capital could be no lower than 5%). The contingent capital instruments would be freely transferable to third-party investors.

3. The specialised mutual fund would not be obligated to hold the investment in any particular bank's contingent capital instrument. It would in fact be encouraged to sell such instruments after a short initial lock-up period into the market to third-party investors (but not back to the issuing bank).

4. To the extent that the specialised mutual fund realised cash from selling the contingent capital instruments to market, the fund would accumulate a cash reserve. This cash reserve would be invested in government securities.

5. The mutual fund would be able to lend these government securities to participating banks against the provision of sound collateral by the participating banks subject to haircuts on the collateral. The investor bank would pay a commitment fee for such a facility and a substantial margin, if it drew on the facility. Any such loans would be with full recourse by the specialised mutual fund to the participating bank.

6. The specialised mutual fund would mark its assets to market.

7. Participating banks could maintain an investment in the specialised mutual fund of up to 10 per cent of their capital. Amounts above 10 per cent would have to be deducted from core Tier 1 capital. This will induce the participating banks to sell their interest in the specialised mutual fund to third-party investors.

The cost to the banks from such a proposal would be significantly lower than building up a cash fund through taxing the banks. Investments in the specialised mutual fund would remain the property of the banks, and such investments could be sold at some future point in time. So a cost to banks arises if and only if the market value of the specialised mutual fund declines. In contrast, building up a fund through taxing the banks is equivalent to a 100 per cent write off of the investment in the fund. Given the lower cost, it should be feasible to build up a larger fund more quickly than would be the case with a tax-based proposal.

References

Adrian, Tobias and Hyun Song Shin, 2008a. *Financial Intermediaries, Financial Stability and Monetary Policy*, Proceedings of the Federal Reserve Bank of Kansas City Symposium at Jackson Hole, pp. 287–334.

Adrian, Tobias and Hyun Song Shin, 2008b. 'Liquidity, Monetary Policy, and Financial Cycles', *Federal Reserve Bank of New York Current Issues in Economics and Finance* 14 (1): 1–7.

Akerlof, George A. and Robert J. Shiller, 2009. *Animal Spirits: How Human Psychology Drives the Economy, and Why It Matters for Global Capitalism* (Princeton, NJ: Princeton University Press).

Bank of England (BoE). *Financial Stability Report* (London: Bank of England), semiannual.

Bank of England (BoE). *Inflation Report* (London: Bank of England) semiannual.

Bank of England (BoE), 2008. *The Development of the Bank of England's Market Operations*. October (London: Bank of England).

Bank of England (BoE), 2009a. *Quantitative Easing Explained: Putting More Money into our Economy to Boost Spending* (London: Bank of England).

Bank of England (BoE) 2009b. *The Role of Macroprudential Policy*. November (London: Bank of England).

Bank of England 2009c. Additional information provided to the Treasury Committee by the Bank of England Tuesday 24 November 2009 available at http://www.bankofengland.co.uk/publications/other/treasurycommittee/financialstability/ela091124.pdf.

Basel Committee on Banking Supervision (BCBS), 2007. 'Core Principles for Effective Banking Supervision' (available at http://www.bis.org/publ/bcbs).

Basel Committee on Banking Supervision (BCBS), 2008. 'Principles for Sound Liquidity Risk Management and Supervision' (available at http://www.bis.org/publ/bcbs138.htm).

Basel Committee on Banking Supervision (BCBS), 2009a. 'Revisions to the Basel II market risk framework', July 2009 (available at http://www.bis.org/publ/bcbs158.pdf).

Basel Committee on Banking Supervision (BCBS), 2009b. 'Proposed enhancements to the Basel II framework', January (available at http://www.bis.org/pubs/bcbs150.pdf).

Basel Committee on Banking Supervision (BCBS) 2009c. Group of Central Bank Governors and Heads of Supervision, 'Comprehensive response to the global banking crisis' 7 September 2009. available at http://www.bis.org/press/p090907.htm.

Benston, George J., 1990. *The Separation of Commercial and Investment Banking: The Glass Steagall Act Revisited and Reconsidered* (Oxford: Oxford University Press).

Benston, George J., Robert Eisenbeis, Paul Horvitz, Ed Kane and George Kaufman, 1986. *Perspectives on Safe and Sound Banking: Past, Present and Future* (Cambridge, MA: M.I.T. Press).

Bernanke, Ben, 1983. 'Non-Monetary Effects of the Financial Crisis in the Propagation of the Great Depression', *American Economic Review* 80: 257–76.

Bernanke, Ben, 2004. 'The Great Moderation'. Remarks at the Eastern Economic Association, Washington, D.C., 20 February (available at http://www.federalreserve.gov/BoardDocs/Speeches/2004).

Bernanke, Ben, 2005. 'Productivity'. Remarks at the University of Arkansas at Little Rock Business Forum, Little Rock, Arkansas, 24 February (available at http://www.federalreserve.gov/BoardDocs/Speeches/2005).

Bernanke, Ben, 2009. 'The Crisis and the Policy Response', Stamp Lecture, London School of Economics, 13 January 2009 (available at http://www.federalreserve.gov/newsevents/speech/bernanke20090113a.htm).

Blanchard, Olivier, 2009. *Macroeconomics* 5th edn (London: Pearson Prentice Hall).

Blanchard, Olivier and John Simon, 2001. 'The Long and Large Decline in U.S. Output Volatility', *Brookings Papers on Economic Activity* 1: 135–64.

Brunnermeier, Markus K., 2009. 'Deciphering the Liquidity and Credit Crunch 2007–2008', *Journal of Economic Perspectives* 23(1): 77–100.

Brunnermeier, Markus and Lasse Heje Pedersen, 2009. 'Market Liquidity and Funding Liquidity', *Review of Financial Studies* 22(6): 2201–2238.

Caouette, John B., Edward I. Altman, Paul Narayanan and Robert W.J. Nimmo, 2008. *Managing Credit Risk: The Great Challenge for Global Financial Markets* 2nd edn (Hoboken, NJ: John Wiley & Sons).

Cohan, William D. 2009. *House of Cards: How Wall Street's Gamblers Broke Capitalism* (New York: Random House).

Committee of European Banking Supervisors (CEBS), 2008a. Proposal for a common definition of Tier 1 hybrids. 26 March. available at http://www.c-ebs.org/getdoc/06e25083–2f37–4146-90f3–9e9a40365117/hybrids.aspx.

Committee of European Banking Supervisors (CEBS), 2008b. Technical Advice on Liquidity Risk Management (Second Part) 18 September. available at http://www.c-ebs.org/getdoc/bcadd664-d06b-42bb-b6d5–67-c8ff48d11d/20081809CEBS_2008_147_(Advice-on-liquidity_2nd-par.aspx.

Committee of European Banking Supervisors (CEBS), 2009a. 'CEBS's Statement on stress testing exercise', 12 May (available at http://www.c_ebs.org?News_Communications/Latest-news/CEBS-statement-on-stress-testing-exercise.aspx).

Committee of European Banking Supervisors (CEBS, 2009b). Committee of European Banking Supervisors, 'Consultation Paper on Liquidity Buffers and Survival Periods', July (available at http://www.c_ebs.org).

COM, 2009a. European Commission, Communication from the Commission, 'European Financial Supervision', 27 May {SEC(2009) 715} {SEC (2009) 716} (available at http://eur-lex.europa.eu).

COM, 2009b. European Commission, Financial services: Commission sets out future actions to strengthen the safety of derivatives markets 20 October 2009 available at http://europa.eu/rapid/pressReleasesAction.do?reference=IP/09/1546&format=HTML&aged=0&language=EN&guiLanguage=en.

COM 2009c. European Commission, *Communication from the Commission to the European Parliament, the Council, the European Economic and Social Committee, the European Court of Justice and the European Central Bank: An EU Framework for Cross-Border Crisis Management in the Banking Sector* {SEC (2009) 1389},

{SEC (2009) 1390}, {SEC (2009) 1407} available at http://eur-lex.europa.eu/
LexUriServ/LexUriServ.do?uri=COM:2009:0561:FIN:EN:PDF.

Committee on Payments and Settlement Systems (CPSS), 1997. *Real-Time Gross Settlement Systems* (Basel).

Committee on Payments and Settlement Systems (CPSS), 2001a. *Core Principles for Systemically Important Payment Systems* (Basel).

Committee on Payments and Settlement Systems (CPSS) and Technical Committee of the International Organization of Securities Commissions, 2001b. *Recommendations for Securities Settlement Systems* (Basel).

Committee on Payments and Settlement Systems (CPSS) and Technical Committee of the International Organization of Securities Commissions, 2002. *Assessment Methodology for "Recommendations for Securities Settlement Systems* (Basel, 2002).

Committee on Payments and Settlement Systems (CPSS) and Technical Committee of the International Organization of Securities Commissions, 2004. *Recommendations for Central Counterparties* (Basel).

Corrigan E. Gerald, 1987. *Financial Market Structure: A Longer View* (New York: Federal Reserve Bank of New York).

Corrigan, E. Gerald, 2009. 'Containing Too Big to Fail' Remarks at the Charles F. Dolan Lecture Series Fairfield University 10 November. available at http://www.group30.org/CorriganRemarks.pdf.

Counterparty Risk Management Group (CRMPG), 2008. *Containing Systemic Risk: The Road to Reform* (6 August) (available at http://www.crmpolicygroup.org/docs/CRMPG-III.pdf).

de Larosière, Jacques, 2009. The High Level Group on Financial Supervision in the EU Report (Brussels: EU Commission, 25 February; available at http://www.ec.europa.eu/internal_market/finances/docs/de_larosiere_report_en.pdf).

Derman, Emanuel, 2001. *The Principles and Practice of Verifying Derivatives Prices* (available at http://www.ederman_com/new/docs/risk-price_verification.pdf).

Dewatripont, Mathias and Jean Tirole, 1994. *The Prudential Regulation of Banks* (Cambridge, MA: M.I.T. Press).

Dornbusch, Ruediger, Stanley Fischer and Richard Startz, 2004. *Macroeconomics* 9th (international) edn (Boston: McGraw Hill).

ECOFIN, 2008. The Council of the European Union, 'Immediate Responses to financial turmoil: Council Conclusions – Ecofin Council of 7 October 2008' Document C/08/284.

Economist, 2009a. 'Efficiency and beyond', *The Economist* (18 July): 71–2.

Economist, 2009b. 'The other-worldly philosophers', *The Economist* 18 July: 68–70.

European Central Bank (ECB), 2008. 'The Implementation of Monetary Policy in the Euro Area: General Documentation on Eurosystem Monetary Policy Instruments and Procedures', November (Frankfurt: ECB).

Fabozzi, Frank J. (ed.), 2001. *The Handbook of Mortgage-backed Securities* 5th edn (New York: McGraw Hill).

FDIC, 2008. 'Notice of Proposed Rulemaking: Processing Deposit Accounts in the Event of an Insured Depository Institution Failure and Large Bank Deposit Insurance Determination Modernization', 12 CFR part 360; 73 Federal Register 2364: 14 January.

Federal Reserve Board, 2008. *Monetary Policy Report to the Congress*, July (Washington, D.C.: Federal Reserve Board).

Financial Services Authority (FSA), 2005a. Discussion Paper 05/4, 'Hedge funds: A discussion of risk and regulatory engagement' (available at http://www.fsa.gov.uk/pubs/discussion/dp05_04.pdf).

Financial Services Authority (FSA), 2005b. Financial Services Authority Discussion Paper 05/02, 'Stress Testing' (available at http://www.fsa.gov.uk/pubs/discussion/dp05_02.pdf).

Financial Services Authority (FSA), 2006a. Discussion Paper 06/6, 'Private equity: a discussion of risk and regulatory engagement', November (available at http://www.fsa.gov.uk/pubs/discussion/dp06_06.pdf.

Financial Services Authority (FSA), 2006b. 'Stress testing thematic review', Dear CEO Letter, 9 October (available at http://www.fsa.gov.uk/pubs/ceo/stress_testing.pdf).

Financial Services Authority (FSA), 2007a. Discussion Paper 07/7, 'Review of the liquidity requirements for banks and building societies' (available at http://www.fsa.gov.uk/pubs/discussion/dp07_07.pdf).

Financial Services Authority (FSA), 2007b. Policy Statement 07/19, 'FSCS Funding Review – Feedback on CP 07/05 and made text' (available at htpp://www.fsa.gov.uk/pubs/policy/ps07_19.pdf).

Financial Services Authority (FSA), 2008a. Consultation Paper 08/22, 'Strengthening liquidity standards' (available at http://www.fsa.gov.uk/pubs/cp/cp08_22.pdf).

Financial Services Authority (FSA), 2008b. Consultation Paper 08/24, 'Stress and scenario testing' (available at http://www.fsa.gov.uk/pubs/cp/cp08_24.pdf).

Financial Services Authority (FSA), 2008c. Consultation Paper 08/25, 'The approved persons regime – significant influence function review', December (available at http://www.fsa.gov.uk/pubs/cp/cp08_25.pdf).

Financial Services Authority (FSA), 2008d. Feedback Statement 08/3, 'Review of the liquidity requirements for banks and building societies: Feedback on DP 07/7' (available at http://www.fdsa.gov.uk/pubs/discussion/fs08_03.pdf).

Financial Services Authority (FSA), 2008e. 'The FSA's Supervisory Enhancement Programme, in response to the Internal Audit Report on supervision of Northern Rock' (available to http://www.fsa.gov.uk/pubs/other/enhancement.pdf).

Financial Services Authority (FSA), 2008f. 'Valuation and product control', Dear CEO Letter, 13 August (available at http://www.fsa.gov.uk/pubs/ceo/valuation.pdf).

Financial Services Authority (FSA), 2009a. Consultation Paper 09/03, 'Financial Services Compensation Scheme Reform: Fast Payout for Depositors and Raising Consumer Awareness' (available at htpp://www.fsa.gov.uk/pubs/cp/cp0903.pdf).

Financial Services Authority (FSA), 2009b. Consultation Paper 09/11, 'FSCS: Temporary high balances and implementing changes to the Deposit Guarantee Schemes Directive' (available at http://www.fsa.gov.uk/pubs/cp/cp09_11.pdf).

Financial Services Authority (FSA), 2009c. Consultation Paper 09/10, 'Reforming remuneration practices in financial services' (available at http://www.fsa.gov.uk/pubs/cp/cp09_10.pdf).

Financial Services Authority (FSA), 2009d. Discussion Paper 09/02, 'A regulatory response to the global banking crisis' (available at http://www.fsa.gov.uk/pubs/discussion/dp09_02.pdf).

Financial Services Authority (FSA), 2009e. Policy Statement 09/14, 'The approved persons regime – significant influence function review: Feedback on CP 08/25 and final rules', July (available at http://www.fsa.gov.uk/pubs/policy/ps09_14.pdf).

Financial Services Authority (FSA), 2009f. Policy Statement PS 09/11, 'Banking and Compensation Reform including feedback on CP 08/23, CP 09/03, CP 09/11 and CP 09/16' (available at htpp://www.fsa.gov.uk/pubs/policy/ps09_11.pdf).

Financial Services Authority (FSA), 2009g. Policy Statement 09/15, 'Reforming remuneration practices in financial services: Feedback on CP09/10 and final rules', August (available at http://www.fsa.gov.uk/pubs/policy/ps09_15.pdf).

Financial Services Authority (FSA), 2009h. 'FSA Statement on regulatory approach to bank capital', 19 January (available at http://fsa.gov.uk/pages/Library/Communication/Statements/ 2009/bank_capital_shtml).

Financial Services Authority 2009i. Discussion paper DP 09/4 'Turner Review Conference Discussion Paper' available at http://www.fsa.gov.uk/pages/Library/Policy/DP/2009/09_04.shtml.

Financial Stability Board (FSB) 2009. 'FSB Principles for Sound Compensation Practices: Implementation Standards' 25 September 2009. available at http://www.financialstabilityboard.org/publications/r_090925c.pdf.

Financial Stability Forum (FSF), 2008. 'Report on enhancing market and institutional resilience', 7 April.

Financial Stability Forum (FSF), 2009a. 'FSF principles for cross-border cooperation on crisis management', Basel: FSF, 2 April available at http://www.financialstabilityboard.org/publications/r_0904c.pdf.

Financial Stability Forum (FSF), 2009b. 'FSF principles for sound compensation practices', 2 April (available at http://www.financialstablityboard.org/publications/r_0904b.pdf).

Financial Stability Forum (FSF), 2009c. 'Report of the financial stability forum on enhancing market and institutional resilience: update on implementation', 2 April (available at http://www.financialstabilityboard.org/publications/r_0904d.pdf).

Finansinspektionen, 2009. 'Finansinspektionen stress tests major banks', Stockholm, 10 June (available at http://www.fi.se/upload/90_English/20_publications/ 20_Miscellaneous/2009/stresstester_20090610_eng.pdf).

Fisher, Irving, 1933. 'The Debt-Deflation Theory of the Great Depression', *Econometrica* 1: 337–53.

Flannery, Mark J., 2005. 'No Pain, No Gain? Effecting Market Discipline via "Reverse Convertible Debentures"', in Hal S. Scott, ed. *Capital Adequacy beyond Basel: Banking, Securities and Insurance* (Oxford: Oxford University press): 171–96.

G-7, 2008. 'G-7 Finance Ministers and Central Bank Governors Plan of Action', 10 October (available at http://www.treas.gov/press/releases/hp1195.htm).

G-20, 2008. 'Declaration: Summit on Financial Markets and the World Economy', Washington, D.C., 15 November 2008 (available at http://www.g20.org/documents/g_20summit_declaration.pdf).

G-20, 2009. 'Declaration on Strengthening the Financial System', London, 2 April (available at www.g20.org/Documents/Fin_Deps_Fin_Reg_Annex_020409_-_1615_final.pdf).

Geithner, Timothy F., 2006. 'Implications of Growth in Credit Derivatives for Financial Stability', Remarks at the New York University Stern School of Business Third Credit Risk Conference, 16 May (available at http://www.newyorkfed.org/newsevents/speeches_arcive/2006/ge060516.html).

Geithner, Timothy.F., Ben S. Bernanke, Sheila Bair and John C. Dugan, 2009. 'Joint Statement by Secretary of the Treasury Timothy F. Geithner, Chairman of the Board of Governors of the Federal Reserve System Ben S. Bernanke, Chairman of the Federal Deposit Insurance Corporation Sheila Bair, and Comptroller of the Currency John C. Dugan on the Treasury Capital Assistance Program and the Supervisory Capital Assessment Program', 6 May (available at http://www.federalreserve.gov/newsevents/press/bcreg/20090506a.htm).

Goldman, Laurie S. and Frank J. Fabozzi, 2002. *Collateralized Debt Obligations: Structures and Analysis* (Hoboken, NJ: John Wiley & Sons).

Goodhart, Charles, 2002. 'Myths about the Lender of Last Resort', in Charles Goodhart and Gerhard Illing, eds. *Financial Crises, Contagion, and the Lender of Last Resort: A Reader* (Oxford: Oxford University Press): 227–45.

Greenlaw, David, Jan Hatzius, Anil K. Kashyap and Hyun Song Shin, 2008 'Leveraged Losses: Lessons from the Mortgage Market Meltdown', in *U.S. Monetary Policy Forum 2008* (Chicago: University of Chicago Graduate School of Business): pp. 8–59.

Greenspan, Alan, 1999. Testimony before the Committee on Banking and Financial Services, US House of Representatives, 22 July (available at http://www.federalreserve.gov/BoardDocs/hh/1999/july/testimony).

Greenspan, Alan, 2002. 'Productivity', Remarks at the US Department of Labor and American Enterprise Institute Conference, Washington, D.C., 23 October (available at http://www.federalreserve.gov/BoardDocs/Speeches).

Greenspan, Alan, 2003. Testimony before the Committee on Financial Services, US House of Representatives, 15 July (available at http://www.federalreserve.gov/boardocs/hh/2003/july/testimony).

Greenspan, Alan, 2005a. 'Reflections on Central Banking', Remarks before a symposium sponsored by the Federal Reserve Bank of Kansas City, Jackson Hole, Wyoming, 26 August (available at http://www.federalreserve.gov/BoardDocs/Speeches/2005).

Greenspan, Alan, 2005b. Testimony on the Federal Reserve Board's semiannual Monetary Policy Report to the Congress, Committee on Banking, Housing, and Urban Affairs, US Senate, 16 February.

Group of Thirty, 1989. *Clearance and Settlement Systems in the World's Securities Markets* (Washington, D.C.).

Group of Thirty, 2003. *Global Clearing and Settlement: A Plan of Action* (Washington, D.C.).

Group of Thirty, 2005. *Global Clearing and Settlement: A Plan of Action. Interim Progress Report* (Washington, D.C. April).

Haldane, Andrew G., 2009. *Why Banks Failed the Stress Test* (London: Bank of England).

Hedge Funds Working Group (HFWG), 2008. *Hedge Fund Standards: Final Report* (available at http://www.hfsb.org/sites/10109/files/best_standards.pdf).

Her Majesty's Treasury (HMT), 2008a. *Financial support to the banking industry*, 8 October. News release 100/08. (available at http://www.hm-treasury.gov.uk/press_100_08.htm).

Her Majesty's Treasury (HMT), 2008b. *Special resolution regime: safeguards for partial property transfers* (available at http://www.hm-treasury.gov.uk/d/specialresolutionregime_061108.pdf).

Her Majesty's Treasury (HMT), 2009. *Reforming financial markets*, July (available at http://www.hm-treasury.gov.uk/d/reforming_financial_markets080709.pdf).

Herring, Richard and Jacopo Carmassi, 2010. 'The Corporate Structure of International Financial Conglomerates: Complexity and Its Implications for Safety and Soundness', in *The Oxford Handbook of Banking* (Oxford: Oxford University Press): 172–203.

Huertas, Michael D., 2009. *Hedge Funds, Master Netting Agreements and Rehypothecation: Limiting Systemic Risk through Increased Transparency* (available at http://papers.ssrn.com/sol3/papers.cfm?abstract_jd=1411609).

Huertas, Thomas F., 2006a. 'Dealing with Distress in Financial Conglomerates', Paper presented at LSE Conference, Prompt Corrective Action and Cross-Border Supervisory Issues in Europe, 20 November (available at http://fmg.lse.ac.uk/upload_file/800_T%20Huertas.pdf).

Huertas, Thomas F., 2006b. 'Facing Uncertainty from a Position of Strength', Remarks before Standard & Poor's Global Bank Conference, 16 November (available at http://www.fsa.gov.uk/pages/Library/Communication/Speeches/2006/1116_th.html).

Huertas, Thomas F., 2006c. 'One Down, Two to Go? Challenges Facing the Global Derivatives Industry', speech before the ISDA Regional Conference, London, 19 September (available at http://www.fsa.gov.uk/pages/library/Communication/Speeches/2006/0919_th.shtml).

International Accounting Standards Board (IASB), 2009. 'Report of the Financial Crisis Advisory Group', 28 July 2009 (available at http://www.iasb.org).

International Institute of Finance (IIF), 2008. *Final Report of the IIF Committee on Market Best Practices: Principles of Conduct and Best Practice Recommendations*, (Washington, D.C.: IIF; available at http://www.iif.com/regulatory).

Institute of International Finance (IIF), 2009a. *Compensation in Financial Services: Industry Progress and the Agenda for Change* (Washington, D.C.: IIF; available at http://www.iif.com/regulatory/).

Institute of International Finance (IIF), 2009b. *Restoring Confidence, Creating Resilience: An Industry Perspective on the Future of International Financial Regulation and the Search for Stability* (Washington, D.C.: IIF; available at http://www.iif.com/regulatory/).

International Monetary Fund (IMF), 2009a. 'Contractionary forces receding but weak recovery ahead', *World Economic Outlook Update*, 8 July 2009.

International Monetary Fund IMF, 2009b. *World Economic Outlook: Crisis and Recovery*, April (available at www.imf.org/external/pubs/ft/weo/2009/01/index.htm).

International Organisation of Securities Commissions (IOSCO), 2008. Technical Committee of the International Organisation of Securities Commissions, 'The role of credit rating agencies in structured finance markets: final report' (available at http://www.iosco.org/library/pubdocs/pdf/IOSCOPD270.pdf).

International Organisation of Securities Commissions (IOSCO), 2009. 'IOSCO finalises policy response to the financial crisis', Tel Aviv, 11 June (available at http://iosco.org/news/pdf/IOSCONEWS145.pdf).

Kashyap, Anil K., Raghuram G. Rajan and Jeremy C. Stein, 2008. 'Rethinking Capital Regulation', in *Maintaining Stability in a Changing Financial System* (Kansas City: Federal Reserve Bank of Kansas City; available at http://www. kc.frb.org/publicat/sympos/2008/KashyapRajanStein.03.12.09.pdf).

Kay, John, 2009. *Narrow Banking: the Reform of Banking Legislation* (London: CSFI).

Lucas, Robert E., Jr., 2003. 'Macroeconomic Priorities', *American Economic Review* 93 (1): 1–14.

Milne, Alastair 2009. *The Fall of the House of Credit: What Went Wrong in Banking and What Can Be Done to Repair the Damage* (Cambridge : Cambridge University Press).

Nouy, Danièle, 2007. 'La Supervision indirecte des hedge funds,' Banque de France *Revue de la stabilité financière* 10 April: 105–16 (available at http://www. banque-france.fr/archipel/publications/bdf_rsf/etudes_bdf_rsf/bdf_rsf_10_ etu.pdf).

Organisation for Economic Co-operation and Development (OECD), 2009. 'GDP stabilised in the second quarter of 2009' (Paris: OECD, 19 August; available at http://www.oecd.org/data/oecd/62/27/43514819.pdf).

PFUE, 2008. 'Statement of 27 European Heads of State and Government on the Stability of the Financial System', 6 October (available at http://www.ue2008. fr/PFUE/land/en/accueil/PFUE-10_2008/PFUE-06.10.2008/decla_27_finance. html).

Reinhart, Carmen M. and Kenneth S. Rogoff, 2009. *This Time is Different: Eight Centuries of Financial Folly* (Princeton: Princeton University Press).

Rochet, Jean-Charles, 2008. *Why Are There So Many Banking Crises? The Politics and Policy of Bank Regulation* (Princeton, NJ: Princeton University Press).

Romer, David, 2006. *Advanced Macroeconomics*. 3rd edn (New York: McGraw Hill).

Sants, Hector, 2009. 'Intensive supervision: delivering the best outcomes' 9 November 2009 available at: http://www.fsa.gov.uk/pages/Library/ Communication/Speeches/2009/1109_hs.shtml.

Senior Supervisors Group, 2008. 'Observations on Risk Management Practices during the Recent Market Turbulence', 6 March 2008 (available at www. newyorkfed.org/newsevents/news/banking/2008/SSG_Risk_Mgt_doc_final. pdf).

Senior Supervisors Group, 2009 'Risk Management Lessons from the Global Banking Crisis of 2008' 21 October 2009. available at http://www.newyorkfed. org/newsevents/news/banking/2009/SSG_report.pdf.

Shin, Hyun Song, 2009. 'Reflections on Northern Rock: The Bank Run that Heralded the Global Financial Crisis', *Journal of Economic Perspectives* 23: 101–19.

Shulman, David, Susan G. Brand and Sharon M. Levine, 1992. *The Goldilocks Economy: Keeping the Bears at Bay* (New York: Salomon Brothers United States Equity Research).

Sinn, Hans Werner, 2009. *Kasino Kapitalismus: Wie es zur Finanzkrise kam, und was jetzt zu tun ist* (Berlin: Econ).

Sorkin, Andrew Ross 2009. *Too Big to Fail: Inside the Battle to Save Wall Street* (New York: Viking).

Steinbrück, Peer, 2009. 'Rede anlässlich der Lesung des Gesetzes zur Fortentwicklung der Finanzmarktstabilisierung im Deutschen Bundesrat', Berlin, 10 July (available at http://www.bundesfinanzministerium.de/nn_88/DE/Presse/Reden).

Treasury Committee, 2008. House of Commons Treasury Committee, *The Run on the Rock* 5th Report of the Session 2007–08 Vol. 1, 24 January 2008 (available at http://www.publications.parliament.uk/pa/cm200708/cmselect/cmtreasury/56/56i.pdf)

Tripartite, 2007. Discussion paper, *Banking Reform – Protecting Depositors* (available at http://www.fsa.gov.uk/pubs/discussion/banking_reform.pdf).

Tripartite, 2008a. *Financial stability and depositor protection: further consultation* (available at http://www.fsa.gov.uk/pubs/cp/jointcp_stability.pdf).

Tripartite, 2008b. *Financial stability and depositor protection: special resolution regime* (available at http://www.fsa.gov.uk/pubs/cp/joint_doc_stability.pdf).

Tripartite, 2008c. *Financial stability and depositor protection: strengthening the framework* (available at http://www.fsa.gov.uk/pubs/cp/JointCPbanking_stability.pdf).

Tucker, Paul, 2007. 'Money and Credit: Banking and the Macroeconomy', speech at the Monetary Policy and Markets Conference, London, 13 December (available at http://www.bank ofengland.co.uk/publications/speeches/2007/speech 331).

Tucker, Paul. 2009. 'Regimes for Handling Bank Failures: Redrawing the banking Social Contract' Speech before the British Bankers' Association Annual International Banking Conference: Restoring Confidence, Moving Forward, London, 30 June 2009. available at http://www.bankofengland.co.uk/publications/speeches/2009/speech396.pdf.

Turner, Adair, 2009a. *The Turner Review: A Regulatory Response to the Global Banking Crisis* (London: Financial Services Authority).

Turner, Adair 2009b. 'Large systemically important banks: addressing the too big to fail problem,' Speech before Turner Review Conference 2 November 2009 available at http://www.fsa.gov.uk/pages/Library/Communication/Speeches/2009/1102_at.shtml.

UBS, 2008. 'Shareholder Report on UBS's Write-Downs', 18 April 2008 (available at http://www.ubs.com).

United States Department of the Treasury (UST), 2008. 'U.S. Government Actions to Strengthen Market Stability', 14 October (available at http://www.treas.gov/press/releases/hp1209.htm).

United States Department of the Treasury (UST), 2009. *Financial Regulatory Reform: A New Foundation* (Washington, D.C.: Department of the Treasury, 2009; available at http://www.financialstability.gov/docs/regs/FinalReport_web.pdf).

Wakeman, L. Macdonald, 1981. 'The Real Function of Bond Rating Agencies', *Chase Financial Quarterly* 1: 19–25.

Walker, David, 2007. *Guidelines for Disclosure and Transparency in Private Equity* (London, November; available at http://walker-gmg.co.uk/sites/10051/files/wwg_report_final.pdf).

Walker, David, 2009. *A Review of Corporate Governance in UK Banks and Other Financial Industry Entities: Final Recommendations* (London: HM Treasury).

Wellink, Nout, 2008. 'The importance of banking supervision in financial stability', Beijing 17 November. available at http://www.bis.org/review/r081117a.pdf.

White, Lawrence, 1991. *The S&L Debacle: Public Policy for Bank and Thrift Regulation* (Oxford: Oxford University Press).

Wolf, Martin, 2009. *Fixing Global Finance: How to Curb Financial Crises in the 21st Century* (New Haven: Yale University Press).

Index

Note: Page references in *italics* denote figures and tables.

ABN Amro, 69, 72
accounting
  accrual accounting, 33–4
  generally accepted accounting
    principles (GAAP), 33, 145
  International Financial Reporting
    Standards (IFRS), 140, 145
  mark-to-market, 144
  regulation and, 33–5
"acquire to arbitrage" model, 17, 19
Aegon, 81
alt-A mortgages, 31, 51, 55
Ambac, 55
American International Group (AIG),
  62–3, 163–4
asset(s)
  client assets, 132–3, 162
  eligible as collateral, 101–2
asset-backed commercial paper
  (ABCP), 43, 47–8, 49, 65
asset-backed securities (ABS), 26,
  28, 49
asset price bubble, 5, *6*, 7, 12–13,
  98, 177
asset protection schemes (APS),
  87–8, 113
auction rate securities (ARS), 57–8

bank(s) and banking
  bank recapitalisation (October
    2008), 78–81, 113
  borrowing from central bank,
    98–100
  guarantees for non-deposit
    activities, 132–3
  protection of, 94–5
  stabilisation of, 78
  see also central banks and banking
Banking Act 2009 (UK), 113, 121
banking book, 33, 140, 141–2
Bank of America
  acquisition of Countrywide, 56
  acquisition of Merrill Lynch, 67

asset protection scheme, 87
Bank of Canada, 63, 83
Bank of England, 99
  discount window facility, 82
  economic forecasts, 40, 41
  emergency liquidity assistance to
    Northern Rock, 46
  interest rate policy, 41
  liquidity support, 63–4
  quantitative easing, 85
  resolution method, 121
  Special Liquidity Scheme, 52–3,
    79, 82
Bank of Japan, 63
Barclays, 62, 89, 99
Basel Accord *see* capital regulation
Basel II *see* capital regulation
Basel Committee on Banking
  Supervision (BCBS), 134,
  140, 141–2
Bear Stearns, 51–2
Belgium
  burden-sharing agreements, 68–9
BNP Paribas, 81
  acquisition of Fortis Belgium, 72
  suspension of redemptions at
    sponsored funds, 37
Bradford & Bingley, 70, 75
"breaking the buck" *see* money
  market mutual funds
Buffet, Warren, 67
business cycle, 5, 7, 143

capital regulation, 94, 135, 136,
  149–50, 172
  leverage ratio, 144–6
  minimum capital requirements,
    146–9
  pro-cyclicality of capital
    requirements, 142–4
  quality of capital, 136–8
    core tier I capital, 137–8, 139–40,
      147–8, 188, 194

capital regulation – *continued*
  hybrid capital, 138–9
  tier I capital, 137
  tier II capital, 137, 138
  quantity of capital, 140–1
  trading book requirements, 33–4,
    141–2
    illiquid assets, 142
    incremental risk charge, 142
Capital Requirements Directive (CRD)
  (EU), 140, 143
Carlyle Capital Corporation, 51
central banks and banking
  borrowing from, 98–100
  borrowing from, eligibility for,
    100–2
  borrowing from, eligible
    counterparties, 107–8
  liquidity support, 63–4
  stimulus and stabilisation
    measures, 1–2, 77, 83, 91
  variation in lending term, 103–4
Citigroup, 50, 187
  asset protection scheme, 87
  offer to acquire Wachovia, 68,
    73–4, 116
clearing, 163–4
client assets, 132–3, 162
collateral
  assets backing securitisation issues,
    21–2
  assets eligibility, 101–2
  valuation, 102
collateral budget, 152
collateralised debt obligations (CDO),
    43, 48, 49, 54
  CDOs–squared, 22
commercial paper, 28, 65, 82–3, 107
  asset-backed commercial paper, 43,
    47–8, 49, 65
Committee of European Banking
  Supervisors (CEBS), 90
concentration risk, 156–7
conduct of business, 134–6, 159–60,
    173–4
conduits, 18, 28, 33, 47–8, 49, 50, 145
conflicts of interest, 160–1
constructive ambiguity *see* resolution
contagion control, 187, 190

contingency funding plan, 152, 190
contingent capital, 149, 187–90, 195,
    203n. 9
Council of Economic Advisers (US), 40
counterparty risk, 23–4, 163–4
Counterparty Risk Management
  Group (CRMG), 179
Countrywide, 55–6, 156, 186
credit default swaps, 54, 63
  data warehouse, 25
  notional amounts outstanding,
    23–4
  "tear up" procedures, 53
  unauthorised assignments, 24–5,
    53, 163, 176, 177
  unconfirmed transactions
    backlog of outstanding, 24–5, 53,
      163, 176, 177
Credit Locale, 69
Cuomo, Andrew, 58

"death by dilution", 80, 188–9, 203n. 9
debt-deflation spiral, 5, 37, 76
debt-deflation theory, 199n. 3
deflation, 13–14
Depfa, 69–70
deposit guarantee schemes, 93–4, 95,
    123, 184
  co-insurance, 125
  consumer awareness, 130
  coverage, 123, 132–3
    branches of foreign banks, 130–2,
      204n. 10
    eligibility, 123–4
  deposit pay-off, 117, 185–6
  deposit transfer, 117–18
  funding, 127–8
    ex-ante premiums, 129
    ex-post premiums, 128
    pre-funding, 128, 132, 201n. 5
    risk-based premiums, 129, 132
    size of fund, 129
  home country responsibility,
    130–2, 198n. 4
  host country responsibility, 132,
    198n. 4
  limits, 124–5
  single customer view, 126–7
  speed of payout, 125–6

Deposit Guarantee Schemes Directive
(EU), 126, 201n. 8
deposit insurance *see* deposit
guarantee schemes
derivatives, 19, 23–5
control, 53
leverage ratio and, 145
regulation of market infrastructures
and, 163
supervision, 176–7
Dexia, 68–9
disclosure, 160–2
Drexel, Burnham, Lambert, 202n. 1
due diligence, 160

ECOFIN, 78
economic growth, 9–12
emergency liquid assistance (ELA),
106, 107
AIG, 63
Fortis Belgium, 72
HBOS, 79, 80
Northern Rock, 46
RBS, 79, 80
Erste Bank (Austria), 81
European Central Bank (ECB), 97
economic forecasts, 40, 41
lending, 99, 100
monetary policy, 99, 100
slashing of interest rates, 84–5
European Commission, 44, 121
European Union (EU), 75, 120,
204n. 10
bank stabilisation, 78
Capital Requirements Directive
(CRD), 140, 143
deposit guarantee schemes, 130–2
Deposit Guarantee Schemes
Directive, 126, 201n. 8
speed of deposit payout, 126

Fannie Mae, 31, 51, 58–9, 65–6
Federal Deposit Insurance
Corporation (FDIC) (US), 56–7,
68, 80, 93–4, 116, 127, 128, 185
Federal Deposit Insurance
Corporation Improvement Act
(FDICIA) (US), 121
least cost test, 68

systemic risk exemption, 80,
94, 116
invoked for proposed
Citigroup-Wachovia
transaction, 68, 116
Federal Housing Finance
Administration, 59
Federal Reserve, 99
credit easing, 85
discount window facility, 65,
107, 166
interest rate policy, 5, 6, 11, 13–15,
41–2, 83, 84
liquidity support, 52, 64–5,
66, 82–3
Primary Dealer Credit Facility,
52, 65
role in resolution/rescue of
AIG, 62–3, 107
Bear Stearns, 51–2
temporary liquidity programme, 65
Term Securities Lending Facility, 52
Federal Reserve Bank of New York,
25, 163
fed funds rate *see* interest rates
financial crisis of 2007–2009, 1–3, 5,
37, 39–40, 76–8, 93, 182
containment, 37–9
containment, conditional, 42
containment, unconditional, 76, *77*
financial guarantee insurance
(monolines), 19, 25–6, 54–5, 59
Financial Market Stabilisation Act
(Germany), 80
Financial Services Authority (FSA) (UK)
hedge funds, 29
interim capital regime, 89
removal of co-insurance, 125
remuneration policy, 158
speed of deposit payout, 126
stress tests, 89, 199n. 4
threshold conditions, 113, 121
Financial Services Compensation
Scheme (FSCS) (UK), 47,
75, 126, 128
financial stability, 13
Financial Stability Board (UK), 158
Financial Stability Forum (FSF), 134,
200n. 4

financial systems, 17, 36, 97
  bank-centric framework, 93–5
  transmission mechanism, 5, 6
fiscal policy, 86
forbearance, 114, 145–6
Fortis, 68–9, 72
France
  bank recapitalisation (October
    2008), 80–1
  capital injection into Dexia, 69
Freddie Mac, 31, 58–9, 65–6

G-7, 78, 83, 134
G-20, 83, 91, 107, 134, 166
generally accepted accounting
    principles (GAAP)
    see accounting
Germany
  asset protection scheme, 88
  Financial Market Stabilisation
    Act, 80
  implicit guarantee for retail
    deposits, 73
Glitnir (Iceland), 74
Goldilocks economy, 11
Goldman Sachs (Goldmans), 67, 117
governance, 154–5, 169–71
Great Moderation, 11, 12
Greenspan, Alan, 177

HBOS, 64, 79, 80
hedge funds, 28–9, 176
HSBC, 50
Hypo Real Estate (HRE), 69–70, 73

Iceland, 74, 198n. 4
illiquid assets
  eligibility as collateral, 102
impairments, 33
independent price verification
    see valuation
Industrie Kreditbank (IKB), 43–4
IndyMac, 55–7, 185
inflation, 7–8, 11–12, 14, 40–1
infrastructures, 163–4, 184
ING, 81
  asset protection scheme (Alt-A
    mortgages), 87
innovation, 9–10

interest rates
  central banks' policy, 8, 41, 83–4
  United States policy, 5, 6, 11,
    13–15, 41–2
International Accounting Standards
    Board (IASB), 134
International Monetary Fund (IMF),
    134
International Organisation of
    Securities Commissions
    (IOSCO), 134
International Swap Dealers
    Association (ISDA), 23–4
  standard contract, 163
investment banks, 67, 186–7
investment grade names, 17, *18*
investors, 19, 20, 205n. 11
  dependency on rating agencies, 22,
    32, 160–1
  non-bank institutional investors,
    26–9
  third-party investors, 33, 195,
    205n. 12
Ireland
  state guarantee of all deposits at
    Irish banks, 71

JPMorgan Chase, 187
  acquisition of Bear Stearns, 51–2
  acquisition of Washington
    Mutual, 68

Kaupthing Bank (Iceland), 74
Kreditanstalt für Wiederaufbau
    (KfW), 43

Landesbanken, 43–4
  European Commission ruling on
    state guarantees as
    state aid, 44
Landesbank Sachsen, 43–4
Landsbanki Islands hf (Iceland), 74
large, complex financial institutions
    (LCFI), 182–5, 203n. 9
  probability of failure, 194–6
Lehman Brothers (Lehmans), 37, 39,
    51, 60, 61–2, 162
lender of last resort (LoLR), 52, 62,
    101, 106–7

lending commitments, 90
lending policy, 100–1
  term variation, 103–4
leverage, 35, 144
liquidity, 63–4, 81–3
  buffer, 153, 180
  funding liquidity, 79, 98, 141, 150
  market liquidity, 98, 141, 150
liquidity regulation, 150–4,
      172–3, 190
living will, 190–3
  contingent resolution plan, 192
  recovery capital plan, 191
  recovery liquidity plan, 192
Lloyds Banking Group (UK)
  asset protection scheme, 88
  bank recapitalisation (October
      2008), 79, 80
  enhanced capital notes (ECN), 195
  Lloyds TSB offer for Northern
      Rock, 46
  merger with HBOS, 64, 80
Lone Star, 43
Lucas, Robert, 11–12

macroeconomic policy, 5, 6, 39–42
  reforms, 97, 98
Madoff Investment Securities LLC, 162
marginal lending facility, 100,
      200n. 1
market abuse, 28, 135, 159, 173
MBIA, 54, 55
Merrill Lynch
  takeover by Bank of America, 67
Mitsubishi UFJ Financial Group
  capital infusion into Morgan
      Stanley, 67
monetary policy, 83–5, 97,
      98–100, 104
  impact on economic activity, 15–16
money market mutual funds, 26–8,
      165–6
  "breaking the buck", 64–5
monolines *see* financial guarantee
      insurance
moral hazard, 109
Morgan Stanley
  conversion to bank holding
      company, 67, 117

sale of stake to Mitsubishi UFJ
      Financial Group, 67
mortgages
  alt-A, 31, 51, 55
  sub-prime, 31–3, 43, 51, 54
mutual margining, 24

National Bank of Belgium, 72
netting, 23–4
  see also ISDA: standard contract
non-bank institutional investors,
      19, 26–9
non-financial corporations
  eligibility for central bank lending,
      107–8
  resolution policy, 114–15
Northern Rock, 45–7, 125, 151, 156,
      186

Office of Thrift Supervision (OTS)
      (US), 56
"originate to distribute" model, 17,
      18–19, 45

Parmalat, 30
Paulson, Hank, 65, 66
Peloton Partners, 51
Pfandbriefe (covered bonds), 69
price stability, 11, 12–13
pricing
  as macroeconomic tool, 104
pro-cyclicality *see* capital regulation
productivity, 9–10

rating agencies, 19, 29–33
  disclosure, diligence and, 160–1
  monolines and, 54–5
  regulation, 160–1
ratings, credit, 54, 101, 102, 171
recession, 12, 102, 193
recovery
  shape of recovery scenarios, 91,
      105–6
regulation, 134–6, 164–7
  accounting and, 33–5
  capital *see* capital regulation
  conduct of business regulation,
      134–6, 159–60, 173–4
  disclosure, 160–2

regulation – *continued*
  economic stress and, 105
  governance, 154–5
  initiation of, 113–14
  liquidity *see* liquidity regulation
  market infrastructure, clearing and
      settlement, 163–4
  money market mutual funds, 27–8
  remuneration, 158–9
  risk management, 155–8
remuneration, 158–9, 170
resolution, 109–11
  bridge bank, 118–19
    IndyMac, 56–7
  constructive ambiguity, 115, 117–22
  consumer-only protection, 109–10,
      115, 116–17
  coverage, 114–22
  deposit pay-off, 117, 185–6
  deposit transfer, 117–18
  liquidation, 117
  loss given resolution, 60, 68, 74–5,
      109, 111, 117–19
  open-bank assistance, 119, 121, 184
  probability of, 111
  receiver, 117
  resolution authority, 111–13
  temporary public ownership (TPO),
      119
  trigger for resolution, 111, 169, 173
  universal protection, 115–16
reverse stress testing, 157–8
Rhineland Funding *see* Industrie
      Kreditbank
Riksbank (Sweden), 83
risk, 193–4
  assessment, 111–12, 140–1
  concentration risk, 156–7
risk management, 155–8, 170–1
risk premium, 12–13
Royal Bank of Scotland (RBS)
  asset protection scheme, 87–8
  bank recapitalisation (October
      2008), 79, 80

Sachsen LB Europe plc *see*
      Landesbank Sachsen
savings and loan (S&L) crisis,
      165–6, 186

Schumer, Charles, 56
search for yield, 17, *18*, 35
Securities Exchange Commission
      (SEC), 28, 29
securitisation, 19, 20–3
  issuance, United States, 1996
      to 2006, 21–2
  mortgage-backed securities
    correlation of defaults on
        underlying mortgages, 31–2
    importance of ratings, 29,
        30–1, 161
    sub-prime, 31–3
    super senior tranches, 32
settlement, 163
  continuous linked settlement
      (CLS), 179
  delivery versus payment, 179
shadow banking system, 17–20,
      47–50
single customer view *see* deposit
      guarantee schemes
Société Générale, 81
soft landing, 7, 12, 15–16
Spain
  guarantee of bank debt (October
      2008), 81
special purpose vehicles (SPV), 20–1,
      197n. 3
Stanford Financial Group, 162
stimulus, 1, 2, *77*, 83–6, 91
stress testing, 104–6, 148, 157, 172
  EU stress test, 90
  FSA interim capital regime, 89
  reverse stress testing, 157–8
structured investment vehicles (SIV),
      18, 28, 47–8, 49, 50, 145
subordinated debt, 119, 189, 202n. 2,
      202n. 3
sub-prime mortgages, 43, 51, 54
  securitisation, 31–3
supervision
  large, complex financial
      institutions, 183
  macro-supervision, 25, 176–81
  micro-supervision, 152–4,
      168–76, 181
  risk-based supervision, 168, 169
Swiss National Bank, 63, 83, 87

Switzerland
  capital injection into UBS, 81

tail-risk insurance, 87, 89
Taylor rule, 5, 11, 14
technology, 9–10
Thornburg Mortgage, 51
threshold conditions, 113–14
"too big to fail", 111, 112, 120, 137,
    182–3, 185, 187, *188*, 203n. 10
"too complex to contemplate", 52,
    112, 183–4, 187, *188*, 203n. 10
"too small to save", 74, 112, 115–16,
    203n. 10
trading book
  accounting, 33–4
  capital requirements, 141–2,
    143–4
transfer pricing, 157
Troubled Asset Relief Program (TARP)
    (US), 65–6, 70–2, 80, 117
  stress testing, 89–90

UBS
  capital injection from Swiss
    government, 81
  losses announced (February
    2008), 51
unemployment, 1
United Kingdom
  Banking Act 2009, 113, 121

bank recapitalisation (October
    2008), 78–80
Credit Guarantee Scheme (CGS),
    79, 80, 82
deposit guarantee limits, 124
fiscal policy, 86
funding schemes for deposit
    guarantees, 128
monetary policy, 84, 85
United States
  deposit guarantee limits, 124
  disclosure regulations, 160
  economic growth, 9–10
  fiscal policy, 86
  impact of capital requirements and
    regulation on banks, 165–6
  monetary policy, 85
  resolution of failed institutions,
    184–5

valuation, 155–6
  collaterals, 102
  derivatives, 145
  independent price verification, 35
  level III assets, 35

Wachovia, 68, 73–4, 116
warehousing risk, 22–3
Washington Mutual, 68
Wells Fargo, 73, 116
WorldCom, 30